The Hidden Curriculum
in Higher Education

The Hidden Curriculum in Higher Education

edited by
Eric Margolis

ROUTLEDGE
New York and London

Published in 2001 by
Routledge
29 West 35th Street
New York, NY 10001

Published in Great Britain by
Routledge
11 New Fetter Lane
London EC4P 4EE

Routledge is an imprint of the Taylor & Francis Group

Printed in the United States of America on acid-free paper
Design and typography: Jack Donner

Library of Congress Cataloging-in-Publication Data

The hidden curriculum in higher education / edited by Eric Margolis.
p. cm.
Includes bibliographical references and index.
ISBN 0–415–92758–7 — ISBN 0–415–92759–5 (pbk.)
1. Education, Higher—Curricula—Social Aspects. 2. Curriculum planning—
Social aspects. 3. Educational anthropology. I. Margolis, Eric, 1947– .

LB2361 .H53 2001
378.1'99—dc21   00–062818

*As always, my dedication
is to Mary Romero*

Contents

Acknowledgments

The editor would like to thank Mary Romero and Sandra Acker for their editorial assistance. Marina Gair was indispensable as a research assistant and helped shepherd this project through all of its many phases. The visual ethnography seminar, especially Guy Mullins, Luis Fernandez, Marina Gair, and Lydia Montelongo, helped develop the notion of making the hidden curriculum visible through photography. Guy Mullins deserves special thanks both for videotaping the interviews reported on in chapter two, and building and maintaining the web site that allowed chapter authors to read each other's work in various drafts and thus helped this collection become more internally consistent than the usual edited volume. Most of all I would like to thank the chapter authors who conducted the detailed research that made this collection possible. It was a pleasure working with all of you.

Peekaboo 1

Hiding and Outing the Curriculum

Eric Margolis, Michael Soldatenko, Sandra Acker, and Marina Gair

Most of those who write on hidden curricula focus their attention on "curriculum." We want to begin by making a few observations on the concept of "hidden." In her important article, "What Should We Do with a Hidden Curriculum When We Find One?", Jane Roland Martin identified two sorts of hiddenness: "Something can be hidden in the sense of which a cure for cancer is hidden or in the sense in which a penny in the game Hide the Penny is hidden." Is the curriculum yet to be discovered or has it been hidden by someone? Martin also noted that a curriculum can be revealed to some, while remaining hidden to others: "Until learning states are acknowledged or the learners are aware of them, however, they remain hidden even if sociologists, bureaucrats, and teachers are all aware of them. Thus a hidden curriculum can be found yet remain hidden, for finding is one thing and telling is another" (Martin 1994, 162). This discussion is helpful, but does not go far enough in investigating hiddenness.

We hide to conceal or protect. To secrete. We hide our wealth in a hoard, we hide our feelings, we hide our intentions. In Edgar Allan Poe's short story "The Purloined Letter," a seasoned investigator has been called upon by the French police to lend his intuitive skills to solving a mystery. He asks the police about their search for critical clues: "I presume you looked to the mirrors, between the boards and the plates, and you probed the beds and the bed-clothes, as well as the curtains and carpets?" To which they reply: "Certainly; we opened every package and parcel; we not only opened every book, but we turned over every leaf in each volume... We also measured the thickness of every book-cover, with the most accurate admeasurement, and applied to each the most jealous scrutiny of the microscope ..." The investigator continues: "You explored the floors beneath the carpets? And the paper on the walls? You looked into the cellars?" To which the police again affirm, "We did." "Well then," speculates the investigator, "perhaps the mystery is a little too plain."[1] In this sense some of the hidden curriculum may be intentionally hidden in plain sight, precisely so that it will remain undetected. Much of the built environment, issues related to the body, the statuses of disciplines, and the ranks of higher education institutions are hiding in plain sight.

We use hides to cover our nakedness. As another important story in Western culture teaches, curricula can be hidden by a general social agreement not to see. The reader will recall in the fairy tale "The Emperor Has No Clothes" that the vain emperor was bamboozled by two tailors who invented a cloth so light and fine that it looked invisible to anyone "too stupid and incompetent to appreciate its quality." When presented with the new garment, the emperor thought, "I can't see anything. If I see nothing, that means I'm stupid! Or, worse, incompetent!" When he paraded naked through the city, "Everyone said, loud enough for the others to hear: 'Look at the Emperor's new clothes. They're beautiful!'"[2] Only when an (unsocialized) child observed that the emperor was naked was the truth revealed. Some of the ideological content of higher education intends to bamboozle, to pull the wool over people's eyes. Disengaged intellectuals both promote and deconstruct the clever subtleties and fine quality of ideology embedded in literature, television, rock music, fashion design, and so on because to do so seems competent and smart. Universities teach those who produce neither for use nor for exchange but produce ideology: labor management, mass communication, advertising, and the like. In this sense the university curriculum itself may be seen as a "hide" like a duck blind.

The nineteenth-century writings of Wilhelm Dilthey (1961) revealed human existence as a process of interpretation. Given that, one might consider curriculum itself to be a hiding place, a cache. Meanings are hidden in texts. Hermeneutics (the science of interpretations) emphasizes the non–apparent meanings of texts—meanings that may not even be understood by the authors. Because we humans tell ourselves lies and come to believe them, meanings can be hidden from us. Similarly, cultural meanings are hidden in symbolism; meanings that may involve obscure allusions and connections lurking in texts but remaining beneath the surface. It is also possible, as Vance Packard (1957) alerted us, that there are "hidden persuaders" that subliminally convey messages. Perhaps they can only be revealed by hermeneutic psycho- and socioanalysis. Fruitful work can be done in the secret garden of the curriculum where sexuality, power, and knowledge lie coiled like serpents. Moreover, at least in the West, knowledge is guilty knowledge. One turns away from certain curricula, hides his or her face in shame, hides his or her eyes. This process is one essential part of what Elliot Eisner (1985, 97–98) called the null curriculum—that which is left out.

Another widely beloved story contains parallels relevant to the hidden curriculum. Elements of curriculum might be thought of as hidden behind the scenes, like the mechanisms run by the bumbling Wizard of Oz. Hidden curricula that are more or less overt—sometimes called the "other curriculum"—fit this model. Leadership, entrepreneurship, manners, and class dispositions—the qualities once called "finishing"—and certain glib pseudointellectual styles are elements of this hidden curriculum. These aspects are what Dorothy Smith (1990) termed "the relations of ruling": elements of superstructure, including the curricula of class consciousness, whiteness, patriarchy, heterosexuality, and of the West. Although these dispositions and relations are taught and learned, the reproduction of what Bourdieu (1973, 40) called *habitus* (discussed below) is very often hidden by a wink. Some of the behind-the-scenes machinery of social stratification is considered "legitimate," and in fact we "pay no attention to the man behind the curtain." There are infernal mechanisms as well.

We hide the evidence of wrongdoing. Many kinds of socialization are indeed covert, will not work if made visible, and in fact will produce resistance if revealed. Here we are thinking of intentionally produced forms of subordination, discrimination, and hegemony that benefit some at the expense of others. As Russell Ferguson (1990, 9) noted: "The place from which power is exercised is often a hidden place. When we try to pin it down, the center always seems to be someplace else. Yet, we know that this phantom center, elusive as it is, exerts a real, undeniable power over the whole social framework of our culture and over the ways we think about it." This is clearly a form of "Hide the Penny," and we want to know who did the hiding. We are not talking of oppression-without-an-oppressor, but covert elements of hidden curricula that have been intentionally hidden and which some segments struggle to keep hidden. Curriculum is both a site of and one of the stakes in conflicts between various social groups. These curricula can best be discovered by examining such things as funding, salary levels, the sources of research support, the biases of standardized tests, and additional mechanisms of discrimination and oppression. Like Toto who pulled aside the curtain, some of the work of social science is to reveal the hidden hands and mechanisms that control the social structures—to make visible the powerful who benefit from the oppression of others. Many of the chapters in this volume do just that.

A BRIEF REVIEW OF THE "HIDDEN CURRICULUM"

Critical theorists have focused their attention on primary and secondary education. Clearly, this is an essential arena for the study of training, education, socialization, and social change. However, advancing technological society has prolonged the entire education process from kindergarten through high school to college and beyond. Alongside higher education's extension of function from an option for upward mobility to a requirement for social and economic survival, the structures of post-secondary education are rapidly changing. The old segmentations of elite versus mass education, private versus public, and the traditional disciplines of the sciences, liberal arts, and professional schools have differentiated into far more complicated structures. The advent of computer-mediated communications and distance learning, for-profit universities, and privatized research facilities are making it increasingly important to apply the insights of critical pedagogy to an examination of higher education. The concept of hidden curricula serves as one valuable theoretical framework from which to examine the social functions of higher education.

Functionalist Origins

Phillip Jackson (1968) is generally acknowledged as the originator of the term *hidden curriculum* in his book *Life in Classrooms*. Through observations of public grade school classrooms, Jackson identified features of classroom life that were inherent in the social relations of schooling. He observed that there were values, dispositions, and social and behavioral expectations that brought rewards in school for students and that learning what was expected along these lines was a feature of the hidden curriculum. He argued that the hidden curriculum emphasized specific skills: learning to wait quietly, exercising restraint, trying, completing work, keeping busy, cooperating, showing allegiance to both teachers and peers, being neat and punctual, and conducting oneself courteously (Jackson 1968, 10–33). These features of school life and requirements for conformity to institutional expectations had little to do with educational goals, but were essential for satisfactory progression through school. About the same time Robert Dreeben (1967) argued that the structure of family life alone could not adequately prepare children for the adult world. He examined the norms of school culture and concluded they taught students to "form transient social relationships, submerge much of their personal identity, and accept the legitimacy of categorical treatment" (Dreeben 1968, 147). The organization of schooling, such as having to wait before getting time with the teacher—transmits these ideas to students. Dreeben maintained that the experience of formal schooling not only taught the overt curriculum, but indirectly conveyed to students values such as independence and achievement, useful for their later membership in adult society.

Jackson and Dreeben were drawing heavily on the work of Emile Durkheim, who observed that public schools perform a specific and central form of socialization that other institutions cannot provide. Durkheim ([1925]1961, 147) noted that the family:

> [E]specially today, is a very small group of persons who know each other intimately and who are constantly in contact with one another. As a result, their relationships are not subject to any general, impersonal, immutable regulation. . . . [T]he morality practiced in this setting is above all a matter of emotion and sentiment. The abstract idea of duty is less important here than sympathy.

In contrast, schools were precisely concerned with abstract social connections like "duty":

> In fact, there is a whole system of rules in the school that predetermine the child's conduct. He must come to class regularly, he must arrive at a specified time and with an appropriate bearing and attitude. He must not disrupt things in class. He must have learned his

lessons, done his homework, and have done so reasonably well, etc.
There are, therefore, a host of obligations that the child is required
to shoulder. Together they constitute the discipline of the school. It
is through the practice of school discipline that we can inculcate the
spirit of discipline in the child. (Durkheim [1925]1961, 148)

According to Durkheim, "Society can survive only if there exists
among its members a significant degree of homogeneity; education per-
petuates and reinforces this homogeneity by fixing in the child, from
the beginning, the essential similarities collective life demands"
([1922]1956, 70). Talcott Parsons (1959), in the "The School Class as a
Social System," defended the Durkheimian position that what is essential in a stable and orderly society is the existence of a moral consensus
or a set of common values. Socializing children to hold particular values such as those of "achievement" and "equality of opportunity" is
necessary to this consensus and is the primary function of education.
Parsons contended that schools impart the ideology that inequalities in
income and social class status are consequences of differences in educational attainment, and are thus to be expected. This "winning and losing" notion of achievement maintains that those who do well in school
ought to be highly rewarded. Parsons believed that the sorting and
selecting of students through a selection procedure that gives the
appearance of rewarding hard work and talent neutralizes inequality.
Such an ideological structure positions subsequent differences in occupational or social class outcomes as fair, thus discouraging resentment
by "the losers in the competition." Conflict is thereby avoided and the
whole process serves an integrative function by developing in students
the societal values that will sustain a common American culture.

Marxist Perspectives

These fundamental works of Durkheim, Parsons, Jackson, and
Dreeben, sometimes collected under the heading of *consensus theory,*
provide the foundation for the general definition of the hidden curriculum as the elements of socialization that take place in school, but
are not part of the formal curricular content. These include the norms,
values, and belief systems embedded in the curriculum, the school, and
classroom life, imparted to students through daily routines, curricular
content, and social relationships. Starting in the 1960s consensus
theory came under broad and sustained attack in the field of sociol-

ogy (Mills 1959; Sartre 1960; Marcuse 1960, 1966; Natanson 1962; Van Den Berghe 1963; Horton 1968; Gouldner 1970; Collins 1971). Influenced by Marxism, some branches of subsequent educational theorizing became more critical about the way in which schools serve capitalism and the state and function to mediate and legitimate the reproduction of inequality, including social class, racial, and gender relations.[3] The socialization process was analyzed in terms of its reproduction of stratified relationships, outcomes, and ideological belief structures.

The most influential examination of the process by which schools reproduce these dominant interests was *Schooling in Capitalist America* by Samuel Bowles and Herbert Gintis (1976). In what they termed the "correspondence thesis," these economists demonstrated the relationship between the norms of schooling and the maintenance of the capitalist system. They argued that through formal and hidden curricula schools reproduce the social relations necessary to maintain capitalism: competition and evaluation, hierarchical divisions of labor, bureaucratic authority, compliance, and the fragmented and alienated nature of work. They argued that the reproduction of these skills and attitudes through the educational system corresponds to and prepares students for future stratified work roles. Embedded in the form, content, organization of the classroom, and the evaluation of students is a message system that conditions students to adopt the traits of punctuality, docility, cleanliness, and conformity. The exact message varied according to the social class of the community around the school. Students in upper-middle-class schools got some messages about internalizing the drive to achieve, while those in working-class schools rehearsed the behaviors appropriate for low-skill, low-autonomy work. For Bowles and Gintis, the hidden curriculum is the process of inculcating these behaviors through the natural and everyday features of school life. Although their analysis draws upon and echoes some of the points made by the functionalists, it differs in its argument that what appears on the surface as a necessary and neutral process of social reproduction serves the demands of more powerful institutions and dominant social groups.

Pierre Bourdieu and Basil Bernstein developed structuralist cultural reproduction theories that extended correspondence theory by recognizing culture (hence education) as a more or less autonomous sphere rather than simply an epiphenomenon of the relations of production.

French scholar Bourdieu (1973, 40) asserted that students vary in the nature of their early socialization, bringing to school a characteristic class "habitus" or a system of social meanings and understandings. Habitus derived from family environments may or may not contain the "cultural capital" or "symbolic wealth" that makes educational success a likely outcome (Bourdieu 1973, 73). Students of middle-class parents are advantaged because schools privilege the social, economic, and cultural capital they bring with them. These students have often attended nursery schools, have access to piano lessons and computers, and in general have been exposed and continue to be exposed to enriching social experiences throughout their school career, developing a reservoir of cultural and social resources. The skills, knowledge, and cultural grammar middle-class students from the dominant culture acquire via such exposure gives them an advantage in decoding and moving comfortably about the school system. By taking for granted such knowledge and treating it as equivalent to "talent" or "intelligence," schools perpetuate an uneven distribution of cultural capital as well as economic capital. In the process, they endorse and normalize particular types of knowledge, ways of speaking, styles, meanings, dispositions, and worldviews.

Bernstein (1977), too, writing from Britain, "emphasizes the mediation of the family between class origins and school as the critical source of class inequality" (MacDonald 1980b, 21). His examination of social class–based linguistic codes was enormously influential within the sociology of education. Schools generally work within what Bernstein called an "elaborated code," one that is compatible with the ways of using language in middle-class households. Kathleen Weiler (1988, 11–12), like other analysts, saw many commonalities between the ideas of Bourdieu and Bernstein:

> Thus for Bernstein, as for Bourdieu, different class language and knowledge lead to different educational paths; schools, by employing and legitimating the language and culture of the existing dominant groups, act to reproduce existing class structure.

Weiler (1988, 11) considered both writers to present an implicitly functionalist view of schooling: actual experiences in classrooms are not investigated directly, and students and teachers are passive recipients of the reproduction process. Several feminist writers from Britain,

Canada, and the United States have built on *and extended* ideas from these theorists, in particular noting the extent to which it is the work of mothers that is crucial to the culturally reproductive processes of schooling (David 1993; Griffith and Smith 1987; Lareau 1989; Smith 1990). Dorothy Smith (1990, 235), for example, one of Canada's foremost feminist scholars, commented that mothers, especially those from the middle-class, consciously produce in their young children "a good vocabulary or such competencies as knowing how to return a brush used for one colour to the pot of that colour so that the different colours do not get all mixed together. It is the investment of mother's work and thought in activities of these kinds which prepares children for school."

British Sociologists of Education

The 1970s was the formative decade for critical sociology of education in a number of countries. In Britain, for example, prior to the late 1970s most of the research sought to investigate the relationship between social class origins and educational outcomes, producing an important body of work, often informed by a conflict view of society, but nevertheless one that was somewhat limited by its positivism and tendency to ignore matters within the school itself. A few early exceptions were studies by Hargreaves (1967) and Lacey (1970), who drew from anthropology to venture into ethnographic studies of the differentiating processes of the school (e.g., streaming—the equivalent of tracking in the United States) that tended to reproduce social class divisions. In 1971, the publication of *Knowledge and Control*, edited by M. F. D. Young, marked a more general change of direction, raising serious questions about how schools processed and defined knowledge. The volume ushered in the loosely bounded movement known as the "new sociology of education." As Sandra Acker's review of the literature demonstrated (1994, 15ff.), these sociologists renewed attention to the reproductive functions of the curriculum in its formal and informal guises. Ignoring the functionalist term *hidden curriculum*, the British scholarship nonetheless investigated similar issues and built on the two theoretical perspectives discussed earlier: the Marxist *social* reproduction analysis of Louis Althusser (1971) and Bowles and Gintis (1976) and the *cultural* reproduction theories of Bernstein (1977) and Bourdieu (Bourdieu and Passeron 1977) (see MacDonald [later Arnot] 1980a, 13–14). Developing in parallel and sometimes in tension with these theoretical developments were ethnographic studies of schools that took their theoretical approach from the symbolic interactionism of George Herbert Mead and Herbert Blumer (Ball 1981; Burgess 1983; Woods 1979, 1983). These studies emphasized ways in which different types of schools created cultures and subcultures and shaped student and teacher perspectives and interactions.

Two important ethnographic studies of the 1970s came out of the neo-Marxist wing of the new sociology of education: Rachel Sharp and Anthony Green's study of primary schooling, *Education and Social Control* (1975); and a study of working-class boys by Paul Willis, *Learning to Labour: How Working Class Kids Get Working Class Jobs* (1977). Sharp and Green drew on phenomenology as well as neo-Marxism. They continued the analysis of differentiation pioneered by Hargreaves and Lacey, but examined it at the classroom level, identifying processes whereby children's identities became "reified" (rigidly characterized, labeled, often according to social background) despite teachers' ideological adherence to a liberal and progressive pedagogy. In order for the progressive pedagogies to proceed, the teacher relied on the "normal" children keeping themselves occupied, a "bedrock of busyness" (Sharp and Green 1975, 122), while the teacher worked either with the problem children or with the bright ones who formed an elite, sharing "intersubjectivity" with the teacher herself. While on the surface there was encouragement of individualism, the reality was that the classroom was a stratified society that paralleled society at large. Willis's study was probably the most well-known on both sides of the Atlantic and influenced the approach termed "resistance theory." Willis introduced a theory of cultural production that emphasized the agency that some working-class young men displayed in constructing a culture in opposition to the regime of schooling. In "celebrating" this culture, they succeeded in the short run in defying the efforts of the school to force them into conformity, but ended up confirming their own destinies, so to speak, in restricted forms of manual labor.

Willis was heavily criticized for equating working-class "kids" with working-class boys. The racism and sexism expressed by these lads was deemphasized in his account in comparison to their affirmation of working-class male culture. Willis was in good company, as British sociology of education remained male-centered until about 1980 (Acker 1981, 1994), a phenomenon also observed in North

America and even among leftist sociologists of education such as Bowles and Gintis (Gaskell 1992, 26–27).

By the early 1980s British sociologists of education, together with counterparts elsewhere, were rapidly modifying class analysis to incorporate gender inequality. A number of influential anthologies were published in the 1980s that included both empirical studies and theoretical analyses of gender (e.g., Arnot and Weiner 1987; Women's Studies Group 1978; Deem 1980; Spender and Sarah 1980; Walker and Barton 1983; Arnot and Weiner 1987). Madeleine MacDonald [Arnot] (1980a; 1980b) set forth a project based on neo-Marxist understandings supplimented by feminism to examine how schooling functioned to reproduce stratified gender relations. Angela McRobbie (1978) and other scholars undertook qualitative studies of working-class girls parallel to Willis's work. Mary Fuller (1980, 1982) looked at the forms resistance took when practiced by black girls.

One study that explicitly named the hidden curriculum was Kathleen Clarricoates's (1978) charmingly titled article "Dinosaurs in the Classroom." Clarricoates described the ways in which teachers sought to capture the interest of recalcitrant boys by shaping the early grades' curriculum around the boys' interests (which, at the time of her study, was dinosaurs). Teachers counted on the girls' putting up with topics that interested the boys, but failed to challenge the boys' disdain for anything perceived to be a girls' topic (such as "flowers" or "houses"). Clarricoates illustrated the ways in which gender inequities were confirmed as a "natural" outgrowth of school policies and pedagogies. The interest in school-supported differentiation and its relationship to occupational outcomes persisted in studies such as Sheila Riddell's (1992) *Gender and the Politics of Curriculum*, which examined ways in which the process of subject choice in secondary schools confirmed class and gender divisions. Similar concerns with the ways in which the hidden curriculum (whether or not labeled as such) shaped and limited girls' aspirations could be found in Canada (Gaskell 1992) and the United States (Valli 1986). By the late 1980s, it was increasingly commonplace to consider the intersections of race, class, and gender (Brah and Minhas 1985; Bryan, Dadzie, and Scafe 1987; Wright 1987; Mirza 1992, 1993) and attention was paid to the normative order of heterosexuality in the school and its consequences for gay and lesbian students (Holly 1989; Kelly 1992; Mac an Ghaill 1994; Trenchard and

Warren 1987). By the mid-1990s, interest in the socialization processes in schools appeared to be declining, as the dominant theme in British sociology of education turned to the analysis of the implications of government educational policy "reforms."

Critical Theorists in the United States

A number of American critical curriculum theorists and sociologists were exposed to (and influenced) the new sociology of education in Britain through their participation in a series of influential conferences starting in the late 1970s held at Westhill College, Birmingham, England.[4] Theorists including Michael Apple, Jean Anyon, Henry Giroux, and Peter McLaren engaged in the project of describing how hidden curricular practices provided qualitatively differential forms of schooling to students from different social classes. Challenging the ideological perspectives of early curriculum movements, Apple and King (1977, 86) pointed out that:

> Deeply embedded in their ideological perspective was a "strong" sense of control wherein education in general and the everyday meanings of the curriculum in particular were seen as essential to the preserving of the existing social privilege, interests, and knowledge of one element of the population at the expense of less powerful groups.

Apple went on to ask how the educational system preserved a social order stratified by class, gender, and race: "A fundamental problem facing us is the way in which systems of domination and exploitation persist and reproduce themselves without being consciously recognized by the people involved" (Apple 1982, 13). Students encounter norms, values, and beliefs through the rules and practices that form the daily routines and social relationships in the classroom and the extended school. This hidden curriculum, grounded in industry's attempt to control labor and increase productivity, must also foster faith in the putative "neutrality" of schools and the supposed "natural" environment of education and tolerance (Apple 1982, 12; Marcuse 1969).

In a particularly telling study, Anyon (1980) studied fifth grade classrooms differentiated by social class, and observed variations in the physical, curricular, evaluatory, pedagogical, and interpersonal characteristics of each environment. Anyon demonstrated how these variations contribute to the development in the children of certain potential relationships to physical and symbolic capital, to authority, and to the process of work. In light of such studies, critical pedagogues also came to identify those things both intentionally and unintentionally excluded from curricula because of their controversial nature, because they represent different values, or because educators are uninformed and relevant materials are nonexistent.

From the 1970s onward, educational researchers from the United States and elsewhere in the world advanced the discussion from labor force correspondence to consideration of gender, race, conflict, resistance, and the political function of schooling (Anyon 1980; Martin 1994; Kessler, Ashenden, Connell, and Dowsett 1985; Everhart 1983; Giroux 1981, 1983a; Grant and Sleeter 1986; Kenway and Willis 1997; McNeil 1986; Thorne 1993; Weiler 1988; Weis and Fine 1993; Wexler 1992; Willis [1977] 1981; Young 1971).

In the United States, gender role reproduction was examined in works by Kelly and Nihlen (1982), Grant (1992), and Thorne (1993). Gail Kelly and Ann Nihlen (1982, 167) specifically discussed the hidden curriculum in connection with the reproduction of gender divisions, considering "the messages implicit in the authority structure of the school, its staffing patterns, and the ways in which the curriculum is transmitted, and the systems of rewards and 'correct' behavior." Linda Grant (1992) studied the ways in which different groups of children experienced different hidden curricula, even within the same classroom. White girls were closely tied to their teachers and encouraged to develop academic and social skills, intellectual competence, and deference. African-American girls in the same elementary school classrooms were encouraged to emphasize social competence alone, and they played roles in the classroom such as "go-between" (between the other students and the teacher) and "enforcer" (helping the teacher control the class). Grant made connections between these differentiated skills and typical job market patterns. Barrie Thorne (1993) conducted a closely observed study of children's behavior in classrooms and playgrounds, unearthing ways in which the language and practices of the classroom confirmed the separation of the sexes. In an approach reminiscent of Jackson's original identification of hidden curricular processes, she commented:

> The practices of school staff are complex and often contradictory, sometimes reinforcing and sometimes undermining social divisions and larger patterns of inequality. The organizational features of schools also work in both ways. . . . Several basic features of schools that distinguish them from neighborhoods—their *formal age-grading*, their *crowded and public* nature, and the continual presence of *power and evaluation*—enter into the dynamics of gender separation and integration. [italics in the original] (Thorne 1993, 51)

Apple turned to an examination of covert curricular forms. Through the curriculum, students' activities, increasingly specified as rules, processes, and outcomes, are integrated through and rationalized by the material itself (Apple 1982, 155). Apple asserted that the recent history of education in the United States was a continuous search for a general set of principles that could guide educational planning and evaluation. These principles are products of the social, political, and economic values of the dominant groups as well as the demands of the market. Thus, education was organized to assist in the production of the technical/administrative knowledge needed to expand markets, control production and labor, create greater artificial needs, and increase dependency on consumption (Apple 1982, 22). Educators searched for the "most efficient method" (Apple 1982, 12), and the curriculum became increasingly planned, systematized, and standardized. Moreover, the content of curriculum was reduced to that which can be measured by standardized texts (Apple 1988). As a result teachers become mere accessories to the educational machine. The same set of curricular principles led to the construction of "legitimate knowledge," as expressed in textbooks. Legitimate knowledge proceeds from the complex power relations and struggle among identifiable class, race, gender, and religious groups (Apple 1993, 46). Teaching literacy, for example, becomes the overt and covert shaping of students to accept things as molded for their consumption. "Literacy was often there to produce economic skills and a shared system of beliefs and values, to help create a 'national culture'" (Apple 1993, 44).[5] Indeed this is, to borrow from Peter McLaren (1988, 223), "a pedagogy of submission."

Henry Giroux (1983a, 48–60) defined four approaches to the concept of the hidden curriculum: traditional, liberal, radical, and dialectical critique. We have already discussed the first three approaches: the *traditional approach* (Jackson, Dreeben), which accepted uncritically the existing relationship between schools and the larger society; the *liberal approach* (Anyon, Martin), which located the hidden curriculum in specific social practices, cultural images, or forms of discourse that reinforced discrimination and prejudice but could potentially be uncovered and eliminated; and the *radical perspective* (Bowles and Gintis), which focused on the political economy of schooling and regarded the social relations of the production process as the determining force in shaping the school environment. Giroux's fourth approach, *dialectical critique* (grounded in the work of Paulo Freire and represented by authors such as Apple, Giroux, hooks, Macedo, and McLaren) is closely associated with the radical approach in that it rejected the one-sided structuralism and pessimism of the political economy posture. It postulates that hidden curricula is plural and that contradictions open spaces for students and teachers to resist mechanisms of social control and domination and to create alternative cultural forms. This fourth approach is sometimes termed *resistance theory.*

Resistance Theorists

Critical theorists from the United States and Great Britain came to recognize that hegemonic ideology and practice is deeply and essentially conflicted. Because culture is lived and produced, they argued, schools cannot be understood as simply places where students are instructed, organized, and controlled by the interests of a dominant class. Students are not merely passive vessels but creatively act in ways that often contradict expected norms and dispositions that pervade the schools (Apple 1982, 95). Therefore to comprehend schooling, it must be understood as an arena of conflict, compromise, and struggle (Apple 1982, 23–31). In books like *Talking Back* (1989) and *Teaching to Transgress* (1994), bell hooks used her own experience to illustrate how individual students and teachers can recognize and thwart socialization regimes. Paulo Freire (1973, 1982, 1994) developed a large body of literature centered on literacy, the development of critical consciousness, and what he termed a "pedagogy of hope." Donaldo Macedo explored similar themes alongside Apple, Willis, McLaren, hooks, and Giroux. These resistance theorists would like us to counter any functionalist reading of the educational system by calling attention to the important role of agency, resistance, and contestation.

Henry Giroux (1983a, 61–63) for instance, built upon Apple's point that the hidden curriculum must be about both reproduction *and* transformation. He linked the structure of hidden curricula to notions of liberation, grounded in values of personal dignity and social justice. Schools therefore become sites of domination and contestation. This does not mean that the terrain is evenly shared between the forces of domination and resistance, or that all forms of oppositional behavior have a radical significance. Given that acts of resistance vary, each oppositional act must be analyzed to see if it constitutes a form of resistance (Giroux 1983a, 110).

Resistance theorists provide cultural space for possibility. They do not want to see the educational system as a reflection of the capitalist order with students and teachers as mere pawns moved by the logic of capital. The original functionalist approach as well as correspondence theory were rejected because they directed us to see the school only in reproductive terms and negated the possibility of contestation. Similarly, right and left functionalism denied the conflicted nature of education within the wider social, economic, and political order. For instance, the act of reading can be at one and the same time a form of regulation and exploitation *as well as* a mode of resistance, celebration, and solidarity (Apple 1993, 53). For this reason, Apple argued that the dominant society's hegemonic control is a dialectic not reducible to the simple interests of the dominant class (Apple 1982, 29).

The philosopher Jane Roland Martin (1994) proved logically that there is no universal agenda, that socialization exists only in particular context. Apple (1982) then emphasized that hidden curricula involve various interests, cultural forms, struggles, agreements, and compromises. Students are not simply passive receptacles but active players in the systems that attempt to socialize them. Students negotiate, accommodate, reject, and often divert socialization agendas. Hidden curricula occur at multiple places and times during schooling. Nonetheless, we can trace how both the form and the content of the curriculum reproduces structures of power and oppression. As Apple noted, however, we should not conceive of the curriculum as a thing, such as a syllabus or course of study. Rather, we should understand it as a symbolic, material, and human environment that is ongoingly reconstructed (Apple 1993, 144). Critical theorists correctly sought to keep open the possibility of human action and democracy. Nevertheless Apple and Giroux are dubious about the nature of resistance. Apple, for instance, recognized that contestation can be contradictory. It might serve to reinforce and reproduce existent power dynamics, as it did in Paul Willis's study. The process of contestation "may act in contradictory ways that may ultimately tend to be reproductive" (Apple 1982, 25)—a point supported by Giroux (1983a).

Kathleen Weiler (1988) provided an empirical example of the contradictions embedded in resistance by showing how high school students resisted efforts by feminist teachers to make them more conscious of gender inequities. Their resistance is not simple obdurateness, but is grounded in their complex subjectivities, which combine classed, raced, and gendered elements. The white, middle-class women teachers were most comfortable with white, middle-class women students (akin to the intersubjectivity noted by Sharp and Green). In affirming a feminist interpretation of a discussion or class reading as "correct," or in supporting "the girls" in a dispute, the teachers are often denying a competing reality of the boys or the working-class students in the class. Thus resistance seems inevitable and its heroic status questionable.

CONCLUSION

The idealism expressed in Giroux, Macedo, and Freire's "politics of hope" may have run its course. In this volume, most of the authors sin on the side of structuralism and functionalism rather than displaying an excessive faith in agency. While sympathetic to the possibility of resistance, they give full weight to the power of institutions to manage contestation, reproduce hierarchy, and resist change. Michael Soldatenko's article, for example, analyzed how the Chicano movement (and by extension the women's, gay, and other ethnic studies movements) was "socialized" from movement to stasis by various hidden curricula in the university.

The concept of hidden curriculum bridges any simple attempt to distinguish social from cultural reproduction or to define a special zone of creativity and freedom. In the following chapters, the authors reveal how the structural production of inequality goes along with the socialization to assent to and believe in that inequality: Kenneth Ehrensal demonstrates how prospective managers are selected and segregated from workers while simultaneously schooled to see their interests in

opposition to workers. Caroline Childress describes a program specifically designed to lower the expectations of dislocated professionals so
they willingly apply for lower-status jobs serving local employers.
Linda Muzzin and Karen Tonso give complementary views of how
women become second-class citizens in professional schools: Tonso
demonstrates how women are systematically excluded both physically
and socially from the world of engineers; and Muzzin explains how
the woman-dominated profession of pharmacy is devalued and disre-
spected in pharmacy schools controlled by international biotechnology firms. Carrie Yang Costello examines how the status and beliefs,
values and attitudes of future lawyers and social workers are conditioned by the physical environment of their schools. Sandra Acker, Eric
Margolis and Mary Romero closely interrogate the personal relationships of thesis advising and mentoring to consider how cultural capital and habitus affect performance in graduate school. Mary Jane
Curry pursues a similar interest in her participant observation of an
ESL classroom where immigrants/refugees are "assimilated" by a
"free" program intended to teach English but more successful at inculcating the value "in the United States you get what you pay for."

This volume only scratches the surface of a very large project. Until
recently, theorizing and ethnographic studies on the hidden curriculum have been limited to primary and secondary schooling. The function of education in primary schooling is to transmit the necessary
values of society, social consensus, and integration; later schooling has
the task of differentiating, recruiting, selecting, and grooming students
for adult occupational roles. While the purposes may appear distinct,
the traditions of the hidden curriculum remain similar: education is an
agency of differentiation and stratification, holding the keys that access
valued cultural elements. Aside from studies such as Bergenhenegouwen's "Hidden Curriculum in the University" (1987), Holland and
Eisenhart's *Educated in Romance: Women, Achievement and College
Culture* (1990), Astin's *What Matters in College?* (1993), and Margolis and Romero's "The Department Is Very White, Very Male, Very
Old and Very Conservative: The Functioning of the Hidden Curriculum in Graduate Sociology Departments" (1998), little has been written directly about hidden curricula in higher education. The lack of
literature raises questions that are at least partially answered in the
studies included in this volume: How does the socialization process
continue in higher education? What new elements of hidden curricula

appear in higher education? What forms do they take? And specifically, how do institutions of higher learning reinforce gender, race, and social class distinctions ultimately producing stratified outcomes? In our attempt to get a theoretical handle on these phenomena theoretically, we sought the collective insights of a variety of contemporary educational theorists—including some of those who developed the concept of hidden curriculum. The next chapter of this volume sums up those views.

NOTES

1. Taken from the online version at http://bau2.uibk.ac.at/sg/poe/works/p_letter.html

2. Taken from an online version of the Hans Christian Andersen story. http://www.geocities.com/athens/2424/clothes.html

3. For a particularly succinct statement of a Marxist position on the relation of education to the state and ruling classes, see "Ideology and Ideological State Apparatuses: Notes towards an Investigation" (Althusser [1970] 1971, 155–56).

4. Conference proceedings were published, including: *Schooling, Ideology and the Curriculum* (Barton, Meighan, and Walker 1980) and *Class Gender and Education* (Walker and Barton 1983).

5. For a detailed exposure of these practices in an ESL class see the Curry article in this volume.

6. Thus the question of contestation is not simply about literacy or texts but about social groups and institutions (Guillory 1987).

7. In another text, Apple returned to the ambiguity of contestation. The controversy over official knowledge, Apple noted, usually centers around what is included and excluded in textbooks. Pressure can be brought to include writers or writings earlier excluded from the text. Apple termed this form of compromise "mentioning." Mentioning may integrate new elements into the selective tradition; however, their close association to the values of the dominant group subordinates them. Thus "[d]ominance is partly maintained here through compromise and the process of 'mentioning'" (Apple 1993, 56).

Hiding in Plain Sight[1] 2
Marina Gair and Guy Mullins

In response to our interview questions, Peter McLaren used Edgar Allan Poe's short story "The Purloined Letter" to point to a lucid characteristic of the hidden curriculum: "The best way to hide something is to put it right in front of somebody's eyes where they are not looking for it ... [the purloined letter] was put in such an obvious place nobody bothered to look there because it was too obvious. That is in a sense a metaphor for what has happened to universities." Much like the purloined letter, the hidden curriculum hides "in plain sight." As with many of the scholars we interviewed, McLaren used a metaphor as a beginning to his analysis and wove theory into his lived experiences as an academic. This chapter was written as a companion to the literature review in the introduction to explore ways in which the concept *hidden curricula* can be explicitly applied to higher education. We wanted to understand how scholar/educators in the academic community perceive and conceptualize the socialization functions of post-secondary school. We interviewed a variety of faculty and administrators, many of whom have contributed to the literature on socialization and hidden curricula in primary and secondary school.

This project grew out of a larger study that utilizes methods of visual ethnography. The research began as an assignment to photograph the hidden curriculum on campus. The collection of photographs provided a broad spectrum of visual imagery of the hidden curriculum; however, much of the data on the subject could not adequately be gathered using still image techniques alone. Physical depictions of certain elements of hidden curricula, including classroom structures, architecture, fraternity and sorority gatherings, and representations of school pride, were somewhat obvious, but a large part of what constitutes the hidden curriculum—social relations like race and gender hierarchy, social class reproduction, the inculcation of ideological belief structures, and so on—was much less visible. Because it proved challenging to capture and illustrate socialization processes visually, we began to further "photograph" the hidden curriculum by videotaping interviews with scholars in the field of education on the topic. The goal of our larger study was to produce *multitextural* documents that utilize visual techniques but are grounded in theory and research, including a video documentary entitled *Right Before Your Eyes: Conversations on the Hidden Curriculum*, and an interactive Internet dialog for "public elicitation" of continuing research.[2]

To date, we have conducted open-ended interviews with twenty-one members of the academic community including university and community college faculty, deans, and administrators. Subjects were selected based on their professional experience and contributions to the literature on socialization and hidden curricula. However, our selection process was strongly determined by lack of funding, which necessitated interviewing easily accessible participants. The video interviews were conducted either at Arizona State University during Spring Symposia visits or on location at professional conferences that we attended. Data collection began late in 1998 and continued through early 2000. The interviews were semistructured, engaging interviewees in a conversational inquiry about the hidden curriculum that lasted approximately one hour. While some general questions were employed for consistency, discussions developed in directions suggested by the interests and experience of the interviewees. Table 2.1 (see p. 41) lists the interview subjects. Interviews were transcribed and coded. The following categories of the hidden curriculum emerged from our analysis of the interviews: (1) perspectives and definitions of the concept; (2) the role of the physical environment; (3) the importance of the body; (4) intentional or overt socialization practices that were not particularly well hidden; (5) socialization functions taught as elements of professionalization, and resistance to attempts at socialization.

COMING TO TERMS:
DEFINITIONS OF THE HIDDEN CURRICULUM

One of the most problematic aspects of the hidden curriculum is in the name itself. Many of those interviewed struggled with the inadequacy of terms for describing how extracurricular information is conveyed in the process of higher education. Just as the term *hidden agenda* conjures up something covert or undisclosed, *hidden curricula* suggests intentional acts to obscure or conceal—a conscious duplicity that may not always be present. However, the hidden curriculum is not something that we must look behind or around in order to detect; in most cases it is plainly in sight, and functions effortlessly. For example, Roxana Ng (Department of Sociology and Equity Studies in Education, University of Toronto) characterized the hidden curriculum as "the way in which business as usual takes place in the university." A similar point was expressed by Alexander Astin (Higher Education Policy, UCLA) in his reference to values and the way that they unconsciously dictate various hidden curricula:

> Values are at the very basis of education. . . . Just having a curricular requirement is a value. We can't escape values; they are embedded in everything we do. What we can do is to ignore the value questions and act as though they don't exist . . . which is what I think we have been doing.

Karen Anijar (Division of Curriculum and Instruction, Arizona State University) also noted the embeddedness of values as a component of the hidden curriculum and specifically highlighted how it operates on a semiotic level: "In the university we have 'excellence' values. . . but the unit of measure by which we are measuring what excellent is, is absolutely obscured for us."

The Donaldo Macedo (Department of English and director of bilingual and ESL studies, University of Massachusetts) definition underscored how socialization penetrates and transforms the individual: "What I see as hidden curriculum is how it's really embedded in the psyche and the discourse and the attitude." Mary Romero (School of Justice Studies, Arizona State University) elaborated the critical process whereby curricula are embedded and naturalized, in other words, "hidden":

> Part of surviving an institution and making it in a profession is learn-
> ing to ignore, or to become part of it, and so that it also all of a
> sudden dissolves, it becomes invisible. So then we also become part
> of the institution.

Interviewees provided a variety of thick definitions for the concept.
Individual interpretations of *hidden curricula* depended largely on two
things: (1) interviewees' political leanings, disciplines, and paradigmatic perspectives; and, (2) their individual experience of hidden curricula in the context of their education, research, and teaching.
Generally, the term was given different meanings depending upon the
functionalist, liberal, humanist, Marxist, or critical postmodernist
paradigms of the interviewees.[3] Most subjects provided critical perspectives of hidden curricula, challenging one-dimensional interpretations of the concept. For example, Anijar made the point that hidden
curricula are plural when she identified the protean nature of the curricula process in her definition:

> I don't think there's a singular hidden curriculum. I think it's some-
> thing that transforms itself like anything else. I don't think it's some-
> thing that's singular or constant. I think it changes, it moves. . . . It
> doesn't remain constant. If it remained constant it would be easy to
> unearth and deconstruct and everybody would know about it and
> where it would occur. . . . It moves and it reconfigures itself like any-
> thing else. It's a process. . . .

Recognizing plurality and process is essential in challenging the early
reproduction theories of Durkheim, Dreeben, and Jackson, who de-
picted students as passive receptacles for unified and unproblematic
social messages. The presence of multiple and conflicting messages opens
up spaces for students and faculty to be active players in the systems that
attempt to socialize them. Michael Apple (Division of Curriculum and
Instruction and Educational Policy Studies, University of Wisconsin,
Madison) in his definition challenged the perception of students and
teachers as simply passive receptacles, and included agency and the development of strategies to avert the institutional requirements of school:

> There is no real hidden curriculum that simply socializes these pas-
> sive beings as if they're puppets whose strings are somehow pulled

by the major marionette at the university. So the way I tend to look about this is that institutions, to use the metaphor I like to use, are "arenas." Where there are various interests, various cultural forms, various struggles, various agreements and compromises, in which students are pretty active players. . . . So when I talk about the hidden curriculum . . . it is one way of talking about the way in which cultural struggles and policies—people's lives—are conditioned by an institution.

Critical postmodern and Marxist interpretations of the topic drew attention to the curricular, ideological, physical, and structural components of schooling that privilege dominant interests and ultimately serve social class reproductive ends. Peter McLaren (Division of Urban Schooling, Graduate School of Education and Information Studies, UCLA) captured this aspect of hidden curricula as *accomplishments* of the university, itself a central institution of the larger capitalist system:

> I guess the hidden curriculum, one could say, consists of the tacit ways in which knowledge and behavior get constructed outside the usual course materials and scheduled lessons in a way to conduce us to comply with dominant ideologies, dominant social practices so that there is an inducement. . . . How does the institutional site that we are working in organize desire? How does it deploy discourses in particular ways? How does it set up the environment? All these factors are important when you discuss the hidden curriculum.

Many of those interviewed underscored the functions of hidden curricula in (re)producing inequality and differential outcomes. Even the grading system reflects ideology, as Donald Blumenfeld-Jones (Division of Curriculum and Instruction, Arizona State University) explains: "We think that we need to compare people to each other to give those who have better grades—meaning more cultural capital, more school capital—that translates into more material capital for them."

However, some definitions of members of the academic community corresponded with Jackson's (1968) and Dreeben's (1968) observations, conceptualizing hidden curricula as necessary socializing mechanisms that shaped desired behavioral outcomes. For administrators like Elizabeth Miller (Director, Center for Teaching Excellence,

Texas A&M), socialization was a central feature of college: "From day one we talk about traditions, traditions, traditions. And how the Aggie is this and the Aggie is that and the Aggie is the other. A lot of our ethics are taught through that." Miller's functionalist perspective emphasized the hidden curriculum as a necessary element of social reproduction, serving an essential integrative function and inculcating students with desirable societal values.

An analysis of the various interpretations of the hidden curriculum points to the redefinition as more than an issue of semantics, but a critical assessment of whether or not socialization is "hidden" in the sense of attempting to deceive, or simply an embedded, accepted component of the educational process that has not been directly examined. While each interviewee unpacked the term and framed the concept to capture the realities of its effects, taken collectively, there was little departure from two early definitions of "hiddenness" employed by Jackson (1968) and Vallance ([1973/1974] 1983). No single definition emerged from the interviews, nor was anything radically new added. This suggests that while complex, the concept is relatively well defined and understood.

In moving from the literature on kindergarten through high school, to the observations made by interviewees in this study of post–secondary education, it became clear that while certain applications may be different, as Anijar stated: "The specifics of where it [in a public school situation or a private school] appears in each instance might be different but there really is no difference from what is going on in an elementary school." In identifying hidden curriculum in higher education, Romero underscored the persistence of structures that discipline and socialize:

> Hidden curriculum I see as the values and norms that get embedded into the way that we structure our courses, the way that we structure our curriculum, the way that we structure the organization. And I think a lot of these elements may be established as intended, as well as unintended.

Applying this to the curriculum of the School of Justice Studies where she teaches, Romero explained how values and norms get incorporated:

There are certain faculty that would emphasize justice issues in terms of social justice in terms of an understanding of collective justice in terms of larger society and there will be other faculty that will emphasize individual rights versus group rights. You can see how part of that hidden curriculum gets into our larger public debates over affirmative action, use of vouchers in funding public schools.

Blumenfeld-Jones noted the "authoritarian hierarchical structures" that distinguish persons in the classroom as "expert talkers and there are inexpert listeners." We can again look back to Philip Jackson's early work, which made an important point reiterated in our interviewees' definitions and understandings of the topic: "Life in college classrooms is surely different from life in lower grades, but beneath the obvious differences lies a basic similarity. In a fundamental sense, school is school, no matter where it happens" (1968; 1990, xxi). For the most part, the hidden curriculum remains an embedded and largely ignored element of academic life.

THE HIDDEN CURRICULUM AS MANIFESTED IN THE PHYSICAL ENVIRONMENT

A number of interviewees drew attention to architecture and the physical environment as elements of the hidden curriculum that functioned as socialization factors. Like Bill Williamson (1974, 10–11), a British sociologist, who wrote "educational attitudes of dominant groups in society still carry historical weight and are exemplified even in the bricks and mortar of the school buildings themselves," interviewees reflected on the built environment of their institutions, and suggested that buildings, the physical arrangement of classrooms, occupation of physical space, and other architectural structures honor certain histories and convey political agendas. In making this point, Blumenfeld-Jones linked the structure of the university buildings to the structure of curriculum.[4]

Looking at the building you are to have a certain attitude towards education and towards that institution that's embodied in that building. When you walk through the doors—through the arched door with the gothic work on the wood, and the stone work, and the

windows and all of that—you are to feel a certain something. The
way in which you structure an institution tells you about the desires
and agendas of that institution.

Interviewees that noted the embodiment of attitudes, emotions, and
dispositions toward education and learning in physical structures
almost always pointed to the divisions among disciplines. Architectural investments were noted in schools of engineering, business, and
the physical sciences. By contrast, the humanities and social sciences
were cited as examples of disciplines housed in vernacular buildings
with less stature on campus and less prominence in terms of physical
space (e.g., temporary structures or basements). The following quote
by Blumenfeld-Jones captures this observation:

> Most university administrations favor tremendously the natural sci-
> ences and mathematics. . . . I'd like to say it'll be a cold day in hell
> before Education gets a building as beautiful. So I'd say if you want
> to look for the hidden curriculum here [ASU], it is where does the
> money go for what kind of buildings—who gets the facilities?

The people we spoke with argued that emphasis in the built environment is largely a result of the rise of corporate culture on campus
and a push toward vocationalization and specialization. Disciplines in
the American academy have increasingly developed businesslike organizational cultures. For some scholar/educators in this study, not only
has higher education become a less independent subsector of the economy, but curricula—both formal and informal—are overdetermined
by the logic of exchange. In a higher education manifestation of Bowles
and Gintis's (1976) "correspondence thesis," one of the main purposes
that hidden curricula serve in the university is to prepare people for the
corporate world (Chubb and Moe 1990; Cohen 1993; Etzkowitz, Webster, and Healey 1998; Lucas 1994; Nelson 1997; Parsons and Platt
1973; Slaughter and Leslie 1997; Spring 1972; Shor 1980; McLaren
2000). Some of those we interviewed believe that informal curricula
and the belief system associated with capitalism reproduces individualism, competition, and a "natural" hierarchy based on what Parsons
(1959) described as the "winning and losing" notion of achievement.
The consensus is that even in the physical environment the hidden cur-

riculum implicitly orders and qualifies particular kinds of knowledge, meanwhile marginalizing "other" disciplines as "low status" and as providing less marketable knowledge. Collectively, scholars whom we interviewed expressed fears that what qualifies as worthwhile knowledge will more often be defined on the basis of its marketability rather than on its social functions.[5]

Most of those interviewed were skeptical of the blurring distinctions between university education and training for capitalist divisions of labor. They argued that corporate culture and the push toward vocational specialization in higher education has grown more dominant over the past several decades. Douglas Kellner (Graduate School of Education and Information Studies, UCLA) described professional socialization agendas as largely influenced by the habitus of corporate culture:

> I would agree that part of the hidden curriculum of the current structure and organization of education is bringing the marketplace, corporatization and business into the university and into schooling. . . . They see the corporate model as the model for schools.

In addition, our interviewees' critiques of the link between the physical environment and the curriculum frequently noted social stratification. Anijar called attention to specific messages of exclusion and inclusion written on the walls (i.e., graffiti and posters) and types of bodies enclosed within the walls:

> The buildings themselves tell you who belongs in there . . . what's on the walls tells you who belongs in there and who doesn't. Some people are in and some people are out. Some knowledge is privileged and some isn't. Yet we want to seem like we are inclusive and embracing.

Physical environment also structures the level of interaction between faculty and students, as observed by Romero:

> Our classrooms are not in the same building as our offices. Since classrooms are very spread out over a large area, the kind of interaction that might occur between students and faculty going to class in the same building where faculty have their offices, does not occur.

Christine Sleeter (director of Master of Arts in Education, CSU-Monterey Bay) identified a structural link between physical space, curriculum, and social stratification that is produced by the particular funding formulas in California:

> With the UC (University of California) system it's like a tracking system serving predominantly white middle- to upper-class students and getting a richer funding formula. And the CSU (California State Universities) serving predominantly working-class students of color and getting a poorer funding formula. . . . In order to get money from the state you have to be able to demonstrate that you're using the space you have in certain ways.

The physical environment of the classroom is codified as "student work stations" measured by square footage:

> What that does, is it translates into a conception of teaching as students come in and sit in fairly close rows. And if you want to have forms of pedagogy that involve people in either moving around . . . other than sitting in almost airplane seats, it starts running up against the constraints that were put into place for how you get funding to have this space in the first place.

Limited physical environment for teaching and learning restricts educators' choices of pedagogy and may influence some to abandon innovative programs and revert to restraining the minds and bodies of the working-class student:

> [W]hat begins to appear to me is that monies are available for taking largely working-class, in many cases underprepared students, who are coming into higher education, having kind of a batch processing curriculum, almost following the egg crate design that . . . you're supposed to put people in it for a certain amount of time, deliver a curriculum, test them over that curriculum and move them on.

THE HIDDEN CURRICULUM AS MANIFESTED IN THE BODY

The body itself, and the way in which it is schooled, were identified by several interviewees as sites for investigation of hidden curricula. The following section further explores the manifestation of the hidden curriculum in the gendered, racialized, class-based bodies of students and faculty. The body is a crucial socializing force that symbolizes gendered and racialized social meanings. Women and academics of color talked about regularly having to maintain a duplicity of being (DuBois 1989) in order to function in the university setting. Anijar offered the following example of how academic culture creates expectations of class-based gender behavior and presentation of self that worked to privilege and reproduce class status:

> When I was finishing my dissertation my advisor told me that when I go on my interviews. . . . I have to do sort of a wardrobe transformation because how I would dress would not be acceptable within the academy because it comes out of a certain social class. She said on my interviews I am to never eat spaghetti because you can't eat it without being sloppy. If everybody else is drinking, I ought not to be drinking because then it might be constructed that I am an alcoholic . . . even if I was sick from eating because they do the three meals a day I should eat because I am female and I don't want anyone to think that I have an eating disorder.

Eating too much or eating too little is less likely to be noticed or to carry the same negative consequences for the male body as it does for a female one. Other women and academics of color noted that they frequently found themselves alienated from university settings if their class and social status background was not congruent with that of the academic environment. Like Karen Anijar, they described dropping (or suspending as necessary) incompatible class habits, as well as feeling pressure to modify behavior and appearance because of gender, race, and ethnicity. Romero elaborated on the intersectionality of race, class, and gender with an example of how the hidden curriculum framed the Latina body as a site incompatible with Ivy League expectations.

> I remember very distinctly as assistant dean at Yale trying to get an idea of what would be the appropriate dress to wear to a particular activity. One of my colleagues, a white woman, said, "Just don't wear anything ethnic." I never thought of myself as wearing anything ethnic. But then I thought: Is it my earrings? Is it my jewelry? Is it my hair? The way I wear my hair? Should I be cutting my hair? Should

I be wearing it so it's tightly matted to my head? Or is there a particular kind of makeup? All that becomes a part of fitting the norm. That same year I recall an undergraduate Chicana I ran into as I was walking across campus. She shocked me by her comment. She said, "You know, today I almost went and got my hair cut, but I decided not to." I said, "Why?" She said, "Well it occurred to me that Dean Romero has frizzy hair so it's okay. I don't have to cut my hair." It never occurred to me that even my physical presence, my body, my hair would be part of being a role model to students who didn't have that image on a campus for them.

Michael Apple noted that within the one institution, different messages were received by students of color and white students:

As it becomes increasingly white, those people of color who come feel as if there is no community for them. So their hidden curriculum is very different than the hidden curriculum of dominant groups. They see very few people like themselves there, the lived culture of the institution makes them feel like *"the other."* What we have then is a group of people who basically come from families that have made it.

Romero described gendered and racialized bodies as functioning as visible signs of status and hierarchy that are sometimes reflected in white students' disrespect and rejection of women and faculty of color: "In talking to my colleagues, particularly white colleagues and even more so, male colleagues, I certainly get challenged more in terms of grades." This is a pretty open secret of campus life—the differing experiences that gender and race have on the act of teaching were acknowledged by several of the white academics interviewed. For instance, Peter McLaren commented:

I know that white students have raised questions with colleagues of mine who are African American or Latino/Latina in ways that they would never question a white professor in class. They just wouldn't think of questioning a white professor. Asking them to justify and almost testing them in ways they would never test a white professor.

Roxana Ng (Department of Sociology and Equity Studies in Education, Ontario Institute for Studies in Education, University of

Toronto) has written poignantly about how her anti-racist pedagogy produced opposition.[6] One white male student who was supported by various individuals in her institution filed a complaint, the handling of which demonstrates how sexism and racism disempower feminist and minority faculty:

> I was asked to teach this course on cross-culture education where I incorporated into the course both stuff on racial and ethnic minorities as well as gender issues. And halfway through the course a student was really mad and he complained that I was a biased teacher. . . . He complained to the chair of the department. And the chair asked to see me and he says there was this complaint. First of all, he said there were complaints. So I said, "How many?" He finally said it was actually only one student that complained. But somehow one student complaint overruled everybody who was actually getting something out of the course. There's kind of an implicit—almost agreement—among men in this context as students, as administrators. And I was told actually halfway through the year to change my curriculum.

The visibly gendered, class-based, and racialized body is clearly an important element of the hidden curriculum as it is transmitted through the interactions of students, professors, administrators, researchers, and scholars.

THE HIDDEN CURRICULUM OF INTENTIONAL PRACTICES

Many interviewees remarked that higher education institutions maintain overt socialization practices that are not really hidden because the outcomes are intentional. Higher education institutions intentionally configure their socialization practices to reproduce particular research interests, habits of mind, and social roles. In comparing interviewees' comments, it is clear that intentional socialization agendas vary across settings and depend on the way each university or department frames its work. For instance, Miller described Texas A&M's "other curriculum" that reinforced tradition as a fundamental aspect of campus identity:

> I think the hidden curriculum is probably one of the most important curricula that we have. We have unannounced curriculums that are

very important. . . . Texas A&M is a very tightly knit, very high tradition university, and that's one of the things that really knits us
together. There is an *esprit de corps* that is quite unique. A kind of
culture there is quite unique: "it's a kind of a one for all, and all for
one." It's kind of a three musketeers thing and it really spills over in
everything we do.

Another example was provided by Romero, who also observed overt
socialization practices that led to the development of distinct definitions of self as a leader:

At Yale, students impart a hidden curriculum as a message that you
are a leader. You are going to be leading the country. Thinking originally, thinking creatively, and learning new knowledge is important.

Apple described an intended hidden curriculum embedded in the University of Wisconsin's institutional mission to counter its radical past:

My own institution has a long history of radical political activity and
cultural experimentation. And for many people that's a little threatening. So parents want to hear publicly that there is an official hidden
curriculum at the institution which is don't worry when your children come here, they will be fine.

Higher education in the United States ranges from two-year community colleges to the Ivy Leagues, from general liberal arts programs
to graduate and professional education. Linda Darling-Hammond
(professor of education, Stanford University) argued that the overall
institutional mission can be revealed by analyzing the smaller socialization agendas:

Not all higher education institutions are the same. Some really see it
as their mission to provide access to a wide range of people, to really
create opportunity in the society, and many state universities configure their responsibility that way [but] not all of them do. But you can
also find public institutions that behave just as though they were private institutions in the way that they think of admissions, manage
financial aspects of the university, and see their mission as either a
teaching mission, a developmental mission, or a select and sort mis-

sion. And I think that plays out in the way universities make decisions about incentives for professors and rewards for teaching versus rewards for research, as much as it plays out in things like admissions policy.

Some institutions define themselves as "access expanders" for students, who for reasons of race, class, gender, economics, immigration, and language status would not have access to higher education. Such institutions focused their intentional practices and socialization agendas on producing support systems for their students. Others see themselves as elite finishing schools for the best and the brightest. Institutional differentiation along the lines Darling-Hammond discussed is a central feature of higher education's role in the reproduction of social stratification. This area of intentional socialization functions mentioned by our research subjects has not been well studied to date. However as traditional "brick and mortar" institutions are forced to compete with "virtual" colleges that provide on-line courses and distance learning, socialization will likely become an important marketing feature. This would be a fruitful area for a major research project.

NEGOTIATING PROFESSIONAL SOCIALIZATION AND RESISTANCE

Throughout the interviews we found that membership in any academic profession was discussed as an induction process requiring more than competence in a respective field. Moving from novice to professional was described as inculcating particular norms, perspectives, accepted tastes and attributes, jargon, attitudes, and institutionalized practices, as well as embracing certain ideologies.[7] The following statement by David Berliner (dean of the College of Education, Arizona State University) captures the general viewpoint: "You learn very quickly what you have to do to survive in any social situation. When you're trying to belong to a club and there are rules and it takes you a while to learn the rules. So the hidden curriculum is just that set of rules that's not made obvious." Also consistent across the interviews was the belief that the socialization process is more *"successful"* for those aligned with the values of particular institutional settings.

The alignment process requires submitting to a distinct class-based consciousness in order to acquire necessary symbolic capital (Bourdieu

1973, 1977; Bourdieu and Passeron, 1990). As indicated by the comments throughout the study, this consciousness includes race and gender. These elements of the hidden curriculum ultimately serve not only in the reproduction of both hierarchy and marginalization, but alienation as well. Speaking of their personal experiences or making observations of various institutional practices, many academics described how hidden curricula in higher education assimilate individuals into the class structure, practices, and values of an established predominantly white, male-oriented, middle-class academic environment.

The experiences and observations as shared by scholars in this study suggest a tension between acquiring the cultural capital which symbolizes membership in the academy and maintaining individual, cultural, and ideological integrity. It was clear that many of the scholars we interviewed had learned to maneuver throughout their careers with what Colin Lacey (1977, 14) called a "strategic compliance": bending to institutional constraints, but choosing to retain oppositional beliefs and ideologies. This delicate balance is implied in David Berliner's observation:

> What you want to do is get people to change the world and speak out as faculty members, and change the world of students, but at the same time the people who pay your salary are people who are in fact the established power structure of a society. And how do you do that in a way that allows for both change, personal growth, being a public intellectual, and not alienating the people who hold your purse strings. That's very tricky.

In describing her efforts to transform the curriculum, Ng reminded us of the risks and consequences of social opposition:

> You need to be conscious when you are challenging the system so that you're not doing it kind of naively. Through a lot of negotiations and struggles, people like myself have carved out spaces to do a different kind of work. . . . We carve out spaces, and the question then is how you actually operate in those spaces.

Although there was broad consensus among the academics included in this study regarding the tendency for hidden curricula to

reproduce dominant frames of reference through professional socialization, many held out the possibility of pedagogies of desocialization
and opposition. Throughout the interviews, they provided notions of
how higher education must also be conceptualized as an arena of resistance. They stressed the need for dissent, compromise, and even out-
right rejection of certain socializing influences. Several reflected on their
own praxis, illustrating the importance of developing cultural transformation by way of "antistructures" or "countercurricula" to challenge the prevailing social and ideological arrangements of the
university. Apple suggested the following strategy:

> At universities the hidden curriculum must be brought to an overt
> level, it must be thought about, it must be talked through and the
> kinds of norms and values you want to organize the workplace. . . .
> All of that should be brought to a level where people can participate
> in it, struggle over it, talk about it but it's got to be done in a way
> where people feel they can speak honestly and where the norms that
> are supposed to be usually hidden are democratic, participatory, and
> organized around critical intellectual and pedagogic work.

Sleeter and her colleagues at CSU appear to be engaged in such praxis
by recognizing that the funding formula restricts space and works
against their philosophy of education. They began a dialogue to explore ways to retain their vision of building a multicultural institution.

While many of those we interviewed seemed well aware of the
limits of resistance and the overwhelming reproductive power of educational institutions, several discussed the possibility that hidden curricula could be changed or expanded to include other values.[8] For
instance, Miller argued that her university's hidden curriculum
included more than capitalist concerns:

> [What] we're trying to teach in these hidden curriculums or unan-
> nounced curriculums is that there is more to life than just money. . . .
> the main thing is that we want you [students] to be passionate about
> life and make a difference. Just one person can make a big difference.

Macedo proposed adding courses in ethics and the foundations of
democracy to graduate schools of education:

They have a curriculum that is designed mostly for the development and creation of technicians along the lines of domestication to serve a particular social order. So for instance to finish a doctorate, you are usually required to take a course on statistics. Methods of research are mostly quantitative research [but] qualitative research also may be required. But there's no course whatsoever . . . that would require a student to engage in understanding and studying what it means to be ethical. And it seems to me that one of the prerequisites of becoming a teacher is the understanding, a fuller understanding, of what it means to be ethical.

Critical scholars openly advocated opposition to dominant regimes of knowledge and noted that counter-hegemonic movements exist and continue to challenge the academy. While certain nontraditional perspectives have gained recognition, or at least tolerance in the modern university, acceptance into the mainstream academic culture simultaneously enables the system to control and perhaps pacify alternative ideologies. Nevertheless, some interviewees promoted cultural transformation by way of "antistructures" or "countercurricula," identifying these as vital resources challenging traditional socialization practices. Drawing attention to the emerging emphasis on service-learning, Darling-Hammond argued that social responsibility was becoming incorporated into the curriculum:

I think there are many places now that are struggling with what does it mean to be educated. And what is the responsibility of the higher educated segment of a society to contribute to the welfare of others, to contribute to the welfare part of society. It gets manifested in some places, in for example, the growth and expansion of service learning courses, internships of various kinds. . . . I think what is important in the institutions I've worked in and the programs that I'm involved with is to prepare people to go into teaching who see themselves as having an ethical responsibility. Who see themselves as having responsibility to the welfare of the children they're going to teach.

This chapter briefly introduced a number of themes drawn both from the direct experience of a small sample of higher education faculty and administrators, and from the concentrated theoretical consideration they have given to issues of curriculum and socialization.

Many of their theoretical propositions—the role of the physical environment, the importance of the body, intentional or overt socialization practices, professionalization, and resistance to hidden curricula—are also the basis for the case studies that make up the bulk of this volume. In the chapters that follow, researchers gathered data and analyzed in detail specific postsecondary educational settings. These case studies both confirm the general observations in this chapter and demonstrate the usefulness of the concepts for concrete empirical investigations.

NOTES

1. The authors gratefully acknowledge the editorial assistance and intellectual contribution of Mary Romero in this work. The authors would also like to acknowledge the encouragement, labor, and insights of Luis Fernandez and Lydia Montelongo. Finally, this chapter would not have been written without the mentoring of Eric Margolis and the foundations he established toward applying audio and visual media to the research process.

2. Our intention was not to provide the same product in different media, but to use aspects of each to provide a "thick" understanding of the topic under study. Drawing on the foundations of Eric Margolis (1994) toward applying audio and visual media to the research process, we determined that videotaped interviews recording the accounts and contemplative observations of participants would yield more multidimensional data and comprehensive understandings of the functioning of hidden curricula. In addition, the weaving of scholar educators' theories and experiences forced us to address "the messy empirical features of the lived reality" (Margolis, 1994, 124).

3. This typology was developed by Henry Giroux (1983a, 48–60). The introduction to this volume includes a review of the literature on hidden curricula and details these paradigms.

4. For a full development of the importance of architecture and the built environment in socialization, see chapter three, "Schooled by the Classroom: The (Re)production of Social Stratification in Professional School Settings," in this volume.

5. This peculiar tension between the demands of business and social relationships is discussed in detail in several chapters in this volume. For instance, Linda Muzzin examined the influence of international drug companies on Canadian pharmacy schools and the ways in which corporate research demands overshadow the social need for well-educated pharmacists; Kenneth Ehrensal looked at how managers are educated to see their interests as different from workers; Mary Jane Curry showed how immigrants and refugees were schooled to the "pay as you go" ideology of corporate America.

6. For a detailed analysis of her experience see Ng (1997), "A Woman Out of Control: Deconstructing Sexism and Racism in the University."

7. For a study of the role of faculty advising and mentoring see Acker's article "The Hidden Curriculum of Dissertation Advising" and Margolis and Romero's piece "'In the Image and Likeness. . .' How Mentoring Functions in the Hidden Curriculum" in this volume.

8. For an able discussion of how the university manages oppositional movements, see Michael Soldatenko "Radicalism in Higher Education: How Chicano Studies Joined the Curriculum" chapter eleven in this volume.

Table 2.1: Interview Subjects

Joe Johnson, Professor, Division of Education and Counseling Psychology, University of Missouri, Columbia

Elizabeth Miller, Director, Center for Teaching Excellence, Texas A&M

Donald Blumenfeld-Jones, Associate professor, Division of Curriculum and Instruction, Arizona State University

Chris MacCrate, Coordinator, Development of Faculty Senate for Teaching and Learning, Estrella Mountain Community College

Sam DiGangi, Associate professor, Division of Special Education, Arizona State University

Mary Romero, Professor, School of Justice Studies, Arizona State University

George Watson, Professor, Department of Political Science, Walter Cronkite School of Journalism and Telecommunication, Arizona State University

Richard Shweder, Professor, Division of Human Development, University of Chicago

Michael Apple, John Bascom Professor of Curriculum and Instruction and Educational Policy Studies, University of Wisconsin, Madison

Linda Darling-Hammond, Charles E. Ducommun Professor of Education, university and executive director of the National Commission on Teaching and America's Future Professor, Stanford University

Roxana Ng, Associate professor, Department of Sociology and Equity Studies in Education, Ontario Institute for Studies in Education, University of Toronto, Canada

Donaldo Macedo, Professor, Department of English; director of Bilingual and ESL Studies, University of Massachusetts, Boston

David Berliner, Dean, College of Education; Professor, Education Policy Studies and Psychology in Education, Arizona State University

Milton Glick, Senior Vice Provost, Arizona State University

Karen Anijar, Assistant professor, Division of Curriculum and Instruction, Arizona State University

Peter McLaren, Professor, Division of Urban Schooling: Curriculum, Teaching, Leadership, and Policy Studies, Graduate School of Education and Information Studies, University of California, Los Angeles

Douglas Kellner, Professor, George F. Kneller Philosophy of Education Chair, Graduate School of Education and Information Studies, University of California, Los Angeles

Gene Glass, Associate dean for research; Professor, Education Policy Studies, Arizona State University

Alexander Astin, Allan Murray Cartter Professor, Higher Education and Work; director, Higher Education Research Institute, Graduate School of Education and Information Studies, University of California, Los Angeles

Christine Sleeter, Professor, Coordinator—Master of Arts in Education Program; director, Advanced Studies in Education, California State University, Monterey Bay

Joel Spring, Professor, Department of Educational Studies, State University of New York, New Paltz

Schooled by the Classroom 3

The (Re)production of Social Stratification in Professional School Settings

Carrie Yang Costello

Do I feel comfortable here at the law school? Sure. It's, well, a comfortable sort of place to be—I mean, I can grab a cappuccino at the café, and go right out into the courtyard and hang out with some friends—studying, yes, but also just talking, arguing, enjoying the sunshine. I like to hang out here. I'm very comfortable; I feel right at home.

> —Grant (a straight white man of upper-middle-class origins)

At first I used to feel weird walking around the halls, like I didn't belong. I couldn't really believe I was here. Now I'm used to it, but sometimes I still kind of look around myself and think, "you really did it, girl," and it's sort of weird, but good.

> —Cheryl (a straight African American woman
> of lower-middle-class origins)

I hate this place. Just walking into the building depresses me. I avoid hanging around this place, and try not to let it get to me.

> —Wei (a gay Asian man of upper-middle-class origins)

That schools tend to reproduce patterns of social stratification is a classic theme in the sociology of education (e.g., Becker 1961; Bourdieu and Passeron 1977); that they do so in a recondite rather than forthright manner is the central premise of the literature on the hidden curriculum reviewed in the introduction to this volume. Several of those writing on hidden curricula have remarked on the importance of the physical environment (Apple 1993; Muzzin, chapter eight this volume). This chapter builds on these observations and fills a gap in the literature by closely analyzing and comparing the built environments of two professional schools at the University of California, Berkeley: the Boalt Hall School of Law and the School of Social Welfare. Both were ranked among the top ten schools in their respective fields by *U.S. News and World Report* "Best Graduate Schools" (1998). In the course of my research at the two professional schools, I undertook more than four hundred hours of participant observation, focusing in part on the schools' settings—documenting them photographically and observing students' reactions to them. In this chapter, the goal is to describe how the physical set and setting function to convey socialization messages, with an eye toward understanding how the schools (re)produce race, class, gender, and other hierarchies.

Studies of professional socialization typically focus on the influence of professors as role models of values, purveyors of methods, and conveyors of substantive knowledge (e.g., Black 1997; Eisenberg 1999; Guinier, Fine, and Balin 1997). There is an unfortunate tendency for socialization scholarship to paint a picture of the world in which people are shaped only through direct interpersonal interaction; this is mirrored in the hidden curriculum literature by a focus on pedagogy. But as cultural scholars are aware, people are influenced in important ways by the material world in which they live (e.g., Crabb and Bielawski 1994; Calvert 1992; Peiss 1996). Sociologists have long acknowledged that individuals' identities are shaped by their physical surroundings. Durkheim himself noted that "[a] child's taste is formed as he comes in contact with the monuments of national taste bequeathed by previous generations" ([1897] 1951, 314). Accordingly, Michael Apple has posited that the hidden curriculum should be understood as being in part constituted by the material environments of schools (1993, 144).

Even a casual observer of a typical college campus is likely to notice that some "neighborhoods" look opulent—commonly sports arenas and the physical science buildings—while other facilities appear shabby and run-down—perhaps including the humanities and social science buildings. Some individuals are clearly aware of and able to "read" the socializing messages sent by these variations in the campus-built environment; for example, see the statements of education professionals interviewed by Marina Gair and Guy Mullins in chapter two of this volume. However, it is important to note at the outset that while everyone is constantly subject to the socializing influence of their surroundings, most people are typically unaware of being so influenced (McDowell 1999). It is this fact that makes the influence of schools' built environment a paradigmatic example of how certain curricula remain hidden, even though they are in plain sight.

Of course, physical settings do not function as socializing agents *sua sponte*; they are things. The people who design, ornament, and maintain them are the true sources of socializing messages, and the settings are merely the means by which these messages are propagated. Yet physical structures persist and continue to affect the people who inhabit them long after those who designed and built them have passed from the scene. For example, the Berkeley School of Social Welfare is housed in Haviland Hall, a facility built for the School of Education in 1924. Haviland Hall was designed by the university architect to convey the authority and prestige of the field of education through neoclassical architecture, and it continues to impart to social welfare students today that they gain prestige by association with classical Western culture. On the other hand, new generations of students may "read" structures in a manner that differs from that originally intended, as meanings change over time. Haviland's grand stairways, classical pediments, and formal entryways, meant to celebrate and embolden Anglo teachers in the 1920s, may alienate students of color pursuing social work degrees in the twenty-first century.

I chose to study schools of law and social work because of the interesting contrast they present. As noted by Martin, "A hidden curriculum is always *of* some setting, and there is no reason to suppose that different settings will have identical hidden curricula" (1994, 125, emphasis in original). It was the potential difference in the hidden curricula of the two schools that interested me. Law is a traditionally male profession and social work a traditionally female one; wealthy white males are overrepresented among the legal client base while women, children, people of color, and especially the poor constitute much of the social work client base. Despite these differences, however, white men from privileged class backgrounds are disproportionately successful in the two professions, although the effect is more pronounced at the law school and in legal practice. These puzzling facts are among those that the present analysis can help to explain.

HIDDEN CURRICULA OF THE SETTING

In the course of my research, I attended classes with first-year students at the Schools of Law and Social Welfare as a participant observer, and during the first confusing days I was struck by the importance of the physical settings. Before students began to know their professors and peers, they got important cues regarding their new professional roles from the architecture, decor, and level of maintenance of the facilities they entered. Later, as students became familiar with the school facilities, they stopped paying as much overt attention to their surroundings, directing their attention to personal interactions and academic tasks instead; however, the settings continued to provide socializing cues that the students continued to absorb. I will now analyze some of these cues by comparing in detail several aspects of the school facilities: entryways and hallways, artwork, and classrooms.

Entryways and Hallways at Boalt

Because the law school building in fact comprises an original core and two major additions constructed on substantially sloping grounds, negotiating it can be perplexing. An individual entering the law school for the first time is likely to feel rather lost, finding himself or herself dumped unceremoniously into one of many intersecting hallways. A student entering at ground level through the doors facing the Borden Family Courtyard can travel downstairs at the west end of the building to find herself or himself on the ground level of the original Boalt Hall facility, or may travel upstairs and eastward to exit at ground level once again from the North Addition. The effect is disorienting.

During the period in which I carried out my research, rooms in each section of the law school were numbered according to unrelated schemes, adding to the confusion. The warren of the Boalt hallways served to discomfit the uninitiated while giving the initiated a sense of mastery as they moved from place to place with swift self-assurance. Getting lost was initially a source of embarrassment and anxiety for the first-year students; later, after they could negotiate the halls easily, the confusion of neophytes was a source of amusement for them. One student joked to me when I asked him for directions that "Boalt has been organized so as to cause the maximum possible confusion for [first-year students]" (Field note, August 20, 1997).

Besides confusing the novice, the hallways of Boalt serve to impress. The hallways of the original building core are wainscoted with a rich honey-toned wood called *terminalia superba*, imported from the west coast of Africa (Epstein 1997, 207). The floors also give a grand impression, being ornamented by linoleum parqueted in a striking checkerboard pattern. Across from the major lecture halls, benches of *terminalia superba* are inset into the walls for the comfort of waiting students; heating grilles cunningly set into their bases warm the students' feet. Luxuries like these convey to students that their status is high, warranting every convenience.

In addition to giving an impression of richness, the hallways of the law school give an accounting of wealth. Along the central corridor between the registrar's office and the library there are long panels of donative plaques, arrayed beneath a quotation from Roger J. Traynor reading: "[T]he law will never be built in a day, and with luck it will never be finished." A bench is located across the corridor so students can contemplate the list of donors at their leisure. The Capital Campaign Donor Wall acknowledges charity and rewards school loyalty, and since it lists law school patrons according to the amounts of their donations, it also advertises wealth. The largest donations are listed at the top of the wall, conveying the message to students that being willing and able to give money is admirable, and being willing and able to give a lot money is even more admirable.

Reading the names on the wall, students also learn something about the nature of admirable donors: they are mostly male, and apparently mostly white. To give a typical example, there are forty-nine listings in the $25,000 to $34,999 donation category: thirty-nine of these are male and only one is female (the rest are couples or law firms); and there are no Asian or Latino last names among them (Lobby, May 1, 1997). The dominance of the Capital Campaign Donor Wall by white males conveys several messages to students. The first is a reminder that the law has traditionally been a white male preserve. Even so, substantial numbers of women and/or people of color have graduated from Boalt over the past quarter century, but very few appear to have made substantial (financial) contributions to their alma mater. Students may surmise either that female alumnae and alumni of color feel alienated from Boalt and do not desire to donate money to it, or that while they hold fond feelings for Boalt in their hearts, they have not achieved the financial success of their white male peers who do donate. Either possibility might give nontraditional Boalt students pause.

The Capital Campaign Donor Wall is only one vehicle for the acknowledgment of munificence at Boalt. At the time in which I began my research, the administration was causing a virtual plague of memorial plaques to be visited upon the walls. Central law school facilities have traditionally been known by the names of key donors who paid for their construction: the law school itself bears the name of John Henry Boalt, the library is named the Garret McEnerney Law Library, and the moot courtroom is the Luke Kavanagh Moot Court. But during the recent construction of the North Addition, patrons of Boalt were permitted to make smaller donations in order to have facilities named after them, and in 1996 it seemed that every room at the law school acquired a name. A small sample of these would include the John Stauffer Charitable Trust Lecture Hall, the Leo and Nina Pircher Seminar Room, and the Carl J. Stoney Lobby (this last being a rather pathetic short empty corridor leading from the library).

Nor were classrooms and corridors all that had donors' names affixed to them. Professors' offices themselves were subject to memorializations such as "A Gift of Marvin M. Grove in Honor of Professor Stefan Reisenfeld." Even individual library carrels had memorial plaques attached. The socializing messages emitted by this profusion of donative plaques tended in two directions. On the one hand, they gave an impression of wealth, privilege, and historical continuity. They suggested that alumni donors were honored, and that students should aspire to achieve honored status by being able to make a large donation to Boalt someday. On the other hand, their proliferation was irritating. Just as sports fans feel that something sacred has been commercialized when Candlestick Park becomes 3Com Park or the Orange Bowl becomes the FedEx Orange Bowl, students who watched the name plaques going up felt that they were a variety of sanctioned graffiti intruding into their private sphere. In an amusing prank, one student lampooned the plaques by pasting up pseudomemorial signs in humorous places: the "Sheryl Howell Women's Bathroom," the "Bobby Mockler Blank Wall," and the "Daniel Tellahalian Family Trust Big Brown Marble Bear" (Hallways, October 29, 1996).

Hidden curricula could also be read from materials posted by the administration on bulletin boards. One such set of bulletin boards, maintained by Career Services, sent messages to students about the careers that were intended for them. The board announcing hiring by law firms was full and busy; that announcing public service jobs was sparsely populated and slow to change. This conveyed to students that law firms were where the action was. In fact, even some of the flyers posted on the public service jobs board sought constructive engagement with the presentation of law firm jobs as serious and public service jobs as "fluffy." The headline on one read, "Not Just Another Pretty Law Firm: The United States Department of Justice . . . The Nation's Litigator" (Hallway, August 26, 1996). In seeking to reverse the gendered polarity of public and private sector legal jobs by deploying macho language against a negatively valued feminine image of law firm practice, this flyer conveyed to students that a strongly masculine habitus is paramount in the realm of law, even in the public service sector.

Other bulletin boards were used for posting grades. At first glance, the importance of these boards seems understated: located around the corner from the main circulation path, the boards list grades according to student ID numbers only. A deeper examination reveals that these obscuring factors in fact emphasize the importance of grades by indicating a need for security. This administrative assertion of a need to safeguard grades is underlined by the fact that the grade boards are enclosed behind locked Plexiglas panels. The implication is that if it were not for the triple level of protection provided by location, encryption, and bolting, students might be deprived of crucial information, or have sensitive information about them revealed or even stolen in the fierce competition for grades.

An Asian student eagerly informed me about the "commandeering" of another bulletin board (Field Note, April 28, 1997). For years, student organizations such as the Asian and Pacific Islander Law Student Association (APILSA) and Law Students of African Descent (LSAD) had had bulletin boards assigned to them in the basement of the original section of Boalt Hall. During the Northern Addition renovations, these bulletin boards were removed, supposedly for aesthetic reasons. Student activists of color felt that this removal was politically motivated, and appropriated a centrally placed bulletin board in the name of the "Color Coalition" (comprising APILSA, LSAD, La Raza, and the Native American Law Student Association). "Color Coalition" was written on a banner in magic marker and thumbtacked to a bulletin board near the Moot Court scheduling board. The contrast between the neat, orderly arrays of the administrative bulletin boards and the Color Coalition's rather haphazard arrangement of flyers and slogans made the administrative boards look formal, official, and enduring and the commandeered board look amateurish, chaotic, and ephemeral. The impression generated was that student politics are puerile.

Entryways and Hallways at the School of Social Welfare

The corridors of the School of Social Welfare conveyed a hidden curriculum with a nature quite different from that of the law school. If a novice entering the law school for the first time gained an impression of wealth and power, an initiate entering the School of Social Welfare for the first time received an impression of grandeur in decline. Ascending Haviland's classical grand staircase, one enters a large foyer of gracious proportion—and coated with peeling paint. Haviland Hall is a simple yet elegant rectangular building of four floors, each with classrooms lining a central corridor. Designed by the university architect, John Galen Howard, Haviland Hall was built in 1924 to serve as the home of the School of Education. It is in essence a hand-me-down to the School of Social Welfare, indicating the school's relatively low status. When originally occupied by the School of Education in 1924 it was probably quite lovely, and its original beauty persists in places such as the stairwells, with their attractively vaulted ceilings and wrought-iron ornamental railings.

For the most part, however, the bloom is off the rose at Haviland Hall. Its hallways offer a cautionary tale about life lived under institutional functionalism. The corridors mirror those of poorly maintained public schools and government facilities everywhere: bland beige walls, ceilings of graying acoustical tile, fluorescent lighting, and mismatched furniture. The difference between the linoleum floors at Haviland and Boalt is emblematic. While the law school decorators transformed linoleum into an elegant surface by crafting it into glossy parqueted checkerboards, the floors at the School of Social Welfare displayed linoleum to its worst advantage: brown and beige speckled tiles were selected to conceal dirt, but their dingy color and scratched surface left them appearing constantly dirty anyway. The Haviland hallways conveyed to students the class message that they, like their clients, would need to value pragmatism rather than luxury and to conserve valuable resources. In keeping with this ideology, there were no donative plaques on the walls; they might appear in poor taste to the social welfare community because they valorize wealth rather than substantive or spiritual contributions to the school.

Instead of displaying beauty through rich materials or impressive formalism, charm was displayed in the hallways of Haviland through individual reverent aesthetic gestures. For example, the door of one faculty member was enlivened by a colorful collage of drawings of women and girls wearing traditional ethnic garb and laid against a backdrop of boldly patterned fabric. This collage, created by the professor herself, served not only to ornament and beautify the door, but also to display appreciation for women in all their diversity. Comparing this door with that of a typical law faculty member, it appears that the corridors of Haviland socialize students to value self-expression and political engagement, while Boalt students are socialized to respect order, formality, wealth, and self-restraint.

Like the law school hallways, the corridors of Haviland Hall contained bulletin boards displaying scheduling information, book jackets from professorial publications, employment information, and the like. Unlike the law school, the School of Social Welfare's administrative bulletin boards did not feature neatly laser-printed headings and schedules. They more closely resembled the Color Coalition's commandeered bulletin board: titled by hand and covered with colorful flyers. In fact, the student organizational bulletin board was more rigorous in appearance: its titles were computer printed and the information it carried methodically arranged. Whereas the contrast between administrative and student boards at the law school suggested a hierarchical relationship between the wealthy institution and amateur students, the administrative bulletin boards at the School of Social Welfare gave the impression that the administration's resources and capacities were the same as those of the students. This analysis leads to two conclusions: first, that the relative status of the professions of law and social work is apparent in the law school's greater resources; and second, that displays of hierarchy valued at Boalt are devalued at the School of Social Welfare.

One thing that was visible in the hallways of Haviland but not of Boalt was student work. The M.S.W. students were occasionally required to make class presentations accompanied by visual aids, and the posters they produced were displayed in the hallways in a manner reminiscent of high school. This high schoolish impression was heightened by the graphically naive style of the posters, with their hand lettering and cut-and-paste collage assembly. If these posters were placed in a corridor at Boalt, they would look "unprofessional" because they do not aim to display intellectualism, access to resources, or upper-class aesthetic sensibilities. What would seem "professional" at the law school would appear as gauche self-aggrandizement at the School of Social Welfare. The fact that student work was displayed in the halls for all to see underlines the differing socialization messages sent to students about how they will be evaluated by the two schools. At Boalt, the importance of hierarchical grading by professors is emphasized by the grades' encryption and protection. At the School of Social Welfare, on the other hand, student work is put on display for all to see and evaluate. Rather than a private and hierarchical process between professor and student, the evaluation of work is a public community affair. The display of student posters at Haviland conveys to students the ideal that professional learning and work are a communal process.

Artwork at Boalt

The corridors of Boalt Hall were decorated not with student posters, but with fine artwork. Artwork serves not only to ornament otherwise bland spaces, but also to convey messages about the institution that displays it. By choosing to display artwork in the fine arts tradition, the law school administration sent a message to students "sustaining [upper] class continuity" (DiMaggio and Useem 1982, 182). The corridors of Boalt are embellished with a number of portraits of respected alumni and former professors. The individuals pictured are generally white males, accompanied by potent signifiers, including judicial robes and Latin epigrams such as *"Simplex vir legibus eruditus a discipulis dilectus."* (This translates as "A simple man, an author and scholar beloved by his students." Like many phrases in the law, it sounds much more impressive in Latin.) These portraits convey to students that the law is a domain of white male authority, which may make students who are not white and male feel like interlopers.

During the period in which I carried out my observations, there hung a single prominent portrait of a person who was not both white and male. In the corridor connecting the lecture halls of the original segment of the law school hung a portrait of Elizabeth Josselyn Boalt, whose donation in the name of her husband, the attorney John Henry Boalt, led to the founding of the law school in his name. While given pride of place to honor her monetary generosity, the portrait of Mrs. Boalt incorporates a number of signifiers sending the message that she sits outside the realm of law: she wears a delicate lavender dress instead of formal robes or a dark suit, and is posed in a domestic setting, with a piano and flowers to give a suitably feminine touch. Thus while a portrait of a woman hangs at the heart of Boalt Hall, her place outside the legal sphere is made quite clear.

Besides the portraits, the law school hallways contain one sculpture. This is an abstract statue of a roaring bear (the golden bear is the mascot of the University of California). Between its simple lines and its aggressive posture, it manages to embody the lawyerly traits of assertiveness and restraint, modeling the fact that the two traits are not incompatible. The bear, sculpted by Bufano, was donated by the Class of 1948 to memorialize one of their members, Martin Bordin, a popular man who died young (Epstein 1997, 184). It represents an interlinking of fraternal love and respect with school loyalty, characterizing the "old boy network" of Boalt alumni for current students.

While the hallways are sparsely ornamented with formal portraits and the marble bear, the inner sancta of the law school are decorated with Boalt's collection of nineteenth-century English legal caricatures. These black-and-white prints hang in upper-level administrative offices and line the walls of the faculty lounge. Humor is one of the key signifiers of a shared habitus, and the depictions of English solicitors, barristers, justices, and clients constitute an elaborate in-joke. I myself could not see what was funny about the prints perhaps one-third of the time, indicating that my habitus was not as deeply attuned to the lawyerly ideal as were those of the Boalt professors who were able to read all the etchings easily. Such rarefied artwork is difficult for those unfamiliar with nineteenth-century English law to interpret; hence its display prevents visitors to the inner sancta from feeling they have penetrated its mysteries. Moreover, it emphasizes and (re)enforces the Anglo-Saxon and male origins of the legal tradition.

Artwork at the School of Social Welfare

Upon ascending the grand staircase and entering the impressive main doors, one's first impression is that Haviland Hall displays the same sort of artwork as does Boalt Hall. A portrait of one Alexis F. Lange, executed on a heroic scale, takes up an entire wall of the high-ceilinged foyer. Like the formal portraits at the law school, it is a painting of a white man wearing the impressive dark robes of academic authority. Ironically, like the classical facade and elegant staircases of Haviland Hall, the portrait of Professor Lange was handed down from the

School of Education. The students I interviewed did not know that Professor Lange was not a representative of the School of Social Welfare (Hallway and Commons Room, March 10 and 11, 1997). For them, the portrait of an unknown "D.W.M." (dead white male, in student parlance) was another architectural trope that established the building's respectability. They understood academic power to be symbolized formulaically: "Doric columns + wrought iron + large portrait of random D.W.M. = respectability." And it is interesting to note that despite their cynicism, the students' vision of reputability wore a white male face.

Other than the portrait of Lange, Haviland's ornamentation was largely provided by displays of student work and the staff's doorway decorations. Vernacular craftwork was featured rather than fine arts. Traditionally, crafts are considered to be feminine, and hence domestic and of lesser import than the fine arts. For the students, artwork such as the collage of women previously described conveyed the message that the appropriate demeanor for a social worker is warm rather than formal, expressive rather than impassive, and approachable rather than distant—stereotypically feminine characteristics.

Like the individual decorations on office doors, the works of art selected for public display by the School of Social Welfare were virtually the inverse of the artwork at Boalt Hall. They displayed women, children, and people of color—for example, a painting of a brown-skinned woman spinning thread hung in the library and a collection of photographs of "Children of the World" hung in the Social Welfare Commons Room. This picturing of people other than white men had a number of socialization functions: it indicated that such people are deserving of respect; it suggested that women, children, and people of color constitute the social worker's client pool; and it modeled how social workers should shape their environment (e.g., through displays of artwork) to make their clients feel comfortable.

It is important to recognize that white males need not be discomfited by their omission from representation among those portrayed in Haviland Hall artwork, because this artwork pictured the social work client base rather than social workers themselves. The absence of Anglo-Saxon men suggests that they are unlikely to appear as clients in need of social workers' professional services. This heightens the status of white males, who in reality do receive services from social workers in many settings (e.g., drug and alcohol treatment programs, homeless shelters, elder care facilities, mental health centers, etc.). The obscuring of the status of white men as welfare clients is the mirror image of the invisibility of women and people of color as judges and attorneys at the law school. Both (mis)representations heighten the status of white men, which is an essential element of the hidden curriculum at elite institutions.

Classrooms at Boalt

In contrast to the institutional display of artwork, intentionally freighted with symbolic cultural messages, the arrangement of classrooms may appear to be dictated purely by function. But the arrangement of classrooms literally shapes the process of professional school socialization. At the law school, the lecture halls are arranged amphitheatrically or, as Michel Foucault would put it, panoptically (1979). In the law school lecture halls, the professor stands at a podium on a stage, and the students sit in rising arcs of seats before him (or, occasionally, her). The professor can see each student, but the students' eyes are fixed front and they cannot see one another well. In addition, elevated position frequently conveys social superiority, so the lecture halls' arrangement establishes a power hierarchy.

Students in a law school lecture hall sit in arcs of assigned numbered seats so that the professor can use a seating chart to call on them to speak. This arrangement of a central figure of authority overlooking a periphery resembles Bentham's design for a prison, the Panopticon, as described by Foucault: an annular building ringing a central observation tower. According to Foucault:

> Bentham laid down the principle that power should be visible and unverifiable. Visible: the inmate will constantly have before his eyes the tall outline of the central tower from which he is spied upon. Unverifiable: the inmate must never know whether he is being looked at at any one moment; but he must be sure that he may always be so. (1979, 201)

Like Bentham's inmates, law school students are locked into places where they are under constant surveillance and subject to examination at any time. As Foucault explains, this is an extremely efficient arrangement for the functioning of what he terms the "disciplinary mechanism" (1979, 197), which entrenches power and hierarchy at the same time as it trains those who are subject to its workings. Hence the very architecture of the law school lecture hall functions to instill discipline, hierarchical relations, and respect for power and authority in law students.

Boalt Hall also contains a few rooms for seminars, which are open to upperclasspersons (second and third-year students) only. Seminars cover substantive areas on the periphery of legal practice, and attract few students when compared to core upper-division courses such as corporations or tax law. The seminar rooms are designed for small groups, but like other law school classrooms they convey to students that they are deserving of comforts such as custom benches, swivel seats, and thick carpeting. What is strikingly different is that while a desk podium is still provided for the professor, she or he sits with the students "in the round" in these classrooms, significantly reducing messages of hierarchy. This may be read as flattering to upper-division students who are exploring a legal specialty, since it indicates their elevated status by sitting beside the professor. Nevertheless, since only a small percentage of the teaching at Boalt occurs in seminar rooms, their less hierarchical arrangement appears as a deviation from the norm.

Classrooms at the School of Social Welfare

Unlike at the law school, where small circular arrangements of seats appeared as a deviation from the norm, at the School of Social Welfare all classrooms were arranged this way. There were two variants of the circular arrangement at Haviland Hall: classrooms in which students sat around conference tables, and classrooms in which chairs with small attached desks were arranged around the periphery of a room. In both cases the circular setting conveyed the nonhierarchical socialization message that what occurred in the classroom was a communal responsibility. Conference tables comprised rectangular or rhomboid units that could be arranged in different ways to facilitate a variety of community structures, from small groups to class discussions. Since the conference tables were frequently rearranged from class to class, students were trained to take responsibility for flexibility in social organization, learning styles, and practice skills. This was a markedly different message from the fixed and traditional hierarchy conveyed by the law school lecture halls.

While the rearrangements of the conference tables conveyed a certain fluidity to the students at Haviland Hall, this fluidity was not without constraint. The tables were always arranged at least loosely in the round—never into rows or as random individual tables—structurally suggesting that the top-down hierarchy of rows and the anarchic individualism created by random table placement were both unacceptable alternatives. The circular arrangements structured the operations of power in the social welfare classroom in the proscribed way: communally.

Because the panoptically arranged law school lecture halls deployed disciplinary mechanisms in such a clear and obvious way, the rare circular arrangement of law school seminar rooms seemed less infused with power relations. At the School of Social Welfare, however, the circular imperative in classroom arrangements shaped the circle, not as an absence of hierarchical power, but rather as the full presence of horizontal power relations. Whereas at Boalt each student was constantly responsible to the disciplining gaze of the professor, at Haviland each student was continuously responsible to the disciplinary gaze of every other student. If the law school classrooms were panopticons, the social welfare classrooms were omniopticons. The circular arrangement removed hierarchy while shaping an even more effective disciplinary mechanism than the law school amphitheaters could produce. Social welfare students employed communal disciplinary tactics such as shunning to reform students who displayed an inappropriate habitus, which helps to explain why social welfare students conformed to group norms to an extent even greater than that of their law school counterparts.

Besides conveying a message of group responsibility for learning, the arrangements of conference tables were evocative of bureaucratic settings, since bureaucracy and conference tables are inextricably linked in our cultural imagination. The classrooms at Haviland Hall socialized students to work in bureaucratic settings, and particular bureaucratic settings at that. The mismatched tables and chairs that sat in many of the classrooms created an impression of scant resources. While such motley classrooms did not resemble the boardroom of a wealthy corporate charity (such as a museum of fine arts), they did bear a resemblance to the conference rooms of poorly-funded government facilities and public service organizations. Thus the built environment socialized students to professional roles and lowered expectations as to what they could realistically expect to encounter on the job. To compare these rooms to the classrooms at Boalt, it is evident that the law school socializes students to expect a professional career of much greater wealth, authority, and prestige than does the School of Social Welfare.

Additional Facilities

The hidden curricular lessons conveyed by the corridors, artwork, and classrooms of the two schools were similarly inscribed in their other facilities. For example, the contrast between Boalt's Belli Commons and the Social Welfare Commons Room made clear the disparate social statuses of the two professions. The Belli Commons was an elegant café where students' tastes were shaped by a European menu of lattés and cappuccinos, croissants and foccacia sandwiches; the Social Welfare Commons Room offered only mismatched furniture and a few vending machines. Similarly, the libraries of the two schools sent contrasting messages to the students ensconced within them. The law school library was impressively large, comprise several wings, each containing formidable displays of legal tomes and well-appointed study areas. The library at Haviland, on the other hand, was housed in a single room, its once-grand iron grillework and classical plaques marred by dense functional rows of steel bookshelves. In sum, whatever facilities students encountered confronted them with hidden curricula, and while each individual sign or symbol might be subtle, the total effect was powerful indeed.

DISCUSSION

A close analysis of the physical environments of the Boalt Hall School of Law and Berkeley School of Social Welfare reveals distinct hidden curricula embedded in bricks and mortar, furniture and paintings. The hidden curriculum at Boalt prepares students for privilege and exclusivity. It socializes them to adopt role expectations of power and authority, wealth, comfort, and an appreciation of upper class culture. Through its artwork, it reflects the taken-for-granted assumption that the law wears a white male face. The law school's built environment reproduces the expectation of private sector work, intellectual assertiveness, emotional restraint, discipline, and hierarchy. These socializing messages are targeted to, and much more easily received by, white male students who hail from a position of class privilege. Students such as Grant, quoted at the beginning of this chapter, feel both empowered and "at home" at Boalt Hall. Students with different faces and different cultural capital, however, may not feel the same sense of ease in the corridors of the law school. Some, like Cheryl, feel like imposters, and others, like Wei, feel alienation or a vague sense of unease.

The Haviland Hall facilities send conflicting messages. On the one hand, they send a message about the dignity of professional status and the necessity of discipline in a manner similar to that of the law school through the building's classical architecture and heroic portrait of an older, robed white man. These factors tend to advantage white men from privileged backgrounds in a manner similar to the impact of the law school setting. On the other hand, the Haviland Hall facilities send messages about limited resources and class aspirations, and about the values of empathy, modesty, tolerance, public service, and communal responsibility. These messages about limited resources and a communal orientation are associated with the school's private (domestic) spaces and with arts and crafts depicting women, children, and/or people of color. Factors such as these make students who do not have race, class, gender, or other privileges feel at least somewhat "at home."

Closely examining the physical settings of two professional schools reveals the curricula that were hidden in plain sight, and helps us to explain how the schools (re)produce patterns of social stratification. The messages conveyed by the settings help explain both the fact that white men from privileged class backgrounds are disproportionately successful at the two schools, and the fact that this disparity is more pronounced at the law school. Although they are often unconscious of doing so, professional students absorb the messages conveyed by the built environments in which they find themselves, and are socialized to conform to the hidden curricula thus conveyed. The dispositions they are socialized to adopt have little to do with the knowledge base or overt skills of the professions, but like the formal curriculum, the hidden curriculum must be mastered in order for the students to find success as attorneys and social workers.

The Hidden Curriculum of Dissertation Advising[1]   4

Sandra Acker

Few writers analyze hidden curricula in undergraduate or professional education, and even fewer examine graduate schools from this perspective. In fact, graduate schools offer several layers of more-or-less hidden curricula, ranging from relatively overt requirements of the program to conventions of the discipline to more covert notions of what makes a good student. We might think of the hidden curriculum of the graduate school as being like an iceberg, with the more overt requirements above the water and the rest submerged, though visible to a keen eye or with the appropriate equipment.

Students enter graduate school having done well in their prior studies and expect to continue succeeding. Many are profoundly disoriented by the greater degree of independence and originality expected of them. Course assignments are fewer but bigger, assigned readings more difficult, professors less indulgent, and peers more competitive. Although many graduate students will not become professors, the assumption that guides much graduate work, especially at the doctoral level, is that students are in training for an academic career. The degree of disorientation depends on many things, such as the quality of the undergraduate institution and the cultural capital possessed by the student.

Because conventions in graduate work vary considerably from country to country, the literature on graduate education must be read with care. For example, when writers from Britain or Australia consider what is there called postgraduate education, they have in mind a system where the Ph.D. "research student" begins work on his or her dissertation almost immediately, usually under the guidance of a single supervisor. In the United States and Canada, students generally enroll in courses for several years, take a major examination, and then move on to the dissertation stage. They may need to obtain a master's degree or satisfy equivalence requirements before becoming a doctoral candidate.

In all countries, conventions governing the dissertation phase vary among subject fields. These include the likelihood of the student working on a project related to the advisor's own research; the extent to which she or he can expect funding; the rapidity of progress through the dissertation phase; the tolerance for personal narrative in the written account; the structuring of chapters; the formality of writing style; the ease of publication of findings; and the ethics of including the advisor's name in publications. All these practices have to be taught or "caught" by students in each field.

The doctoral student has to become attuned to at least two aspects of socialization: the conventions of the discipline and the practices of the department. Sharon Parry and Martin Hayden (1999, 37) call the two aspects the disciplinary and the organizational cultures of the department. In the first case, students are being socialized or "disciplined" into a research culture (Green and Lee 1999). Students are learning, in Pierre Bourdieu's (1973) phrase, the habitus of a particular field—the set of essentially cultural understandings that allows them to consider themselves and be considered by others to be bona fide sociologists, or anthropologists, or biologists. Departmental practices are more akin to politics. What characterizes a "good student" in Department X? What, exactly, is required and how much flexibility is there about it? This level of the curriculum is lodged within the deepest level of the iceberg. Some students appear to "catch on" and do what is required of a successful graduate student, while others seem endlessly to flounder (Acker, Transken, Hill, and Black 1994).

In this chapter I focus on one specific area within the hidden curriculum of graduate education, the process of what is usually called dissertation advising in the United States and dissertation or thesis supervision in Canada, Britain, Australia, and New Zealand.[2] My sources are somewhat eclectic: the research literature; my own experience as a university teacher working in graduate departments of education since 1972 in Britain and Canada; a research project on supervision in education and psychology carried out with colleagues in England from 1989 to 1991;[3] and a taped focus group discussion with a group of eight graduate students and ex-students and two faculty members in education in a Canadian university in 1997.

In the sections that follow, I consider two examples of the subtleties of the process of dissertation advising: finding an advisor and negotiating with an advisor. Both are examples that seem quite obvious until closely examined; both raise questions about power and positioning. I then make some remarks about the impact of different characteristics of students and their location within the institution.

FINDING AN ADVISOR

In the British study, students found their supervisors through two quite distinct processes, which we came to call *warm* or *cold* entry. In the *warm* entry process, students researched the specialties of different institutions and individuals within them. Having narrowed the field to one or more potential supervisors, they would try to meet that individual or individuals before applying for admission. If the student had been previously enrolled for a bachelor's or master's degree in the same institution, the student and proposed supervisor already knew each other. Other students, especially those pursuing their studies part-time, simply enrolled at a conveniently located institution (*cold entry*). Then a supervisor who most closely shared their interests was assigned to them.

The experiences of the Canadians in the focus group were very different. In the institution where this discussion was taped, the norm is for students to do a year or more of course work, and then have to persuade a faculty member to act as dissertation supervisor. Master's students need an additional faculty member and doctoral students two others to make up a thesis committee. For part-time students it might be quite a few years before this moment arrives. Students are assigned on arrival to what are called advisors, but these advisors are not necessarily expected to supervise their dissertations—a situation that sometimes caused confusion.

Some students had been advised or learned somehow that course selection would be important in terms of sizing up and establishing rapport with potential supervisors; others did not know this information or figured it out too late. Several then had the task of trawling through faculty members trying to find someone who shared their interests or would agree to work with them. It was clear that this search could be traumatic and embarrassing. One student expressed considerable bitterness in her account (and others reflected her sentiments to a greater or lesser degree):

> I'm interested in [names three areas]. And I found it so difficult to find someone who had an interest in most of those things. I mean, I went to all of those people who I thought would be there, and they all said, "Oh, I'm really interested in what you're doing, but I just don't have any time to be on your committee." So I went through I guess a month of continually phoning people, running around the building, and it really is hard on your psyche. Even though some people were nice and some people were just downright "I don't know you from Adam, I'm not taking anyone else on, and I'm not particularly interested in what you're doing" . . . and you feel just so crucified. At the end of it you're so afraid to pick up the phone or face somebody again. You walk in and you say, "I'm here, I'm an independent worker. I don't need much help. I won't take much of your time. Please, just take me on. You don't even have to be there for the defense. I have to have a supervisor!". . . I thought that the most difficult part was finding someone to agree to be my supervisor because you feel sort of like you're grovelling.

Another student confirmed this view: "I think that's so true, though, what you're saying about feeling like you're grovelling." She, and others, questioned whether there was not a responsibility on the part of the department, of the faculty members, to provide supervision, given that they admitted these students in the first place. Although they had some sympathy with faculty being overloaded and not rewarded in tenure or promotion terms for taking on supervision, that sympathy had definite limits. A different student was sceptical about professorial "busyness":

> That's a big bone of contention for me. It really bugged me how professors constantly talk about how busy they are to a point where I personally didn't want to ask anybody for anything, and that ultimately can hold you way back. It can really limit your experiences because you feel guilty all the time . . . you have to think about it for so long before you go and ask for a letter of reference.

At one point in the discussion, a faculty member tried to explain how she experienced students trying to find a supervisor:

> I feel quite bad sometimes when people approach me and almost invite me to reject them. . . . It's when you get a phone call from somebody you've never heard of and they leave a message on your voice mail. They don't tell you what the topic is. They say, "I'm looking for a supervisor or a committee member, please phone me." And you think, "Why me? Why should I? I've got enough to do. Who's this person?" Sometimes the sort of techniques people use almost backfire for them.

Clearly students and supervisors start from different positions and interpret finding a supervisor in very different ways. Supervising a student, especially through a doctoral dissertation, is a long and arduous task, one faculty do not want to agree to unless they can predict a high likelihood of success without undue stress for themselves. As Margot Pearson (1996, 307) commented, some discussions of supervision appear to give the supervisor responsibilities that are simply immense. They become responsible not only for helping students organize their work and giving them feedback but for explaining institutional procedures; troubleshooting with the committee and other faculty; editing and proofreading; providing information and advice over finances and housing; inducting the student into the professional culture of conferences, networks, and publications; supporting the student through personal crises; finding a job for the student; and remaining an active mentor for years to come. The notion of mentoring is a concept larger than the specific issues of supervision I discuss here.[4]

In part, a confusion between mentoring and advising may be at issue. Some students expect too much, while others expect too little. If faculty see a huge responsibility looming, they may feel that it is important not to take on more students than they can cope with. It is also likely that supervision will not "count," or not count much, in decisions over tenure and promotion or workload; and even if the quantity of supervision is measured, the quality is probably not (Acker and Feuerverger 1996, Hulbert 1994). For faculty, the necessity for students to find a supervisor may be seen as a sign of their progress through the system, an aspect of the partially-hidden curriculum or a rite of passage indicating that the student has been sufficiently socialized into the disciplinary and departmental understandings to master the process. But for at least some of the students, finding a supervisor is a humiliating ritual—grovelling—one that requires abasement and extreme deference on their part.

NEGOTIATING WITH THE ADVISOR

To oversimplify a bit, the advisor's role could be characterized as either manager/director or facilitator. In the first conception, the supervisor's main task is to keep the student moving along the stages of dissertation research by telling him/her what to do. In the second, the role is less overt; the supervisor tries to respond more to what the student wants and needs. The two main conceptions match respectively what could be seen as a technical-rational view of the process (it can be predicted, understood, controlled, improved) and a negotiated-order view (what happens is emergent and depends on interpretations and strategic responses). The manager/director conception is the one found in guidebooks and is a more obvious part of the hidden curriculum. It is helpful insofar as both parties gain a clearer understanding of ways they can proceed and seek consciously to improve their practice. However, the second model is a more insightful one in terms of the actual dynamic relationships involved in advising. This argument is developed further in Acker, Hill, and Black (1994).

What is being negotiated? We can start by considering, for example, negotiations over procedural issues, such as how often advisors and students will meet, what the typical content of a meeting is, how much work the student will be expected to do in what time frame and to what standard; how much direction the advisor should provide and how much further input such as reading and editing chapters he or she should give. Examples of different expectations, negotiated more or less well, can be found in the British research. Here is a case where a student wanted the supervisor to be more focused in his meetings:

> Sometimes they [meetings] haven't worked because I've got eight things to talk about and we talk about the first one and the hour has gone and he's got another student waiting outside. So I sometimes say, "Before you say anything, Bill, there are eight things I was hoping to cover in this session." So in a sense I've been more formal than he has, and that's something I've learned to do. (male student)

In contrast to "Bill" (all names are pseudonyms), this supervisor tried to control everything that happened:

> That's the way I handle all my meetings: what's our agenda, what are we trying to achieve, what's our time line? And I would say, "Okay, I would like to get this on the agenda" and then we would go through whatever it was and then I would say at the end something like, "Are we okay now?" or I might say, "Look I think we're pressed for time, I think we ought to wrap this up. Given what we said at the outset is there anything we need to get done before you leave? Would you please make a note of what we've agreed and send me a copy." (male supervisor)

Another student was clearly unhappy with the meetings with her supervisor but could not work out how to change the situation:

> There's a feeling that I need to perhaps have some set time where I could say, you know, or she could say to me, "You have three quarters of an hour of my time" . . . I'm feeling for almost a clue for her to say, you know, "I've had enough of you now" or "That's the end of the session" and there isn't any. (female student)

Despite their typical lack of clarity, procedures for conduct of meetings seem straightforward when compared to some of the other questions that arise (or lurk, unaddressed) during the process of advising, such as how much should be expected from an advisor or how close the relationship should be between student and advisor. Complications also arise from the social location of the main players—both in terms of their identification as "students" or "supervisors" and also in terms of differential resources and perspectives related to gender, class, race, and other such attributes.

A particularly difficult question is how close the personal relationship between the student and the supervisor should be. In general, both the faculty and students in the British research said they preferred a professional relationship, with some distance, but in practice some relationships were close while others were almost nonexistent. One male supervisor told us: "I don't actually see it as my function to be their support and soul mate and someone who will get them through the next five years of general living. I don't think that's my job," while another male supervisor went to the opposite extreme: "They've all got my home telephone number. They come and visit me . . . some stay with me . . . I get very close with them."

One woman student had hoped for a closer relationship with her female supervisor, saying sadly, "There was a time when we were quite close, but then she really clouted me away." Another woman student expressed similar hopes:

> [In the meeting] we talked about Melanie [the supervisor] because she's been going through a bad patch, so I think, but that felt good because it felt like somehow I was getting a bit closer to her, that she was opening up a little bit to me, and that was like a kind of little self-disclosure that made her seem . . . a bit more human as it were. I felt much better.

A third female student had a number of problems with her supervisor, who seemed to be indifferent, distracted, and inaccessible. The alternative to indifference seemed to be harassment:

> Fiona [another student] is a bit different because she, I think they get on very well because she's superbly beautiful and she's very charming and I think when she arrived Simon [the supervisor] was very interested in her, and so he got her a research assistantship and she's designed a program and he's been working very closely with her. I think she has different problems with him in that he will be calling her up at all times of the day and even when she's at home, and wanting her to work, you know, all hours of the day and night.

Several commentators point to the difficulty managing the degree of potential intimacy in the advisor-student relationship, especially when there is a hint or more of sexuality. Colin Evans, in a study of university foreign language departments in Britain, speculated on the parameters of the gender imbalances common in universities. In modern language departments, the students are mostly young women and the faculty middle-aged men, but "the sexual elements of this relation are almost never acknowledged. . . . The whole gender question is an emotional and intellectual no-go area." Participants retreat, he suggested, into a father-daughter role relationship (Evans, 1988,

134–35). Calls to incorporate "caring" more centrally into teaching (Noddings 1988), easily extended to supervision, require some attention to "the delicate balance between too much and too little loving care" (Booth 1994, 36).

Most of the pairs in the British data consisted of a male supervisor and either a female or male student. Female supervisors (themselves a minority among the supervisors) tended to supervise female students; there were just a few cases of female supervisors and male students. One was particularly interesting as it seemed to embody the potential difficulties and contradictions inherent in this pairing. The participants seemed unsure of whether they should be acting as man and woman or supervisor and student. The male psychology student, John, was unhappy that another prospective supervisor had left the university and Catherine, the substitute, was clearly second best in his eyes. His interview was full of contradictions. He praised Catherine's intelligence and gave her credit for solving major problems with his work. Then he compared her to the supervisor who had left, and said Catherine didn't really come up to that sort of standard: "It's hard to describe, you know, but in times of real anger, I've sort of like, really felt down and you think oh God, she's just so bloody stupid." He also had other criticisms of her: she lacks humor and "is a very nervous character . . . smoking cigarettes, drinking cans of Coke, God knows how much . . . there's always a can of Coke there, she must get through more caffeine, God knows."

John saw Catherine virtually every day: "I never let it go for more than, say, a couple of days really. I mean I always see her, even socially, you know, go for a drink or something." He said he's been away for weekends with various people in the department and she is included in the group. He discussed "a weekend by the sea, and we hired a car and I drove up with Catherine, and we just had a weekend there . . . we used to go for a drink occasionally . . . never just me and her, it was usually a group of people, say, from the department . . . there's certainly no distance socially. I mean, I feel completely relaxed with her." Nevertheless, John asserted that Catherine is too busy and not available enough: "Like I say, she's a workaholic, and like a lot of the time I have to go through and explain things to her which I've already explained and like she's forgotten about or at least forgotten the gist of it." He even complained about her reluctance to come to his office:

I'm on this floor, I'm on the third floor and she's on the second. . . . And you know, it's a case of, I've only seen her in my office twice or something like that. And it would be nice, once in a while, if she just popped in and just said, "How's it going, what are you doing?"

In trying to make sense of this supervisory relationship, the gender dynamics are hard to ignore. Age may also play a part. John is twenty-seven, while Catherine is about six years older. Had she been still older and a more commanding figure in her field, some of the ambiguity might have been reduced. As it is, John does not seem quite sure whether Catherine should be regarded as an authority figure, a girl-friend, a friend, or a mother. We see here the operation of contradic-tory norms and negotiations around power, gender, reciprocity, and intimacy.

DIFFERENTIAL LOCATIONS

Barbara Grant and Adele Graham (1994, 165) refer to "unequal underpinnings" of the supervisory relationship, given that the disser-tation is "likely to be the student's major work focus while it is one small aspect of the supervisor's current workload." Like Grant and Graham, I think this model of "sovereign power," similar to a class conflict model, contains important insights but is also problematic—the advisors themselves are embedded in work relations that do not necessarily empower them, and many of the students themselves have an expectation of "upward mobility" into an academic position in time. Also, the students and advisors are united in their wish for a suc-cessful outcome. Where the model is helpful is to remind us that dif-ferent parties are differently located in the structures that make up graduate education, and that their perceptions and vested interests will inevitably be correspondingly different.

While acknowledging the importance of locating perspective in "advisor" and "student" frames, we must move beyond seeing all advisors, or all students, as interchangeable. This conceptualization is a major flaw in the literature. Diversity among students can stem from idiosyncratic characteristics or ways of interpreting their situation (Acker, Transken, Hill, and Black, 1994). It can also stem from what I will call "registration status"—essentially whether they are full- or part-time students. It can stem from a myriad of other features of people's lives related to the operation of gender, race, class, age, and other attributes.

Below I expand first on the importance of registration status, mainly as it emerged in the British research project but with some support from the Canadian focus group discussion. Then I look at some of the complications that emerge when we take into account relations of gender and other positions and resources. In the process, we will see that "power" no longer seems simply vested in the advisor.

In the British research, what stood out in shaping student perspectives, rather to our surprise, was whether the student was registered full-time or part-time, and if the latter, on what basis (Hill, Acker, and Black 1994). Part-time students might be either "detached"—usually working full-time outside the university and whose contacts apart from the supervisor were minimal—or "semi-detached"—in the university working full time, usually on a faculty member's research project, and simultaneously registered as a part-time student.

Of course the variables were not independent; for example, full-time students were more likely than the others to be young, in psychology rather than education, and to have funding for their studies. But there was far from a perfect correspondence between registration status and other characteristics. The importance of registration status was that it stood as a representation of where the student was located vis-à-vis the academic world. It strongly shaped expectations for supervision and how students coped with indifferent supervision if they encountered it. Full-time and part-time "semi-detached" students were more likely to voice dissatisfaction than part-time students, even though part-time students got little by way of material benefits from the university (they were rarely given desks, lockers, or access to other facilities; they knew few other students or faculty members). Detached students usually had other sources of self-esteem and support, however, and they were not so dependent on supervisors and the graduate student experience for validation. Some who were making little progress blamed themselves or stressed how little the degree mattered as they were so enjoying their research experience. Full-time students complained more about not getting sufficient supervisor time and they often had financial worries. Semi-detached students were characterized by their marginality in both the student world and the faculty one.

Their progress on dissertations was impeded by their work responsibilities; yet they were not accepted as equals to faculty members and many expressed discontent with their ambiguous situations.

I had not expected similar issues to arise in the Canadian focus group. Nevertheless, there were parallels. Some students in the focus group talked about how difficult it was for them to find a supervisor or know the ropes when they lived at a distance or could not "be around" for other reasons. One student commented:

> When I look back there was a real difficulty, and I think it's common to students that do their work here on a part-time basis, and that is that there isn't a relationship building among students and among faculty. So you don't know faculty that well and they don't know you that well in terms of developing bonds and knowing where your different interests and faculty interests are.

Another student explained that because she lived in another province, she took courses for two consecutive summers before she was able to do her residence year. She stressed how difficult it was to meet people and "it's really just by luck that you happen to encounter a course where people are instrumental in furthering you along your way." She went on to say:

> The problem when you come as a summer student is that often the advisor that you have been assigned isn't there in the summer. That was the case with me. I came for two summers, but my advisor was never present in the summer. And he doesn't answer E-mails, so when I E-mailed him from [her home] I never got any response. So I just said well, maybe he's not interested. I found out subsequently that he just is not a good E-mailer, he doesn't like to read it.

A third student added to the conversation:

> I think we undervalue the [effects of] being outside, like living in [suburb], for other people too who are outside of [the city where the university is], you can't underestimate the value of just being on the premises, being seen, being able to be on these committees and whatever else, and getting to know people not just through courses but through a number of things.

This discussion suggests pressing questions about where students and supervisors are located on various dimensions. The literature on graduate student supervision has been remiss in looking at race, class, and age, for example, and almost as unlikely to notice whether students are fully engaged in their study or are part of what Leonard Baird (1990) calls "the forgotten minority," those who are studying part time. In writings by black feminists, there are certainly indications that they survived graduate school despite, rather than because of, the response they found there (Bannerji 1991; Carty 1991; hooks 1988; see also Margolis and Romero 1998). A study of a large U.S. Midwestern university concluded that minority women had fewer professional socialization experiences than majority women; that is, they were less likely to report being mentored, holding research and teaching assistantships, coauthoring papers with faculty or being introduced to wider academic networks by the faculty (Turner and Thompson 1993; see also Margolis and Romero, chapter five). In their study of twenty-six women students of color in American graduate sociology departments, Eric Margolis and Mary Romero (1998) go further in concluding that not only are the women disadvantaged by a socialization process based on a white, male model, but the entire process confirms and reproduces social differences in the academy based on gender and race.

An American study of graduate students in engineering, history, and economics found that students from the United States, with their more fluent English, were more likely than international students to be teaching assistants, which gave them helpful experience for the future as well as office space (Friedman 1987). In engineering departments, research associateships were more likely to go to the students from abroad, but advantages were not always apparent because they worked in groups where the professors did not give much individual assistance. American students had more outside sources of support and were better integrated with student peers. Nathalie Friedman's (1987) study as well as Joanna Channell's (1990) research in Britain found that faculty saw international students as highly problematic, mainly because their greater needs and expectations for close supervision resulted in extra work for the supervisor. Similar sentiments were expressed in our British supervision project interviews. Tanya Aspland and Thomas O'Donoghue's (1994) interviews with five international students in Australia found that these students were disappointed and disillusioned about what they saw as inadequate supervision. These students paid much higher fees than other students and some believed they were not getting "value for the money." Prejudices and deeply embedded cultural assumptions held by supervisors about "Asian women" also entered into the relationships (Aspland 1999).

Age and class feature less often in the literature. Because many of the students interviewed in the British study were older—for example, former or current school teachers studying for a higher degree—they were aware that academic careers might not be open to them, even when they desired them. It was curious to find individuals in their forties refer to themselves as "geriatric" or "oldsters" (Acker, Transken, Hill, and Black, 1994). Most, although not all, of the interviewees who made such references were women, probably reflecting the deeply rooted combination of sexism and ageism that flourishes in the academy as well as elsewhere (Carpenter 1996).

Tensions based on ethnicity or social class seem even more rarely explored. Josephine Mazzuca (2000) reports on the complex strategies employed by Italian-Canadian women graduate students to negotiate (and often segregate) their family and student lives. Most rarely spoke about their families to their student peers. They also found the individualism and competitiveness of graduate school at odds with the collective ethos encouraged in their communities. Similarly, students who hail from less advantaged backgrounds may downplay their origins in order to pass as part of the elite in the academy (hooks 1988; Smith 1993). Patricia Clark Smith (1993, 132, italics in the original) refers to looking around surreptitiously at academic functions wondering: *"Who's here who wasn't born knowing how to do this?"*

In the supervision research in Britain, a male psychology student in his late fifties explained why he did not want to join the academic world: "I've never been interested in academia as such because academia smacks, to me, of a club, it's a bloody club. When I went down to that conference it was a middle-class club . . . with everybody telling everybody else how wonderful they were. That's not for me." A woman psychology student transferred to a different supervisor after repeated conflicts with the first one. She resented the way he had altered her topic, his high-handed manner, and his inclination to take rather than give, despite his "brilliant mind." She disliked his giving her orders: "Go and read this, do that, do the other," because "you just felt like you were sort of like an office girl." She added: "And, you know, I'm a sort of working-class girl and he's this sort of like private school, you know, type lad, and do you know what I mean, he's just much more articulate than I am." In contrast, another woman student got along well with the same faculty member, with whom she shared leisure interests as well as a similar class background: "We do most of the time get on. He's young for a supervisor and he still has an interest in sport and things so we can talk about a lot of issues. It's very relaxed most of the time."

In the Canadian focus group, one of the students raised questions of class and ethnicity:

> I know it's important, the personal, but a lot of our behavior is also influenced by our ethnicity, our class position. And if most of the faculty are from, say, middle class, can there be tension because of the different social structures that we come from? Or do we go back to the idea that maybe it's a rite of passage and whatever class we're from we have to learn sort of middle-class kind of behavior in order to get the supervisor and the committee members.

Another student took up her point:

> I think it's true that it makes a difference for me, coming from a certain ethnic background, a working-class background, but especially around the ethnicity, where family is really central. So that I might in a conversation mention something about that and right away feel like, "Oh, why did I do that?"

She told an anecdote about a group of students being invited by a faculty member into his home and how comfortable she felt because although the specific ethnic background was different, it was also one "where family and community [are] really important." This faculty member "has got his mother living there and two sisters and a brother, and it really is validating for me. He's okay with it. . . . It is important."

Of course, it is difficult to tease out individual characteristics that put a student at ease or otherwise with advisors. We can surmise that a combination of characteristics—class, age, gender and others— work to produce comfort or diffidence. I have not exhausted the list of possibilities. For example, I have not discussed students who are gay or lesbian, who are disabled, or who are single parents, all groups who may feel uncomfortable in certain supervisory relationships. Nor have I said much about the characteristics of advisors. There is some writing that points to difficulties that faculty from minority ethnic backgrounds have with students who do not recognize their authority in the classroom and about the ways in which they are silenced in the academy (e.g., Bannerji 1995; Karamcheti 1995; Ng 1993). Minority faculty are also overworked by efforts to mentor minority students (Tierney and Bensimon 1996). Power relations are not simply questions of *"me faculty, you student."* Grant and Graham (1994) suggest we use a Foucauldian view of power instead. Students and faculty are inserted into various discourses of the academy and of social life more generally (as we have seen most vividly with the story of John and Catherine) and thus the "rule of supervisory power is neither complete, nor is it unmediated by the students: both the student and the supervisor are acting subjects who may act on the actions of the other" (Grant and Graham 1994, 168).

DISCUSSION

One theme in this chapter has been that the graduate student experience is far from homogenous. I have given examples that focus on the particular characteristics of the student and the advisor and the negotiation that takes place throughout the relationship. There is much more that could be said about the context in which those activities take place, which would involve further study of the impact of departmental culture, disciplinary conventions, institutional type and location, government research policy, and the state of the economy and the academic labor market. Enough has been said to show that the relationship at the core of producing a doctoral dissertation, that between student and advisor, includes aspects of both power and pedagogy and cannot be made entirely predictable or homogenized. Students and advisors should understand that they may operate from very different perspectives that are rooted in their structural location within the academy. Moreover, these perspectives are further influenced, although by no means in simple fashion, by attributes such as gender and class origin. The advisory process is certainly important to the production of the successful graduate student—but it remains elusive, mysterious, and ambiguous, well below the tip of the hidden curriculum iceberg.

If being a graduate student involves extensive learning of norms and practices that are rarely explicitly shared, we may ask why the process is so mystified: What purpose does it serve? On the whole, I agree with Margolis and Romero (chapter five) that the process is one that replicates some of the more conservative aspects of academic life. A perpetual insecurity, a willingness to please even through abasement ("grovelling"), and a sense of one's own inadequacies provide a motor that drives the junior untenured academic, especially in research-based universities, to shape his or her work and personality to match the dominant ethic in the institution. Academics who rock the boat risk a painful immersion in chilly waters (Acker and Webber, 2000). In contrast, those who can make the habitus their own are more likely to enjoy their lives in academe. The hidden curriculum in graduate school is good preparation for the hidden curriculum of pre-tenure academic life. By the time security is achieved, any urge to defy convention has probably gone underground. For its faculty, as for its students, university life remains a microcosm of a class-, gender-, and race-stratified society.

NOTES

1. In this chapter, I use "advising" for general points, but "supervising" when reporting on the research conducted in Britain or Canada, where the latter term was the conventional one.
2. "Students and Supervisors: The Ambiguous Relationship. Perspectives on the Supervisory Process in Britain and Canada." In *Supervision of Postgraduate Research in Education. Review of Research in Education No. 5*, edited by A. Holbrook and S. Johnston. 75–94. Coldstream, Victoria, Australia: Association for Research in Education.
3. The study, conducted by Sandra Acker, Tim Hill, and Edith Black, was a funded, two- year project involving qualitative interviews conducted in 1990 and 1991, producing usable transcripts from sixty-seven students, fifty-six supervisors, and fourteen "others," such as heads of department or administrators. Three departments in each discipline participated. For more details, see Acker, Hill, and Black 1994a; Acker, Transken, Hill, and Black, 1994b; Hill, Acker and Black, 1994.
4. *Mentoring* is more fully investigated in chapter five by Margolis and Romero who examine the experiences of women of color in U.S. sociology graduate programs.

"In the Image and Likeness ..." 5

How Mentoring Functions in the Hidden Curriculum

Eric Margolis and Mary Romero

Mentoring has traditionally been an important apprentice model determining the advancement and success of graduate students. Unlike the more specific role of dissertation advisor discussed in the previous chapter, embedded in the concept "mentor" are a number of interpersonal relations. Two decades ago, Levinson, Darrow, Klein, Levinson, and McKee summarized the mentor's diffuse roles:

- A *teacher*, by enhancing an individual's skills and intellectual development;
- A *sponsor*, by using influence to facilitate an individual's entry and advancement;
- A *host and guide*, by welcoming the individual into a new occupational and social world and acquainting the individual with its values, customs, resources, and role players;
- An *exemplar*, by providing role modeling behavior. (Levinson et al. 1978 cited in Luna and Cullen 1996, 4)

More recently, mentoring has come to be seen as a panacea: empowering faculty, retaining students, improving curriculum and the quality of higher education, and offering particular benefits to minority students and women (Johnson 1989; Rendon and Justiz 1989; Pounds 1989; Rendon 1992; Luna and Cullen 1996; Faison 1996). A few scholars have approached the topic critically, warning of potential drawbacks to the mentoring relationship: it may be overly protective, stifling, egocentric, exploitative of the protégé (Levinson et al. 1996;

Fury 1979); may limit the protégé to a single relationship (Fury 1979); and may benefit the mentor more than the protégé (Rawles 1980; McGinnis and Long 1980 cited in Mirriam 1983, 170). Despite the notice of possible drawbacks, most writers proceed from the perspective of the institutions of higher education to emphasize ways that mentoring helps students (Luna and Cullen 1996). However, mentoring as an institutional practice has rarely been examined structurally or analyzed critically.

Blindness to structural significance and the student's perspective extends to the peculiar homage paid in the literature to the etymology of the word *mentor*. The word *mentor* has come to mean a trusted guide and advisor to the young. Attention has been given to the psychosocial aspects and ways that mentoring involves the "whole person" (cf. Erickson 1963; Levinson et al. 1978). Almost every writer on the issue comments on the origin of the word in Homer's *Odyssey* (Luna and Cullen 1996; Johnson 1989; Knox and McGovern 1988). In that epic, the goddess Athena disguised herself as "Mentor," a nobleman from Ithaca, to act as guide and advisor to Odysseus's young son while Odysseus was away; however:

> To him, on departing with his ships, Odysseus had given all his house
> in charge, that it should obey the old man and that he should keep
> all things safe. (Homer, *Odyssey*, Book 2, line 225)

No authors grasped the dual nature in Homer's description of mentor: to be counselor; to take charge of the household whose duty it was to obey "the old man." In fact, fifteen definitions of "mentoring" culled from the literature of higher education, business, and developmental psychology by Jacobi (1991) do not mention the functions for the institution. However, as we shall demonstrate, mentoring is all about the maintenance and reproduction of existing hierarchy and the status quo; the primary beneficiary is the institution. Mentors are first and foremost agents of socialization; it is this reproductive aspect of mentoring, essential to the activity, that is ignored by most writers on academic mentoring.

Proceeding from Janet Egan's (1989, 200) assessment of graduate school as a socialization process, we examined the structural consequences of mentoring in graduate school. Instead of beginning with institutional concerns like matriculation, supervision, and accountability, we adopted the perspective of those being "socialized"—the women of color graduate students that we interviewed. The present analysis focuses on the structural aspects of mentoring as an essential element of the legitimation and reproduction of academia.

The research reported on here is based on open-ended interviews with twenty-six women of color graduate students in sociology. The details of the sampling procedure and methods are discussed in Romero and Margolis (1998) (see also Romero and Storrs 1994; Margolis and Romero 1999; and Margolis and Romero 2000). In-depth, open-ended, tape-recorded telephone interviews ranged widely to explore the formal and informal social structures of graduate programs. Interviews included discussions of financial and mentoring support; relationships between faculty and graduate students; research, publishing, and teaching opportunities and experiences; and factors that influenced decisions to select programs and shape career plans. We asked open-ended questions about mentoring experiences, including questions about the subject and about their perceptions of the experiences of other students in their program—a process that left the women free to define mentoring as they saw it.[1]

If there is a master narrative in graduate school it is the reproduction of academia itself with its ivory tower, valorization of theoretical knowledge, disciplinary structures, emphasis on discourse and method, and hierarchies of knowledge and rank. Mentoring describes the process whereby people of power embedded in the system personally select and groom their successors—successors who will in their turn safeguard the noble house.[2] From this perspective, the mentoring function is perhaps the most singly important element of the hidden curriculum in higher education. Highlighting the difficulties in mentoring relationships and the experiences of women of color sheds light on the interpersonal dynamics and institutional structures that work against the students who are different from the faculty in the department in some key characteristics. As Mirriam (1983, 167) noted in her review of the mentoring literature, "successful but unmentored men and women are largely ignored in these studies as are other possible explanations for success." This chapter is an investigation of the role of conflict and dissent in the socialization of graduate students, specifically the importance of opposition and resistance in intellectual development. It concludes with an examination of alternative norms and values cultivated through conflict and dissent.

INTERPERSONAL DYNAMICS
AND INSTITUTIONAL STRUCTURES

Despite attempts to institutionalize mentoring programs (Luna and Cullen 1996), mentoring remains outside the institutional rules and it is rarely part of faculty accountability. No faculty can be forced to mentor a particular student, or to mentor them well. Mentoring is not enforceable and cannot easily be monitored, and neither student nor faculty can be held accountable for mentoring or not mentoring. The truth of this is captured in one student's observation: "It's just that there are students that professors would rather work with, rather help, rather make commitments toward and so forth." The presumption of choice and assortative mixing between mentors and students makes it look like a fair and equitable process; but there will never be a mentor for every student. Because part of the game of mirrors that is mentoring is for the mentor to shine by reflection, many tend to avoid the difficult students and select students who are already reflections of themselves (Roth 1955; Plutzer 1991). Two points that capture the essential basis for mentoring come from an interview with a very perceptive African American woman completing her dissertation at a private eastern university:

> I think they discriminate on the basis of class, one, and the second thing is interest. My perspective is so different from theirs that they know that we don't share enough in common to have a good solid working relationship with one another. It's just my bias is not the same as their bias. I think the institution or the people who represent the institution respond to you and make opportunities for you if they think that you're going to use them and make them look good.

From the perspective of the institution the mentor controls the gates to social reproduction. The explicitly personal nature of the relationship between mentor and student means that here the academic system works outside the formal curriculum and without regard to objective measurements like grades and test scores, or the laws and rules governing affirmative action and civil rights. Charles Lawrence and Mari Matsuda (1997, 100–1) remind us of the pitfalls of the subjectivity and personalism that are the hallmarks of the mentoring relation:

[S]ubjective evaluation invites prejudice. At one law firm, the evaluation sheet for associates asked: "is this our kind of person?" When insiders look for someone who "seems like the type of person who does well here," they tend to look for someone like themselves, missing the valuable talents of people who are different.

Moreover, decisions not to mentor are an essential way that the system produces losers. Thus, as in the law firm discussed by Lawrence and Matsuda, this is where the hidden curricula of academic institutions incorporate subjective judgments in a powerful way. The real conflict in finding a common ground for potential mentor and protégé lies in value differences and commitment to the institutional structure—academia, the discipline, the graduate program.

Five of the women that we interviewed described mentoring relations that they had with department faculty and each fit a traditional academic model. The students were single, young, and enrolled full-time, and embraced the career goal of a tenured academic position in a university sociology department.[3] The majority of the women that we interviewed did not fit this model and were not mentored by faculty. Some were international students. Others were older, had established careers in other settings, and approached graduate education with a different set of expectations. These older women of color were frequently from blue-collar, working-class backgrounds: they had different sets of life experiences; they had held full-time jobs for long periods of time; been married (and often divorced); had children and raised families; and a few had served in the armed forces. Interviewing nontraditional students gives us a useful window on student-faculty relations in higher education.

The unmentored students in our study were keenly aware that they violated many of the expectations held by faculty; they attributed this violation to their failure to attract mentors. A Latina from a working-class background blamed her lack of a mentor on her own failure to understand the system:

No one in my family has ever been to college. I didn't understand what graduate school was about. In a lot of ways I didn't understand that one has to kind of affiliate oneself to a professor and establish a relationship [because] that professor is in turn responsible for getting financial support for the student or for advising the student to do this, that or the other thing.

Unprepared to seek a mentor, this Latina student did not position herself to be drawn into a mentoring relationship. Unfamiliarity with the importance of mentoring and how the relationship operates in higher education may result in students missing opportunities.

However, not having a mentor may also be a product of not needing one. When we asked if she had a mentor, one African American woman explained:

> No. Probably because I didn't know that I needed one. I've been a 4.0 student throughout school. And I just didn't think I needed one. I'm sure that if I wanted one I could get one. We have a mentor program at the university. . . . You must remember, now, I'm a very mature student. I worked thirty-four years before I ever went to school; and so what they would offer me might not be what I could use.

Some of the non–traditional students are already in academic careers that are perceived as having low status by graduate faculty in the research-oriented institutions, namely those in positions at universities or community colleges. A Native American student who never had a mentor found the hierarchy stifling but persevered in order to acquire knowledge to help her in her job:

> I think the fact that I'm a little bit older, I'm not a young graduate student. Had I been younger, I would've dropped out. I would've definitely left if I had been in my twenties. But luckily I was in my thirties when I got into the program. I was already teaching at a college. I had tenure at another college.

It was typical that these women came to school with a well-developed research agenda:

> My dissertation topic is something that I've been thinking about from day one. And a lot of the work that I've done for various classes, whenever I've been able to, related it to my dissertation topic or some form of it. I have been collecting materials and talking to people and thinking about it for a long time.

> I started thinking, I should be able to do what I want to do. I'm a grown-up. I'm forty some years old. If I want to write a dissertation

about [X], then by God, I should be able to do that. And so that's what I decided I was going do.

These women recognized that mentors do not serve everyone and that the faculty decision to mentor or not was grounded in faculty and student characteristics, including: age, race, class, gender, ability, and sexual preference as well as political and personality issues. An African American woman completing her dissertation at an east coast university made the link between mentoring and reproducing the status quo:

> Mentoring relationships in this department? Yes. It actually does occur. There's this one professor who basically is one of the old guard who doesn't ever want to change his racist attitudes or his attitudes about smoking in the classroom. He basically operates on this old system of you know one professor, one student. He has a lot of students that work with him but yeah I mean it's really kind of the old fashioned way. You basically develop a working relationship with this person and you're his protégé in a way. So all his students actually have this kind of relationship with him and he's producing somebody who's gonna be like himself.

This student's assessment of the mentoring relationship brought to light the inequities of mentoring relationships that were not offered to everyone, or operated to reproduce the old discipline and its networks.

CONFLICT, OPPOSITION, AND THE FUNCTION OF MENTORING

Much of the literature on mentoring either ignores conflict and dissent or implicitly assumes a teaching-centered model of learning. In borrowing concepts from business models, discussions of mentoring fail to examine what must be core issues in academia: student agency, the development of intellect, and the connection to the great chain of cultural symbols that is scholarship. Mentoring reproduces specific models of academic endeavor, but conflict and opposition are essential to the development of new forms of thought and paradigms. In the process of intellectual struggle, mentoring has at best a suspect role. Scholarship is not all about getting through graduate school or getting an academic job. Moreover, as Peter McLaren and Henry Giroux (1994, 26) noted in a different context: "Mental development can take place under both favorable and unfavorable conditions. . . . people develop cognitively often during attempts to resist—to overcome disadvantageous circumstances." This was clearly evident in one woman's statement:

> The thing that I got out of Yale was my struggle against the institution, my struggle against how sociology was taught there and I think I learned a lot about being critical by struggling against what I thought was inequitable in the department.

The situation faced by women of color graduate students makes an important example because it involved not simply integrating into academia, but changing academic theories, practices, and institutions in profound ways that the institutions and institutional power structures prohibited and sought to prevent. The academic careers of these women were part of intersecting and not always congruent projects stemming from the social movements of civil rights, feminism, and the gay movement, and from insurgent theoretical perspectives like Marxism, postmodernism, multiculturalism, critical pedagogy, and critical race theory. The women that we interviewed entered the academic world at a particular historic moment in the late 1980s and early '90s. Their presence, a product of court orders and affirmative action programs as well as the encouragement of the preceding generations of academics of color, was part of an opening wedge that began cleaving academia in the 1960s and is not done yet. And the increasing presence of such non-traditional students in graduate school portended additional change in sociology.

In the discussions that follow, we turn to an analysis of resistance and opposition to the hierarchical regimes of graduate school that include the status of rank and discipline; patriarchy; and racial, ethnic, and national subordination.

Resistance

In our study, *resistance* seems to fall into the category of feelings that "I don't want to grow up to be like you." An African American woman in an Ivy League university gave this reaction to one of the members of her committee:

I always felt very suspicious of his support because some of it came unprompted and had a weird ring to it. And as it turns out, I sat in on his class and he and I had a big falling out, basically because we fundamentally disagreed on a lot of things and he finally was able to say, "look, I'm neoconservative." And that didn't come out until I took his course, so I felt like he was sort of doing a good deed, you know, by encouraging me. And the problem with that is I didn't really feel like he honestly respected my work. I felt like he was, you know, "this is my civic duty to support this minority graduate student." And I find that pretty insulting.

An A.B.D. Asian American graduate student in an Ivy League university was from time to time invited to luncheons where faculty mentors and their chosen students interacted. She recalled these relationships with scorn:

The four other male students, it was like, you know, when we had these lunches, it was their opportunity to shine for the professor and they were extremely competitive. You know, they were extremely arrogant. I also got a sense of how they treated their students, you know, so it was all very, sort of, authoritarian and, you know, this is an opportunity to impress the boss.

The personalized power relationship of mentor-protégé may be particularly unacceptable to non–traditional students—including those who are working-class, people of color, women, and older students. For some students such closeness represents illegitimate authority, an unwelcome and condescending parental figure, a sexual threat, or a hurdle to be overcome or circumvented. An older African American woman graduate student observed:

I like to keep distance in those relationships. I don't want to add too much personality into it. Because sometimes people can get into arguments on a personal level that they wouldn't get involved with on an academic or professional level. And I've seen that. I've already seen a couple of my female cohorts get into this kind of father-daughter thing, and it might be more difficult. . . . But I really don't want to get involved in that dynamic. I have a father and I have enough with the one that I have.

Three of the students we interviewed—an Asian American, an African American, and a Native American—rejected the traditional taken-for-granted power relations of graduate school. As one asserted:

> I didn't want to go get myself locked into place where they say come in, take sixteen courses, we tell you what sixteen. And do a thesis. We tell you what thesis, and also you're gonna work on your professor's project while you're at it. I really resented that.

In some cases resistance was grounded in a profound dislike of faculty: a distrust of their politics and a wariness of personal relations within or across gender, racial, class, and nationality lines. In other cases, the traditional academic rituals of subordination were denied legitimacy.

Opposition

As part of the development of feminist and nonwhite paradigms for sociology, women of color graduate students and faculty opposed elements of the graduate curriculum and the discipline itself. A black woman spoke for many of our respondents when she criticized the abstract theoretical thrust of her program:

> I mean they place a much higher value and premium on things that are purely theoretical types of studies. And things like that than they do things that I consider more practical and policy oriented. I think that the historical background of Black women—that we are interested in things that we feel like can make a difference in the real world.

A Native American woman's critique not only pointed out the essentialist Eurocentrism of the discipline but the peculiar form of logocentrism embedded in the tyranny of print media:

> It was like saying that all the thinking in the world comes from Europe. People in other parts of the world don't have any ideas. And a lot of it has to do with the fact that you're always in competition with the written word. And what's written down is God. You know it's reified in paper so therefore how can you question this?

The vast majority of the women that we interviewed defined themselves and their intellectual careers in opposition to the department and the types of knowledge that were being privileged and reproduced.[4] They lived their graduate school project in opposition to the dominant forms of knowledge and to the existing hierarchy. Each idea put forth by their professors could not be accepted at face value, but had to be tested against an identity different from "white sociology." They had to bring race into the center of sociological discourse even though it was never central to the canon.

Being in opposition does not simply mean confronting abstract ideas; frequently and most uncomfortably it means confronting one's professors:

> I have never treated these faculty members like they were gods or anything like that. Some students are just terrified of actually confronting them about what we don't like about their work, or what we don't understand, or what we think needs to be developed more fully, or what have you.

For these women, one problem with having a mentor is becoming beholden to that person. At national meetings, associations set up an employment service—colloquially known as the meat market. Frequently one sees protégés all dressed up and trailing behind their mentor with respectful and hopeful looks on their faces. Among some of the women, making it without mentors or assistance became a point of pride: "You know that on some level I don't feel beholden to them for anything because other than admitting me to the program they haven't given me anything. So of course I was very outspoken about my experience." Joyce Ladner set forth the challenge to future generations of sociologists of color with her 1973 volume *The Death of White Sociology*. She began with the following epigram from Lerone Bennett, *The Challenge of Blackness* (1972, 35–36), which said, in part:

> It is necessary for us to develop a new frame of reference which transcends the limits of white concepts. It is necessary for us to develop and maintain a total intellectual offensive against the false universality of white concepts, whether they are expressed by William Styron or Daniel Patrick Moynihan.

Whether the goal of killing white sociology is understood in Kuhnian terms of scientific revolutions, or as the oedipus/electra complex that requires killing the father/mother figure, earning their doctorates without help, or in spite of the faculty, was an important form of opposition. In the account below, this woman explains the racial climate in academia that led her to write articles and send them out to journals *before* showing them to her professors:

> If I failed I wanted it to be my failure. And I was willing to accept that. And if I succeeded at it, I wanted it to be my success because part of what happens, being a minority student, you spend so much time in another world—you sort of start questioning your own intelligence. And you start to wonder what ideas are yours, and what are somebody else's. And so I did not give it to anybody to look at. I sent it in and you know I sent in my first two articles totally. Once they came back with the acceptance and I did the corrections and got them in, that's when my professors saw them for the first time.

These forms of overt political opposition are unavoidable and are clearly a boon to self-esteem but have personal and professional costs for the student. In one Native American student's experience:

> If you don't jump in as a woman of color and start playing their game and turning out white sociology then it just takes you forever. And then you get a really bad reputation as well as a troublemaker and so on.

Failure to show deference and a willingness to engage in political arguments also contributes to the inability of these students to find mentors among faculty who may find this behavior threatening. The following statements by two students finishing their dissertations, one Asian American at a southern university and one Latina at an eastern university, demonstrate this:

> I am very vocal and I am very political. So I had problems first with my political beliefs. I'm considered what you can call probably a progressive person. And I face problems with professors because of my political beliefs. And of course that's related to what I am. A Filipino woman. In one particular class, for example, I had to even to rewrite

a paper because the professor thought that it was too Marxist oriented or too, you know, "left" for him.

Any type of research is a political option you do and depends on your perspective. . . . What I'm trying to say is that they will be interested [in your work] as long as it expresses their own views, too. But as long as it contradicts what they stand for, they don't support it, nor do they see it as valid and so that's a political issue.

These patterns of opposition illustrate the extent to which non–traditional students are far less accepting of the power differentials of academia, including the mentor-protégé relationship. Some women from communities of color or working-class backgrounds may have cultural beliefs and practices antithetical to those promulgated in academia.

The rejection of mentoring and faculty guidance is a complicated issue because these independent women were simultaneously aware that they were missing important elements of their graduate education. An African American woman attending a major Midwest state university explained that no one informed her of funding opportunities, taught her how to write a proposal, or made any suggestions about how to get her work published. She put it ruefully:

No, I've never really had a mentor. And I've really missed that. You know there are some students who get the opportunity to work on a publication or research project with another faculty member. That hasn't happened to me. I'm not sure why that is. Part of it may just be that I'm not the kind of person that asks a lot of other people. Maybe they [mentored students] were more aggressive or more assertive or something. I guess I feel a little slighted. There are some students that have that mentor-student relationship and I've never managed to have that at all. I've always felt like I was kind of out there on my own. Everybody's been perfectly nice and helpful and complimentary, but as far as someone who just really took me under their wing, showed me the ropes so to speak, or that kind of thing [it didn't occur]. I feel like it's been a real individual project for me.

Resistance and opposition is likely a situation to which one is condemned—cast into by gender, culture, age, and race. Certain students live their graduate career in resistance or opposition because it is the only choice in a system that was not made for them. Bonilla, Pickron, and Tatum (1994), in their profoundly oppositional essay on peer mentoring among graduate students of color, direct us toward some alternatives to academic mentoring as usually practiced. These three graduate students in education worked together to shepherd each other through the dissertation process, and in reflecting on this experience describe many of the things that faculty mentors cannot provide. Like the students we interviewed, they describe feelings of fear, frustration, anger, and vulnerability and the need to question academia itself. They recognized that "[t]he major difference lies in the power and status relationship of the faculty-student relationship versus the equality inherent in the peer mentoring relationship" (Bonilla, Pickron, and Tatum 1994, 112).

Similar alternative support networks were reported by numerous women we interviewed. One of our interview subjects, an older Latina from Southern California, reflected on a support group she turned to after being told by her chair that: "people like you don't finish the program. It's a waste for the university and for you and your time. You should go back to your family and just forget about this." She commented:

> I couldn't believe it. I was in shock. I realized that, "wait a minute, you know, all these people, the whole faculty are my enemies. They are not here for me or in the same way that they are here for the younger students." But what I did instead of going and crying on my own—we used to have a women's group, support group of women. It was mostly Anglo women, a lot of lesbian women. Probably there was something that they could understand because they couldn't come out in that department, in that environment. They knew that they [faculty] would punish them in the same way that they were punishing me for being Latina.

While it muddies the conceptual waters to call formal and informal organizations of graduate students "mentors" or "peer mentors," graduate student political organizations and affinity groups are essential both in aiding graduate students and in reshaping academia to be more inclusive and less hierarchical. In organizing, students can move from individual resistance to the kind of organized opposition that produces change. At one university, the concept has been institutionalized by graduate students, as one of our respondents recalled:

We created a position in the department for a graduate student who is a mentor to minority graduate students and he has been in the department for the last two years. And that was thanks to the pressure we put on them [faculty]. The graduate mentor has to be a person of color because that person is going to be sensitive and is going to know how to relate to his own or her own experience, what these minority students might face. We don't want them [new students] to go through the same things that we had to face.

A Native American woman attributed her persistence in the program to a peer relationship with another Indian graduate student:

I almost quit. One time because I just got so fed up with just the whole system. . . . There were some other people at the university that were friends of mine that I went to see. Another Indian graduate student who had a really very similar experience in another department who had graduated had always told me, "You're gonna do it in spite of the university." So it's like being in a little—you know metaphorically—it's like being in a war. . . . That's sort of the mentality that I took on. That I'm going to do this and I'm not going to let them sort of break me or I'm not going to give up.

Peer relationships among students with similar backgrounds and political commitments confirm and enhance the women of color graduate students' identity as scholars, teachers, and researchers. These relationships create a culture of cooperation rather than competition and may serve as the kernel of change in the discipline and academia.

DISCUSSION

From the vantage of the student there are a number of problems that cannot be addressed by more effective mentoring programs. The uncritical advocacy of mentoring programs does not recognize that:

- Mentoring has specific reproduction functions that may not benefit or be appropriate for some students;
- Mentoring empowers the institution and the faculty at the expense of the student and does not recognize student agency or resistance;
- Mentoring is not a cure for structural racism;

- Mentoring offers no meaningful way to change the system;
- Business models based on hierarchy may not be appropriate for academia where the life of the mind depends on criticism, opposition, and resistance as much as on "learning the ropes";
- Mentoring functions as an individual path to upward mobility. It is a different model from a civil rights or group conflict approach of group relations;
- Mentoring assumes that students and faculty share common goals. Some faculty and students reject the hierarchical position or parental affirming and enhancing role.

Embedded in the construction of mentoring are two central issues: (1) the function of mentoring is a device to reproduce existing systems and institutions; and (2) the failure to recognize that women and minority scholars profoundly changes the culture of academia, for they cannot simply be socialized into academics like their white male predecessors. The movement of women, people of color, and gays has been an oppositional movement, not one of inclusion. This project is in opposition to mentoring to reproduce the institution. In *Talking Back*, bell hooks (1989, 58–59) analyzed her graduate school experience in English, similar in every way to the accounts reported by the sociology students in our study:

> During graduate school, white students would tell me that it was important not to question, challenge, or resist. Their tolerance level seemed much higher than my own or that of other black students. Critically reflecting on the differences between us, it was apparent that many of the white students were from privileged class backgrounds. Tolerating the humiliations and degradations we were subjected to in graduate school did not radically call into question their integrity, their sense of self-worth. . . . To them, tolerating forms of exploitation and domination in graduate school did not evoke images of a lifetime spent tolerating abuse. They would endure certain forms of domination and abuse, accepting it as an initiation process that would conclude when they became the person in power. In some ways they regarded graduate school as a game and they submitted to playing the role of subordinate. I and many other students, especially non-white students from non-privileged backgrounds, were unable to accept and play this "game." Often we were ambivalent about the

rewards offered. Many of us were not seeking to be in a position of power over others. Though we wished to teach, we did not want to exert coercive authoritarian rule over others. . . .

Although hooks writes as if she is taking a heroic stance "transgressing" and "talking back," for most of the women we interviewed the situation was far more painful and uncertain. It is not comfortable to oppose the power structure, to suffer much of graduate school alone, to see peers benefit from relations with faculty denied or unavailable to you. One seldom feels heroic or empowered. Much resistance is by necessity what Maddox (1997, 276) termed "expressions of alienated resentment," as exemplified in the following commentary by a Latina attending a west coast university:

> Oh you saw white students working with all different kinds of people in that department. It seemed like every professor would have a pet or a couple of pets that they would take under their wing. One of my office mates was always working and involved in research. And I got to the point where I didn't even like her. Because I could see that going on with her and it wasn't happening with us.

As we asked in our earlier work (Margolis and Romero 1998), How can the hidden curriculum "reproduce" what does not yet exist— that is, women of color sociologists? Mentoring, which functions as a key element in professional socialization, clearly could not be the answer to insurgents seeking to change sociology. In the long run, however, as the role and status of these women change the discipline—as they take their place in the hierarchy—they will be in a position to aid those who come after.

Academia has produced "good old girls" networks, associations of scholars of color, and journals that are parallel to but structurally function in much the same way as the "good old boys" networks, and similarly there are critical and progressive networks that strive to mentor students and reproduce their own structures. It is curious to consider what it means for critical theorists to arrive at tenured positions and be in position to mentor their own critical students who do not thus produce themselves as oppositional theorists but are reproduced in an uncritical way. New networks are routinized; new paradigms become "normal science." Tools for accomplishing this become part of hidden curricula. The larger issue of course is that the dialectic of change both in science and in the arts and humanities predicts that new groups with new ideas will seek to break in and change the disciplines in the future in ways those disciplines try to prevent. Mentoring will always function to limit and slow change.

NOTES

1. Less than half of our sample (43 percent) claimed to have been mentored. For minority students, this seems to be an improvement over earlier statistics. In 1989 Blackwell reported that only 20 percent of African American students had mentors. Our findings of 43 percent were less than Knox and McGovern's 1988 study of Virginia Commonwealth University in which 66 percent of women students had a mentor. Those who had been mentored described faculty behaviors ranging from offering advice about the program and information about the profession to the offer of research or teaching assistantships to warm personal friendships. However, detailed long-term guidance through graduate studies and collaborative research were comparatively rare, noted by only half of those who reported mentoring relationships.

2. As Luna and Cullen (1996, 62) emphasized: "Mentoring should be reserved for developing human potential in terms of improving organizational goals."

3. This is congruent with Acker's concept discussed in the previous chapter that "registration status" is an important axis of differentiation.

4. While no doubt in many departments there were faculty of color and women who shared and encouraged the students' perspective, they do not dominate sociology or the power structure of departments.

Training Capitalism's Foot Soldiers 6

The Hidden Curriculum
of Undergraduate Business Education

Kenneth N. Ehrensal

This chapter is about the education of "white collar" workers. I use this term very loosely to include professionals, technical specialists in and around corporate headquarters, and *managers*—the foot soldiers of corporate power. I find this group particularly interesting because of the way in which they see themselves. In a society where the conventional wisdom states that we do not see ourselves in class terms, these workers, who make up about 15 percent of the labor force, do see themselves as a group separate from and with different interests than blue-collar workers. In many ways, this group's self-image mirrors the traditional Marxist cosmology that the world was divided into the working class (or labor), the managerial class, and the capitalist class. This division of the world is, of course, problematic in that it ignores the fact that managers, like labor, are employees of capital. This leads to the general question that typically interests me. That is, by what processes do white-collar workers come to imagine their interests as linked to the interests of capital, rather than the interests of the broader working-class?

This question is not irrelevant to the study of the capitalist labor process. Clearly, in order to take on their role as organizational agents for capital, a change in their subjective perception of self is required. This chapter will argue that this change in self-perception is a key ingredient to the group of employees' *consent* to the division of labor and the capitalist labor process.

"PLAYING THE GAME"—
PROBLEMS IN MANUFACTURING CONSENT

In his classic workplace ethnography *Manufacturing Consent* (1979), sociologist Michael Buroway argued that consent to the capitalist labor process is derived by "playing the game" of "making out." That is, consent is manufactured through the compensation system. By "playing the game" workers are co-opted into their role in the system. As Buroway (1979, 79) stated: "[o]ne cannot both play the game and at the same time question the rules."

In attempting to apply this schema to white-collar workers, I note that it varies little from early management theorist Chester Barnard's theory of authority ([1938] 1968) and its elaboration in Cyert and March (1963). Here, consent, or "zone of indifference" as it is called by these authors, is obtained through co-optation created through the use of "side payments" derived from "organizational slack." If the individual demonstrates that he or she is willing to play the game, she or he is duly rewarded. This formulation of consent seems reasonable if one focuses only on the control of task performance and levels of productivity; that is, production workers' willingness to meet quotas or white-collar workers' willingness to put in extra hours for the same pay. However, utilizing this scheme is difficult to explain, for example, foremen in General Motors assembly plants have been reported to actually "enjoy" engaging in activity that would draw grievances from their unionized workers (Hamper 1992).

Buroway (1979, 82) made the claim that:

> I am not arguing that playing the game rests on a broad consensus; on the contrary, consent rests upon—is constructed through—playing the game. The game does not reflect an underlying harmony of interests; on the contrary, it is responsible for and generates that harmony. The source of the game itself does not lie in a preordained value consensus but in historically specific struggles to adapt to the deprivation inherent in work and struggles with management to define the rules.

Here I part company with Buroway's analysis. Buroway argued that it is the game itself that both manufactures consent and obscures the relations of production. What I will demonstrate is that the game is played in an arena in which all of the players know the rules long before they hear the starting whistle. That is, consent is first created in people's heads and then reinforced by the playing of the game. Institutions beyond the workplace, such as the media and, as I argue here, schools, function to

> inculcate individuals with the values, beliefs, and codes of behavior that will integrate them into the institutional structures of the larger society. (Herman and Chomsky 1988, 1)

Thus, long before their first day in the workplace, working-class lads "learn to labor" (Willis [1997] 1981), working-class girls "become clerical workers" (Valli 1986), and female undergraduates are "educated in romance" (Holland and Eisenhart 1990).

SCHOOLING AND CAPITALISM

What I will argue is that we cannot understand the control of the labor process, and in particular control of white-collar labor processes, without understanding the role of schooling in capitalism. For it is schooling that creates the subjective arena in which consent will take place. Further on in this chapter, I will argue that collegiate-level business schools are the pinnacle of schooling. But first, I want to examine schooling under capitalism in general. In their essential text, Samuel Bowles and Herbert Gintis (1976, 54) demonstrated that schooling under capitalism is:

> dominated by the imperatives of profit and domination rather than human need. The unavoidable necessity of growing up and getting a job in the United States forces us all to become less than we could be: less free, less secure, in short less happy. The U.S. economy is a formally totalitarian system in which the actions of the vast majority (workers) are controlled by a small minority (owners and managers).

> Making U.S. capitalism work involves: insuring minimal participation in decision making by the majority (the workers); protecting a single minority (capitalists and managers) against the wills of a majority; and subjecting the majority to the maximal influence of this single unrepresentative minority.

Or as Daniel Liston (1988, 16) put it:

> At the risk of oversimplification, this connection can be presented in the following manner: schools produce minimally skilled workers for wage labor, and these institutions "educate" workers to an ideology of compliance.

The general argument in the radical critique of schooling literature runs as follows. The primary dilemma of capital is that roughly 80 percent of the workforce needs to be simultaneously excluded from any meaningful participation in the economy and yet needs to be utilized in the production of goods that brings wealth to a small minority of capitalists. Thus there is both a need for control and an "unfortunate" dependency. The ramification for education is the "factory model" of schooling, with its emphasis on structure, discipline, and order. In schools under capitalism children are taught how to be "on task" and to regulate their work habits, bladders, and bowels to the demands of a time clock.[1]

The rise of large-scale industrial capitalism creates an even larger paradox: the rise of the professional manager. While traditional Marxists conceptually lump owners and managers together, they are, in fact, distinct entities (Roomkin 1989). Thus, we have a group of employees who are at once waged workers of the organization while at the same time, agents of capital's control over the productive process. This separation of ownership from control is further exacerbated as firms grow larger and a greater number of managers are added. It falls on the public school system to supply capital with the necessary labor to take these positions, and requires the schooling system to ensure that while these white-collar workers have the required technical skills, they also have appropriate attitudes to carry out the tasks that will be asked of them.

Socialization to this role is both subtle and incomplete. It starts early in schooling, with the purposeful skimming of the top 10 percent (or so) of students into what will eventually become the "college track" curriculum in the secondary school. Simultaneously, tracking starts the process of socializing these individuals' perception of a world divided into "us and them." This is further solidified by the secondary school experience, where the isolation of the college-bound is accomplished not only in the academic but also in the extracurricular arena.[2]

By the time individuals find themselves in college they have spent a substantial portion of their time isolated from those whom they will later be asked to manage.

MANAGEMENT EDUCATION AS SYMBOLIC VIOLENCE

The central premise of this chapter is that collegiate-level business and management "education" is a form of symbolic violence.[3] In the previous part of this chapter, it has been argued that the public school system under capitalism begins the process of schooling future college graduates to see themselves as a class separate from non–college graduates. Thus it creates the division in the working-class between, essentially, blue-collar and white-collar workers. That division is further widened and then cemented through the schooling of future managers.

The principle by which "symbolic violence" is imposed, according to French social theorist Pierre Bourdieu, is through schooling or what he calls "pedagogic action" (Bourdieu and Passeron 1990). The imposition of cultural arbitraries—in this case, the perceived differentiation of class interests between blue-collar and white-collar employees—and the perceived allying of white-collar class interests with those of the power elite[4] can be seen as the primary role of management "education." Pedagogic action is delegated by those in power to agents who exercise pedagogic authority, the right (through claim to expertise) to transmit pedagogic communication; that is, deliver the message of the cultural arbitraries. This is explored in the following section.

PEDAGOGIC AUTHORITY

Elsewhere (Ehrensal 1999) I have argued that the business school accreditation process acts to establish pedagogic authority. Here I summarize that argument. According to Bourdieu:

> Because every PA [**pedagogic action**] that is exerted commands by definition a PAu [pedagogical authority], the pedagogic transmitters are from the outset *designated as fit* to transmit that which they transmit. . . . (Bourdieu and Passeron 1990, 20, emphasis added)
>
> Every agency (agent or institution) exerting a PA [**pedagogic action**] commands PAu [**pedagogic authority**] in its capacity as the

mandated representative of the groups or classes whose cultural arbitrary it imposes in accordance with a mode of imposition defined by the arbitrary, i.e. as the *delegated* holder of the right to exercise symbolic violence. (Bourdieu and Passeron 1990, 24, emphasis added)

In a commentary in the *Journal of Management Education*, Wanda Smith (1994, 238) explicitly posited that it is the role of (undergraduate) management education to "satisfy management's expectation of anticipatory socialization." She explains:

Business faculty have been given the responsibility of instilling students with the desired technical skills, as well as with anticipatory socialization—exposing them to beliefs and values of organizations of which they aspire to become members. Principally, employers expect business graduates to have developed belief systems and a variety of survival skills . . . prior to joining their organization.

Thus, business professors are imbued with pedagogic authority, and delegated the right *and* responsibility to impose the required ideological training upon their charges so that when graduates join organizations after the completion of their studies, they will accept the system of authority as legitimate.

However, only those who are "designated as fit" may be assigned these roles. This is no trivial point in American business education. Currently there are two non–governmental organizations for the accreditation of business programs and schools—the American Assembly of Collegiate Schools of Business (AACSB) and the Association of Collegiate Business Schools and Programs (ACBSP). While specifics of the criteria for accreditation differ between the two organizations (AACSB accreditation is geared primarily for research-oriented schools, while ACBSP focuses on teaching-oriented programs), each has specific guidelines concerning the credentials of the faculty, the structures of the curriculum, and content of specific courses.

As for faculty credentials, the research-oriented AACSB defines the primary qualification to be a doctoral degree in a relevant business discipline. It then allows for doctoral degrees in "related" disciplines, when they are supplemented with a business-oriented research program. Under the rules, economists or industrial psychologists who received their degrees from faculties of arts and sciences fall into this second category. ACBSP is more "liberal" in its policy, having two categories for faculty—doctorally qualified and professionally qualified. They are less stringent about the discipline of one's doctorate, as long as it is either in a business discipline or a related field. *Professionally qualified* means either M.Phil./A.B.D. in a business discipline, a M.B.A. and industrial experience, or some degree and substantial executive-level experience. In either case, discipline must be maintained (Foucault 1979) and "outsiders" must be eliminated. Further, while not all schools are accredited, most programs are "associate members" of either one or both of these organizations. Therefore their guidelines drive the staffing policy throughout the "industry."

PEDAGOGIC ACTION

Again, according to Bourdieu:

> All **pedagogic action** (PA) is objectively, symbolic violence insofar as it is the imposition of a cultural arbitrary by an arbitrary power. (Bourdieu and Passeron 1990, 5)

> In any given social formation the cultural arbitrary which the power relations between the groups or classes making up that social formation put into the dominant position within the system of cultural arbitraries is the one which most fully, though always indirectly, express the objective interests (material and symbolic) of the dominant groups or classes. (Bourdieu and Passeron 1990, 9)

To understand how business faculty fulfill this responsibility, we must examine how they carry out their *pedagogic work*. Pedagogic work is defined as:

> a process of inculcation which must last long enough to produce a durable training, i.e. a *habitus*, [5] the product of internalization of the principles of a cultural arbitrary capable of perpetuating itself after PA [pedagogic action] has ceased and thereby of perpetuating in practices the principles of the internalized arbitrary. (Bourdieu and Passeron 1990, 31)

Both the overall curriculum and the content of specific courses are also dictated by the accrediting organizations (Ehrensal 1999). The principal purpose of undergraduate business education is to inculcate in students various forms of habitus that are both adaptive to and desired by the organizations with which they seek to find employment. This habitus serves the organization's interests by making the inculcated individuals "self-controlling" actors within the organization, and by elevating the need for various overt control systems (supervision, technological controls, and bureaucratic controls). The inculcation of this managerial habitus is accomplished through several types of pedagogic action commonly found in business school classrooms.

All undergraduate business students are exposed to the same core of courses during the early stages of their business education (Ehrensal 1999). These courses consist of micro- and macroeconomics, a year of financial accounting, principals of management, principals of marketing, and an introductory course in corporate finance. These courses share the following common features:

- The teaching of these courses is highly textbook dependent, that is, instructors rarely, if ever, use primary sources.
- An examination of the various textbooks in the market for any of these courses reveals that they are highly uniform in content, varying only in such features as the level of writing and the use of color and graphics.
- A significant portion of the textbook is dedicated to introducing the student to new specialized vocabulary.
- Typical mass-market texts come with significant amounts of instructor "resources," including detailed lecture outlines and notes; test banks with both objective and essay questions, plus outlines of correct answers for the essays; and instructor's case notes, detailing the correct student responses to end-of-the-chapter case studies and problems.

The world portrayed in business textbooks is one of simplified certainty. There are distillations of management practice and knowledge (both folk and expert), which in the world are highly context-bound, contingent, and probabilistic. In contrast, text knowledge appears to be normative, certain, and based on universal precepts. I will return in a moment to the issues of how and what is included (and what is excluded), but first, I will look at the pedagogic authority of the textbook.

Written in third person passive voice, it does not present what the particular author thinks or believes to be true about management, but rather a litany of what the recognized "experts" have found to be "true." Thus, what is included in the text becomes the received knowledge of the sages, and as management professors Stephen Fineman and Yannis Gabriel (1994, 379) noted in their analysis of rhetorical techniques in organizational behavior textbooks, "[a] text's persuasiveness can depend as much on what is excluded as what is included." Strategic exclusions (the null curriculum [Eisner 1985]) can reduce ambiguity and given the authority of the text, banish particular perspectives from the field. Excluded from the textbooks are any perspectives that question the capitalist project, suggest that organizations are or could be dysfunctional, or suggest that any interests beyond those of the stockholders might be seriously taken account of in the decision-making process.

The second form of pedagogic action is the classroom lecture. This in many ways is more complex than the issues raised by textbooks. Here, both the lecturer and the lecture bear their own (somewhat) independent pedagogic authority. The lecturer often brings two forms of authority with her or him. The first is based upon his or her institutional role. As the faculty of record, with the authority to both present material and evaluate student performance (an issue to be discussed later), the faculty assume an identity transcendent of their particular personalities. In this sense, they share pedagogic authority with all other faculty in all other disciplines. Here, however, we are interested in examining their pedagogic authority to inculcate managerial habitus. In that role, we must examine how business faculty establish pedagogic authority beyond their purely institutional role. It is not uncommon for business faculty to create pedagogic authority by making reference to their connections to the business community. This is done either by reference to the business careers that they had prior to coming to academia or by claims about the business consulting practices that they have. Reference to these is made either when they are talking about their biographies, or as anecdotes in lectures where reference to their experience is meant to illustrate a point being transmitted in the lecture. Thus, in the business school classroom the pedagogic authority of the lecturer is derived through a combination of institutional and personal authority.

The pedagogic authority of the lecture itself is similarly highly complex. In part, the lecture derives authority from its consistency with the textbook. That is, to the degree that it is consistent with the textbook it is deemed acceptable by the student. This is not as problematic as it may seem on its face. All mass-market textbooks in this area come accompanied by extensive supplemental materials for the instructor, including highly detailed lecturer notes that summarize material included in the text as well as "enrichment" materials that reinforce the message in the text, but are not included in it (e.g., blue boxes). Thus, the typical lecture is one that reiterates material from the text, utilizes third party examples—from sources like the lecturer's notes—and often inserts relevant examples from the individual's own experience. To the degree that these are consistent with the messages derived directly from the text, they are seen as having authority.

However, we must recognize that beyond consistency, lectures themselves—consistent or not—bear pedagogic authority. As Bourdieu (1991) pointed out, lectures are a form of the "discourse of authority" and as such are authorized language. They represent the delegation of that authority from higher, yet potentially obscured sources. Thus, the lecturer, in his or her speech act, is not recognized necessarily as speaking for herself or himself, but rather is seen as speaking for the institution itself. Thus, the lecture, like the relationship of the textbook to its author, has the potential to be transcendent of its speaker.

Case Studies

Case study analysis as a form of pedagogic action has its origin in the business school but has, over time, spread to other administrative programs. The case study itself presents the student with a scenario, sometimes based upon reality and sometimes fictional, in which the student is to bring to bear appropriate theoretical and conceptual frameworks for its analysis. In doing so, the student demonstrates that she or he can take the general and universal and apply it correctly to the specific. As Stewart (1991, 121) explained: "The management case study teaches theory by fulfilling two functions: (1) illustration (translating from the abstract to the concrete), and (2) socialization (conveying the paradigm that governs the theory's application)." Stewart (1991, 122) continued:

> The second function of the case study [socialization] is to help bring the neophyte into the community of the discipline. A case study

conveys the theoretical paradigm to new members of the theoretical community by telling a story that shows the paradigm in action. Reading a case study, the neophyte sees not only what problems look like, but also what problem-solvers look like. By setting out the problem in such a way as to suggest how to play the role of the problem-solver, the case is in effect socializing the neophyte.

Stewart's statements about case studies in general can also be applied to the case studies that would be included at the ends of chapters of the typical business school textbook. However, these cases vary in one important way from the more general model of case studies in that they always include specific questions that direct the analysis that the (undergraduate) student will do. Thus, in the early stages of socialization, the directive nature of the questions points the student to the specific theory that they need to apply—very little is left to chance.

The case, as part of the textbook, thus carries with it the transcendent voice and therefore the pedagogic authority of the text. In addition, all textbooks come with instructor's resource material, which includes the answers to the questions at the end of the case. Thus, not only does the question direct the student, but also the answers ensure that the lecturer follows the appropriate line of action in her or his discussion of the case.

Within the classroom itself there may be further forms of pedagogic action. One often finds the use of experiential exercises, typically in the form of role-playing and games. In these exercises, students are asked to demonstrate behaviorally their mastery of appropriate management behaviors in the simulated organizational situations in which they are placed. These are often filmed for review, and always critiqued by the instructor and often by fellow classmates. Behavioral errors are highlighted, not only for the individual's learning, but also in order to heighten social learning among all classroom participants.

In addition to behavioral evaluations that occur in experiential exercises, behavioral modeling also takes more subtle forms in business classrooms. Business faculty traditionally come to class wearing "business attire," with haircuts appropriate for the corporate sector, and usually, among male faculty, without facial hair, as would be appropriate in business. Additionally, it is not uncommon for faculty to require students to come to class in "appropriate" business attire on days when the students are scheduled to give in-class presentations.

Films are also heavily used in business school teaching. Often they are commercially produced training films used to reinforce particular points already made in the lecture material. However, faculty in the field of management frequently use popularly released feature films or television shows that can be analyzed in class using the lens of this or that particular theory. The logic of these exercises is that business school theory can be used to analyze anything in life.

There are also a number of forms of pedagogic action in the business school that take place outside the immediate classroom setting. Among these are "outside" speakers from the business community used either on campus or during site visits, where students meet with business "leaders" at their location. In these activities, classroom lessons are validated and extended. Students observe that real live business people actually *act* and *think* in ways consistent with portraits in lectures and texts. Additionally, these activities allow the student to observe particular modeled behavior in the "real world."

Outside speakers and site visits are often orchestrated by student clubs such as Students in Free Enterprise (SIFE), Society for the Advancement of Management (SAM), and the American Marketing Association (AMA). The goals of these clubs are to promote careers in areas under their purview—SIFE for entrepreneurship, SAM for corporate management, and AMA in the areas of marketing and advertising. These clubs also function to bring newer, less experienced students into contact with students more advanced in their program, thus allowing the junior students the opportunity to see what they should be like at the end of their educational process.

Probably the most powerful form of pedagogic action outside of the classroom is the use of internships in the latter part of students' educational experience. During these internships students spend from 120 to 240 hours gaining "practical firsthand experience of business enterprise" by working in a job for which they receive academic credit. Role-playing of the experiential exercise and the other modeling behaviors is transported to the "real" world of the business organization. In this setting the student's adeptness to perform appropriate behavioral responses to particular organizational situations is judged, not by a professor but by a member of the business community. As interns, demonstrating that one has inculcated the appropriate habitus not only leads to a grade, but often to an offer of employment. Thus, internship evaluations are often seen as external validations of the internal pedagogic actions.

The various forms of pedagogic action within the business school curriculum can be seen as mechanisms for the inculcation of management habitus within the student population. By the time a student successfully leaves a business school program, he or she is a ready foot soldier for the capitalist enterprise.

THE HIDDEN CURRICULUM IN THE COLLEGE OF BUSINESS

In the previous section we reviewed the various forms of pedagogic action used in business school classrooms. The purpose of this pedagogic action is to inculcate business school students with certain cultural arbitraries that benefit the organization in the form of managerial habitus. Now we can examine some specific details of the hidden curriculum that socializes business students:

- *Soviet-style centrally planned economies failed; therefore, any economy that is not based upon free market economics will fail.* Mainstream economics and business texts teach about economic systems by contrasting the ideal free market with (evil) Soviet-style centrally planned economies. For example, in one of the best-selling introduction to business textbooks, a photograph from China accompanies the discussion of planned economies, which has the following caption:

  > *"Volunteers" in a planned economy.* These students are among the 100,000 recruited by the Chinese government to spruce up the city of Beijing for the 11th Asian games. Though called "volunteers," the students probably had little choice, and the banners and overseers give the sense that the government is watching (Pride, Hughes, and Kapoor 1993, 22).

  The text gloss over the fact that most economies are really mixed. They never offer a serious discussion of northern European welfare-based socialist economies, nor of successful socialist economic enterprises such as the kibbutz.
- *Decision making in organizations is the outcome of the application of rational (quantitative) techniques.* A substantial portion of the business school curriculum focuses upon the mastery (memorization) of quantitative analysis tools in finance, statistics, economics, and accounting. Throughout the students' training, professors or texts supply all the necessary information so that the student may

plug in numbers to get the "right" answer. However, simplifying assumptions, issues of imperfect information, or the epistemological/metaphysical issues of these techniques are never discussed. Thus, students come to believe that the application of these techniques in practice is inherently objective and value-free. Articles from critical journals such as *Accounting, Organizations and Society* are not discussed.

- *Decisions made at the top of the organization use rational and objective procedures*. The prescribed capstone course in the business curriculum is "Strategy and Business Policy." Each of the available texts for this course starts by describing a process known as "comprehensive strategic planning," which has its theoretical roots in decision science. Researchers have shown that few if any firms actually practice comprehensive strategic planning, and also that it is a less than effective means of doing strategy. Furthermore, none of the mainstream texts discuss the issues of power and politics that exist during strategy-making, even though the research literature stresses their importance. Why is it taught, then? I contend that it is for the "Wizard of Oz" effect. It is not the overt curriculum that is important but the socialization of lower-status individuals in the organization who will be asked to implement organizational strategy. They will be more effective foot solders if they believe that corporate strategy is rational, and "pay no attention to the man behind the curtain."

- *Unions are illegitimate*. The discussion of labor relations in management or human resource management texts starts with discussion of labor history. After a brief discussion of why workers form unions, the texts devote the rest of the time to discussing "union avoidance" strategies. The messages are subtle, but by the end of their training the typical business student will be avidly antiunion, seeing unions as nothing more then corrupt troublemakers, full of lazy and greedy workers.

- *How to commit murder*. In his essay "Eichmann in the Organization," Jerry Harvey (1988) examined the implications of Hannah Arendt's *Eichmann in Jerusalem: A Report on the Banality of Evil* for understanding the dynamics of behavior in organizations. He discussed the idea that organizations progressively ask their members to commit "little murders" on the way to an all-out holocaust. I contend that the pedagogy of the business school allows its students to practice these little murders in simulated situations. Throughout schooling, the students are asked to discipline unruly subordinates through the analyses of case studies, role-playing, and experiential exercises. These exercises are structured to put the students in the role of the manager and ask them to exercise their organizational authority. They quickly inculcate a number of beliefs. Probably most important is that in a dispute between a manager and a worker, the worker is always wrong, and the organization is always right. Cases, role-playing, and "experiential exercises" reinforce students' right to carry out banal acts of evil, and "internships" hold their hands and prepare them for the time that they are asked to do so in the "real world."

- *Managers and professionals are motivated by intrinsic factors in a job (money is not a motivator).* White-collar workers have *careers*, not jobs; therefore, "investing" in their current job will have long-term benefits. Most discussions of motivation in the undergraduate curriculum draw on the models of Herzberg and McClelland, who associated motivation with the fulfillment of higher-order needs and the beneficial traits of individuals who score high in a need for achievement. Particularly in the works of McClelland, being "not motivated" becomes equated with being lazy. Thus, those who do a job for the sheer pleasure of seeing it done well become idealized as the norm; deviations from this norm are stigmatized.

Undergraduate students are urged to invest in their careers. A key feature of most business school curricula is the internship "opportunity." Here the student is assigned to a company in which he or she works at least twenty hours a week under the supervision of both a manager and a faculty member. The student gains "real-world experience" and receives college credit. Most internships are unpaid or low paying and the students pay tuition for the credits they receive. But it "looks good on the resume."

DISCUSSION

Johnson and Gill (1993, 34) argued that for control systems to be effective they must be expressed through the actions and attitudes of individual managers and employees. They must operate as *self-controls*, which is defined as the controls people exert over their own behavior.

In order for this to happen the norms embodied in administrative or social controls must be "either directly or indirectly . . . internalized by the members of the enterprise and operate as personal controls over attitudes and behaviour."

A substantial part of the "management" portion of a business student's training (particularly in the area of organizational behavior) has as its goal the inculcation of a self-view and worldview that benefit the organization. As noted earlier, the essential process of learning to see oneself as different from other elements of the working-class begins in the public schools. The social construction of the blue-collar "other" becomes fully formed at the business school. Students are taught that the difference between them and blue-collar workers (blue-collar work is portrayed as unskilled, assembly-line jobs) is that white-collar work is inherently satisfying because the work itself is interesting and rewarding. It is essential to the inculcation of self-control that white-collar workers are socialized to identify with their job independent of the financial rewards. They are taught, for instance, that because it will be good for their career, they should always be willing to work more hours than they are actually paid for.

The foregoing analysis illustrated some of the cultural arbitraries that the pedagogic action of management "education" instills. I believe that this analysis makes a strong argument for understanding management education as a form of symbolic violence. If education and in particular management education is a form of symbolic violence, then we can only conclude that consent to the labor process under monopoly capitalism is, in fact, established in advance of "playing the game."

Where does this analysis lead? This is a vexing question for those of us who depend upon appointments in business schools to pay the mortgage. After laying bare the fact that we are the agents in which pedagogic authority has been vested, what can we, as professors and scholars, do to emancipate rather than enslave our students?

Hugh Willmott (1994) suggested transforming the paradigm of management education to one based upon critical action learning. While applauding his approach, I am not optimistic that business schools will, or even could, move in that direction. My analysis indicates that the legitimacy of management education is firmly rooted in serving the interests, as my colleagues often put it, of the business community. In the United States, at least, the common discourse is that business schools have two customers—the students, and the firms that will eventually employ them. To many of my colleagues the second of these is the more important of the two. This being the case, a pedagogy that demystifies the moral and political framework of management practice would lead to a rapid withdrawal of the support that university-based management education currently receives.

As with many other critical pedagogies, the perspective that I offer here will remain marginal to the mainstream of "real" business scholarship. As individuals, we can, of course, act. But doing so will likely be a solitary walk in the wilderness. We can teach our students to "resist well."[6] Teach them of the dark forces at work. So even if they will not be able to avoid playing the game, they will at least know which rules are truly operative. Similarly, we can distinguish between being a professor of management and being a social scientist studying management behavior.[7] This approach will probably not make us many friends among our business school colleagues, but perhaps social isolation is a small price to pay for maintaining integrity.

NOTES

1. For the management ramifications of this dilemma, see Edwards (1979).
2. Clearly, the boundaries in the typical public high school are not perfectly seamless, and leakage occurs; but the college-bound do find themselves academically isolated from the general track students. Moreover, the extracurricular activities offered in the typical high school also tend to draw from different social worlds, thereby reinforcing tracking and social segregation.
3. Jenkins (1992, 104) stated, "Symbolic violence, according to Bourdieu, is the imposition of systems of symbolism and meaning (i.e. culture) upon groups or classes in such a way as they are experienced as legitimate."
4. At this point, a traditional Marxist would rely on ownership of capital to distinguish the dominant class from the dominated. However, under conditions of late-twentieth-century capitalism I find C. Wright Mills's (1956) concept of "power elite" to be much more useful, acknowledging the role of both the "older" capitalist class as well as a newer class of individuals who hold positions of power in government in large corporations, but whose social and economic roots may not be from the aforementioned class (see also Schwartz 1987).
5. A habit or unconscious way of dealing with interactions in the world.
6. I take this phrase from my colleague Mike Elmes who talks often of "teaching our students to resist well."
7. I acknowledge my colleague, Christa Walck, for this idea.

Downward Mobility 101   7

Learning to Be "Flexible" in an Age of Uncertainty

Caroline Childress

In the 1980s and early 1990s an economic downturn and deindustrialization spread across the Northeast and Midwest resulting in the shrinkage of middle-sector employment (Harrison and Bluestone 1988; Levy 1987). Before deindustrialization, manufacturing provided the bulk of middle-sector jobs. As manufacturing jobs moved offshore, those jobs that remained, as well as newly created ones, are mostly in the service-sector. At the high end of the service sector are jobs such as doctors and lawyers; at the other end are low-skill "McJobs" with scant benefits and pay. Unlike manufacturing, where workers may start at low-end jobs and work up to middle-sector jobs, the service industry has no middle layer and therefore cannot provide the same opportunities for upward mobility.

While the disappearance of middle-sector jobs has had a significant impact on a large number of workers, professionals find themselves in a particularly problematic position. The culture of meritocracy and the individual pattern of layoffs make it difficult for laidoff managers and others to recognize the structural changes that explain their individual troubles (Mills 1959; Newman 1988). Prior to deindustrialization, managers followed a career track, usually within one company, in which they were implicitly guaranteed job security. Only those people considered "failures" were passed over for promotion or promoted horizontally rather than vertically (Kanter 1993).

Today, the implicit contract between employee and employer no longer exists (Kanter 1993). As a result of the new "service economy," dislocated professionals encounter an employment market that offers little opportunity for the continuance of the career paths they have come to know and expect. This chapter investigates the hidden curriculum in one federally funded retraining program that was created to help dislocated professionals on Long Island adapt to what Erving Goffman (1952, 451), in his insightful article "On Cooling the Mark Out," described as "the loss of sources of security and status which they had taken for granted." In essence, the program serves to "cool out" the dislocated professional, primarily through the process I term "resocialization for downward mobility."

COOLING OUT THE MARK
AND THE HIDDEN CURRICULUM

Goffman (1952) explicated the process whereby individual "failure" is mediated by those who have a stake in the individual's mollification. Such smoothing over can take several forms, such as stalling, consolation, apologies of self, or the offering of a new framework in which to judge the self. Burton Clark (1960) developed Goffman's theory by examining in detail the "offering of a new framework." The new framework provides the mark with an alternative status, which is less attractive than the status that has been lost. With time and coaxing, lower status may be adopted as a compromise.

Clark suggested that when expectations exceed available opportunities the manifest function of an entire institution may be to "cool out" on a wide scale. He argued that junior colleges in California were instituted to "soften" the blow to students who would either be rejected by state universities or would "fail out." By softening failure, Clark contended, motivation was maintained. While attending junior college, students are inundated with alternative possibilities to higher education. If the staff perceived a student to lack promise in the area being pursued, they engaged in strategies to assist the student in arriving at his or her "true" potential. Pretesting, remedial courses, and the use of the "objective" student records, including grades and test scores, were employed to dissuade students from difficult majors or from the goal of transferring to a four-year institution. Counselors directed students out of transfer programs and into terminal degree programs.

Clark (1960) stressed the importance of concealment for such a cooling out agency. In order for the mark to engage voluntarily in the functioning of the agency, she or he must understand the purpose of the agency to be something other than adjustment to failure. Should it be known the agency is in the business of handling "failures," the mark will not be motivated to participate. In the case of the junior college, the transfer feature is celebrated although the majority of students never transfer to a four-year institution.

The literature on the hidden curriculum has made a similar claim: much that is taught in schools is not explicitly stated and contributes to the production and reproduction of a race, class, and gender hierarchy (cf. the introduction to this volume). This chapter is a case study of a school which as part of the cooling out process resocializes dislocated professionals for downward mobility in an attempt to persuade them to apply for lower-status jobs. Just as Ehrensal (chapter six this volume) argues that the business ideology taught in undergraduate business programs is a form of symbolic violence, my study demonstrates exactly how specific elements of the curriculum in the School of Professional Development are used to produce a new class of workers for local employers (i.e., capitalists). Specifically, the school attempts to produce, from the previously managerial class, a new class of lower-status workers who will accept jobs for which they are overqualified, and underpaid, and which offer little or no job security. By aligning the interests of the students with those of local employers, the school is participating in a form of "symbolic violence" against workers, who are taught to carry the entire burden of economic change without giving critical thought to the responsibilities that capitalists might be expected to bear (Bourdieu and Passeron 1990.)

THE PROGRAM

In 1994, the Suffolk County Department of Labor (DOL) approached administrators of the Workforce Development Center at the State University of New York at Stony Brook and asked them to create a retraining program in response to the high volume of dislocated professional workers on Long Island who were not being reabsorbed into the labor market. The resulting program is called the School of Professional Development (SPD). The majority of clients enrolled in the program receive financial support through the Suffolk County Department of Labor under the Job Training Partnership Act (JTPA). Dislocated workers collecting unemployment insurance are eligible for government funding. The program lasts twelve to sixteen weeks and clients enter in cohorts of ten to twenty-five people.

METHOD

I collected data both from focus groups and participant observation. I recorded and transcribed four focus groups with a total of twenty-one graduates of the program, eleven men and ten women. Each focus group lasted about ninety minutes. Participants ranged in age from thirty-six to sixty-five, with an average age of fifty-one. About half of the women previously occupied service industry jobs while the other half were from managerial or professional positions.[1] With the exception of one stock and options specialist, all of the men had held professional, managerial, or supervisory positions.[2] Because program administrators selected the participants for these focus groups, they were not representative of all clients. However, since participants were likely to be selected as "star" graduates or those most supportive of the program, they were particularly good at articulating the program's philosophy.

Once I developed a general understanding of the philosophy of the program through these focus groups, I entered the sixteen-week program as a participant observer. Although administrators, instructors, and clients were told that I was collecting data for research purposes, I attended courses, completed homework assignments, took tests, and gave presentations along with nine clients. In addition to the courses discussed in the next section, a roundtable was held at midterm. During the roundtable four panelists, human resource representatives from various companies on Long Island, answered questions about the job search process. Quotes from both the courses and roundtable were extracted from field notes.

COURSE CURRICULUM

In his chapter on the undergraduate business curriculum, Ehrensal (chapter six) describes how capitalist ideology is used in university business programs to indoctrinate students into the managerial class. In direct contrast, the curriculum at the School of Professional Development attempted to *remove* these workers from the managerial class in an attempt to persuade them to apply for lower-status jobs.

The overt curriculum consists of three specific areas: computer literacy, career development, and management administration skills. While the name "career development" has a neutral ring to it, it is in these courses that instructors focus most on adjusting the expectations of clients to what administrators of the program believe to be the characteristics of the jobs available to them. Therefore, the hidden curriculum in these courses will be of central importance throughout the chapter.

COOLING OUT THE MARK IN THE SCHOOL
OF PROFESSIONAL DEVELOPMENT

We now closely examine the attempts to "cool out" the dislocated professional. I identified and will analyze three curricular elements of varying importance: the most elaborate, pervasive, and complex of these is "resocialization for downward mobility"; the second form involves the reiteration of power between employee and employer; and the third is what Goffman (1952) termed "stalling."

As mentioned earlier, one way to "cool out" the mark is to offer an alternative status to substitute for the one lost. The SPD creates an alternative career path for the dislocated professional to follow. At the same time, staff assure clients that eventually they will return to their prior professional status. In contrast to traditional managerial routes of climbing ladders, clients are told to take a step down with the hope that later opportunities for upward mobility will come again. In order to prepare the dislocated professional to step down in social status, the staff attempt to lower clients' occupational and income expectations. In addition to changes in expectations, staff teach clients how to display their decreased expectations during interviews and on their resume. I refer to downsizing expectations and the accompanying de-skilling of the self as "resocialization for downward mobility."

At the same time, staff try to mollify dislocated professionals by reiterating the power differential between employee and employer. Staff teach that in the present economy employers hold all the power, in contrast to the relatively labor-friendly environment of the early '80s. This power differential makes any complaints students might have about mistreatment by past or future employers seem irrelevant. The clients, as individuals, have to accept and adapt to this new environment.

The third program element involves "stalling," the term Goffman coined for giving the mark time to come to accept a new status. By offering program participants more time on unemployment insurance via extensions, and encouraging them to stay out of the labor market during their term in the program, participation buys the dislocated professional more time to come to terms with alternative job choices.

RESOCIALIZATION FOR DOWNWARD MOBILITY

While "socialization in later years builds on attitudes and skills acquired earlier, using them as a foundation for later, more demanding learning" (Brim 1966, 19), *resocialization*, as defined by Wheeler (1966, 68), "make[s] up for or correct[s] some deficiency in earlier socialization." When speaking of resocializing institutions, Wheeler wrote of the need to resocialize deviants, as is the case in prisons. Egan (1989, 201) expanded the use of the concept to describe the process of professional socialization in graduate departments, claiming that the aim is to "alter the past rather than merely build on it" in an attempt to correct deficiencies in prior socialization. Similarly, I use the concept of resocialization here to analyze attempts to lower the expectations of dislocated professionals whose jobs have disappeared as a result of bifurcation in the economy. While at least some resocialization in graduate school and prison is expected, this aspect of the program is never stated explicitly. It is one of those aspects of the hidden curriculum that must remain hidden if it is to work and not provoke resistance.

I will discuss two aspects of resocializing for downward mobility: the first entails changing expectations in terms of career goals and income; the second teaches how to apply successfully for lower-status jobs both by restructuring the resume to reflect a less flattering work history and by dissembling during the interview. The incorporation of lower-status skills into the clients' resumes as well as newly learned interviewing techniques were referred to by administrators as the "marketing makeover."

CHANGING OCCUPATIONAL EXPECTATIONS

The first goal of the career development courses is to convince clients to consider jobs for which they normally would not apply. These include those jobs outside the clients' original areas of expertise as well as those offering substantially less in terms of prestige and income than the job from which they were dislocated. Staff routinely refer to those who can envision applying for this new range of jobs as having an "open-mind" while those having difficulty need to "become more open-minded." To facilitate this change, administrators and instructors provide clients with what Dr. Paul Edelson, dean of the School of Professional Development and Continuing Studies, called "a category of acceptable dissatisfaction" (Dr. Paul Edelson, personal communication, July 15, 1996). To this end, all jobs are categorized into one of three types: "survival," "bridge," or "career." At the low end are the survival jobs, including the "hamburger flipping" types that clients would normally never take, but need in order to support themselves and their families. To compensate for this deterioration in job prestige, the term "survival job" takes on a moral tone because the person is "doing what they've got to do" despite the unpleasantness intrinsic to the job. Such jobs are considered temporary.

The "bridge job" is a considerable step above the survival job. Although lower in status than previous jobs the client has held, clients are told that the bridge job offers a point of entry to the next category, the "career job." Thus, the bridge job serves two purposes: first, it offers the client a more acceptable identity than either the survival job or unemployment; second, it holds out hope that once part of a company's internal labor market, the client will be able to move up. Accepting bridge jobs does not preclude the client from seeking career jobs or other more promising bridge jobs outside the current employer.

The third type of job, the "career job," is commensurate with the occupation held prior to dislocation in terms of job satisfaction. While the bridge job may be a means to a career job, administrators of the program know that over time the bridge job may become the client's new career job. For administrators, the goal is to see that the client is satisfied with his or her employment situation.

These job categories are specifically referred to by administrators and used by instructors during career development and current work topics courses. Less explicitly, these job categories are also used during computer courses, as with the following instructor:

> I had a man in my class named Joe [all names have been changed to protect confidentiality] who said he would get a job sweeping the floors of a company and then one day he would walk up to someone and say "You need to press Control-F5" and then the company

would realize how much he knew and he would be *discovered*. He didn't get a job as a sweeper; he got a job as a parking garage manager. You may need to start out lower than you expected, but you'll be *discovered* because you're very smart.

In this story, a client dreams of using a survival job as a bridge to either a bridge or career job. As it turned out, Joe did not need to take that janitorial position, but the story demonstrates the hope that in the future one will be "discovered" for one's true ability.

In another setting, a career counselor administered the SDS (Self-directed Search Test) in order to broaden the range of jobs for which clients might consider applying. In place of the terms above, the term he used was *transitional job:*

> Explore these things [employment options]. Gather information. I think that for a lot of you there are better, more enjoyable jobs for you than you were at. But remember, in the short term you might have to get a *transitional* job to pay the bills. But it doesn't mean you have to trash your long-term goals.

The purpose in introducing these categories of jobs is to have dislocated professionals set aside their long-term career goals "temporarily" in order to meet short-term needs, such as paying the bills. With these concepts the client can hold on to the status of professional because the interruption in career is supposedly only temporary. In the interim, the dislocated professional is provided with a vocabulary of motives to justify working at lower-status jobs (Scott and Lyman 1968). However, this strategy does not address the structural reality of the shrinking middle-sector of jobs or the question of whether such middle-sector jobs will exist in the future.

CHANGING INCOME EXPECTATIONS

On the first day of classes one client shared with several other clients and the instructor during a break that she felt embarrassed about being unemployed: "I haven't been unemployed since I started working at nineteen." In response, the instructor (who taught computer courses) assured her that "It might take time, and you might have to start at a lower pay base, but there are jobs out there."

Later that same day, the career development instructor relayed a similar message:

> INSTRUCTOR: You have to realize that you may never get at the same pay that you had before.

> General groans from the class.

> INSTRUCTOR: Well, at least not at first. You have to realize that in the eighties people were making a lot of money because there was a low supply of talented people, but now there's lots of talented people competing for jobs and it's hard. But you will get a job.

Thus, a similar strategy used by administrators and instructors for changing status expectations—a kind of delayed gratification explanation—was used to lower expectations for income.

Another strategy used by administrators and instructors to lower income expectations involved asking clients to think in terms of the *minimum* amount of money on which they can live, or the *minimum* they would be willing to accept:

> If you can take a lower job, then you can prove yourself [to the company] and move up. You have to be open. You can't say you're not taking this job for more than a couple thousand less than what you were making before. So what is the *minimal* amount you would take to get a job? You have to have *flexibility* and be realistic about what's out there today.

Flexibility is the term that administrators and instructors used to describe this minimizing approach to income needs. At a later date in the same course, we were asked to write our monthly budgets in order to see where costs might be cut. Thus, staff attempted to lower income expectations in much the same way that they lowered job status expectations; clients were asked to set aside their long-term goals and focus on present financial needs.

THE "MARKETING MAKEOVER"

Although clients were constantly bombarded with motivational phrases such as: "open your mind" and "change your paradigm" to encourage them to apply for new types of jobs, inevitably there were some who had already applied for jobs and were unsuccessful in their attempts. The downsized professional is caught in a dilemma in which she or he is "overqualified" for many of the lower-status positions for which companies are hiring and at the same time "underqualified" for higher-status jobs in new fields for lack of experience. Jacob, a sixty-year-old dislocated engineering section manager, articulated this dilemma:

> I did realize at some point in time that I wasn't getting back into engineering and at that time I got into this program. . . . Yet because every new career always wanted experience, and obviously, I didn't have any so it was like a catch-22. I know I can do that job, but nobody will take me in that job or any other job because you're not experienced.

Clearly it is not enough to apply for lower-status jobs. The client has to undergo a "marketing makeover" that transforms, in the eyes of potential employers, a formally skilled worker into an attractive candidate for a lower-status job. The makeover includes de-skilling one's presentation of self both on the resume and during the interview.

DOWNSKILLING THE RESUME

As part of the project of creating an employee marketable for the range of lower-status jobs, clients are required to rewrite their resumes. Staff instruct them on changing the orientation of the resume from chronological to "functional," as described in this focus group:

> JOSEPH: As far as resumes go, I changed mine from a chronological to a functional. So I was an engineering manager at electronics engineering and my specialty was electronic counter measures. So rather than saying electronic counter measures, in the functional resume I would say X amount of years' experience in organization dealing with people rather than saying I was an engineering manager. Because as soon as you say engineering manager, you went to a garment place or went to a gas station or something for a job, they would say, "We don't need engineers." So I would highlight organizational skills. I like to deal with other people and things like that versus the technical aspects so you could fit into a different niche.

GROUP LEADER: Could someone define *functional resume?*

JACOB: It's more generic. It tells what your skills are but it doesn't relate to the specific industry you came out of. [It] doesn't talk about history.

Clients were taught to "generalize," that is, to emphasize skills that translate well to other jobs and industries. Unfortunately, when specific skills are generalized, value is lost. For example, Joseph was no doubt a valuable asset to his former employer specifically because of his knowledge of electronic counter measures. However, when he attempted to translate that intellectual capital to another industry, and *reframed* it as general managerial experience, information was lost and skills were downgraded. Even if this "generalization" makes the dislocated professional more marketable outside his or her original industry, the jobs he or she is now "qualified" to pursue are inevitably of lower pay and occupational prestige. At the same time as the client's resume is "downgraded," the client is less likely to be told, "You are overqualified." Positive phrases like *generalizable skills* and *functional resume* hide an important function of the marketing makeover—the de-skilling of the client—a central socialization message of the program's hidden curriculum.

DE-SKILLING DURING THE INTERVIEW

The program also taught the importance of demonstrating lowered expectations during the interview as discussed in the following quote by Marty, a fifty-eight-year-old dislocated systems engineer:

We came into this room for a practice with interviews and what we were supposed to do was, each person was supposed to think of two questions to ask everybody. Each individual, as you knew them, that would really maybe stop them during an interview. I put some thought into it. I asked questions that was on the border of being gross. I was really trying to reach. I reached at one gal that was, she was laid-off in the banking industry. She was in human resources with one of the larger banks on Long Island and she wanted to go elsewhere and do something different. And I asked her [the] very pointed question of why she would be willing to accept a job that was less responsible, less salary, and less this than what you had for the last fifteen years or something. Somebody asks you that in an interview [and] it can set you back. And I think that that was good practice. Damn good practice.

Staff frequently warn clients that during interviews they will be asked whether they will be satisfied taking a particular job given their prior income and experience. In response, clients are told to assure employers that this job meets their expectations and that they are comfortable with the pay, as demonstrated in this coaching session during a career development class:

> INSTRUCTOR: What if you're asked, "Why are you willing to take a job for $25,000 less than you were making?" How can you convince me, the interviewer, to believe you'll stay?
> CLIENT: I'm willing to learn because it's a new industry so I can start at the bottom to learn it.
> INSTRUCTOR: Based on that, what did you want from us in the future?

During one class in career development, the assistant director of the program came to let us interview her. We were given two weeks to think of tough interview questions that might stump us during an interview:

> CLIENT: I see you have no experience in this area of banking. What makes you think you'll do well in this job?
> ASSISTANT DIRECTOR: I like numbers and working with formulas. I like repetition. I know that there's a high rate of turnover in the banking industry because people get bored, but I like repetition.

The roundtable had a similar purpose, to prepare clients to be interviewed by giving them a chance to ask a panel of human resource representatives about the interview from their perspective:

> CLIENT: When you ask me what my salary requirements are, what should I say?
> PANELIST: It's a personal decision. You need to give a *realistic range on which you can live*. I wouldn't give a number, but a range. You need to say you have *flexibility*.

Similar to the advice given by the program staff, instead of considering the type of industry, the amount of training or skill the job might require, this advice suggests that one should be prepared to settle for the minimum on which she or he "can live."

At one point during the roundtable, a client sought advice from the panelists about her search for a job in computer graphics because it was so different from any of the jobs she had held before:

> PANELIST: It's very important to say, "I'm willing to start at an entry level."
>
> SECOND PANELIST: Target a company that has a division in graphic arts and get a job anywhere and then move over to the graphics department. Get your foot in the door and then transfer into that department.
>
> FIRST PANELIST: Be careful when you go for an entry-level job with another job in mind. You need to show enthusiasm for that entry-level position and that you want to be in that position a while. Otherwise I would feel you'd get bored.

It is not enough to *apply* for an entry-level position; the applicant has to *demonstrate* that he or she really wants that position, even though he or she has sights on another job. Additionally, because entrepreneurial experience might be viewed as threatening to employers, clients were taught to hide this aspect of their work history. Should the employer learn about it, the client must assure the employer that she or he is not a threat. One panelist gave this word of advice:

> There are a lot of entrepreneurs in here [referring to when the clients introduced themselves and gave employment backgrounds]. That's great. It's great. I could never do that. But if you've been an entrepreneur, we are wary because: one, you may leave for your own company. Or two, you may try to run ours. So you need to transcribe [translate] it as experience. Don't put C.E.O. of a company, or president. Instead, put "hired, managed . . . " Don't lie, just don't make it up front. If it comes out in an interview, OK. So, just allay my fears.

If the discrepancy between expectations and skills is too large, employers will be wary of the mismatch, as evident in the following exchange:

PANELIST: We don't ask for salary history anymore, but we ask for a range over the phone. The key is to say you're flexible.

SECOND PANELIST: Over the phone I'll say, "Let's be honest. If you were a VP previously and this is a low position . . . " He must say, "I'm *flexible*."

CLIENT: Can you under-do your salary requirement? Coming in too low?

FIRST PANELIST: Yes, that's bad because you're undervaluing your-self. We had someone who did that and we asked what was wrong.

THIRD PANELIST: You may want to submit a *modified* resume that says you're OK, not the best in the world and then have the won-derful one as a backup.

This is the closest anyone came to articulating the importance of actually de-skilling the resume. If an interviewee offers a potential employer a resume that reflects high-skills yet asks for an entry-level job, the potential employer may sense the mismatch and ask, "What is wrong?" By de-skilling the resume, a client can allay the employer's fears by preemptively countering the overqualification issue. Further-more, if there are lingering questions about overqualification, the client should use the interview to assuage employers' fears by emphasizing one's lowered expectations.

Importantly, the word *de-skilling* is never used by staff. Instead, the *functional resume* is offered as a more successful style than the tra-ditional, chronological one because it is "more generic" and thus can be used with a wider array of employers. Similarly, no one was told "lower your expectations," but to "have an open mind" when con-sidering different jobs. By using such euphemisms, the staff maintained a relentlessly positive tone while pursuing the hidden agenda of cool-ing out the clients.

THE REITERATION OF POWER AND DISCRIMINATION

During one of the career development courses, we were handed a sheet that outlined the cycle of emotional responses to the "trauma" of dis-location, among which were denial, depression, and anger. The staff maintained that people who are not successful at finding a job after the program either do not have an "open mind" or are "stuck in the anger phase." According to the career development instructor, if a client still harbors anger toward prior or potential employers, this will "flow out" during interviews and employers will "not hire a worker who has issues." Thus, as part of the cooling out process, clients are told to get over their anger if they want to find a job. This is remarkably congruent with the meritocratic view that losing or finding a job is not a structural economic issue so much as a personal problem and matter of individual responsibility.

In conjunction with coaxing clients to "let go of their anger" came a threat of sorts. Clients were told that in today's labor market employers have all the power so there is no use questioning their motives or behavior. The following warning from the career development instructor demonstrated the message that was repeated frequently:

> This is not the seventies and eighties. Now the shoe is on the other foot. If you don't want a job, there are twenty others ready to take it.

During one class, a client complained about being taken advantage of at her previous work site. In response, the instructor defended employers: "The whole business environment is like that. They ask you to stay long hours and can because five other people are willing to take your place." This message was similarly implicit at the roundtable. One panelist suggested the clients display their understanding of this during the interview: "Show *flexibility*. Say you're willing to work more than forty hours a week . . . don't ask, 'What are the benefits?' Wait until I bring them up."

While power differential at the roundtable was obviously tilted in the direction of employers, panelists somewhat cynically reframed the situation as an "opportunity" for the clients. One of the clients asked the panelists an apparently vague question: "What do you think about temping?" to which the first panelist eagerly responded by listing the advantages to the employer:

> PANELIST: It's very advantageous to us because there is no turnover on our payroll. You're [the company is] not stuck with unemployment, and you can just say "good-bye." We'll try them out, like engineers and technical people, but we don't hire any managers or vice presidents this way.

SECOND PANELIST: From your perspective, you can also walk away and you can see the culture of the company.

FIRST PANELIST: It's a good opportunity to get your foot in the door so [you] get exposure and experience, and learning good skills in the meantime. We do our own recruiting and advertising ourselves and then we hire and call Payroll Services and the person works for them. Then it can develop into a permanent . . . [she catches herself] Oh, we don't like to say "permanent," we say "direct" employee.

THIRD PANELIST: What's nice is you can work two to three days a week and still look for a job the other days and you may get introduced to new skills and companies.

Downsized clients, who no longer have steady paychecks, medical insurance, or retirement packages are encouraged to view "temp" jobs as an opportunity—contingent, easily disposable, mainly part-time work. They are told to think of such work as a mutually rewarding arrangement. This ideology of encouragement continued throughout the roundtable.

Any discussion of structural issues was quashed, as were attempts to see the situation from the workers' perspective. When the issue of age discrimination was raised by a client during the roundtable, the panelists reacted in much the same way that administrators and instructors had handled such claims. First, they denied that discrimination occurred and then implicitly blamed the client through reference to a self-fulfilling prophecy: because attitude is so important during an interview, if one expects to be discriminated against, he or she will send out negative signals, which is what the interviewer is responding to, not the age of the interviewee. In this "blaming the victim" tactic, the responsibility is turned back onto the client. If the issue is pushed or a blatant example of discrimination is given, the client is told, "You wouldn't want to work for that type of company anyway." This sequence was played out as follows:

CLIENT: A lot of people here are over fifty. And I have experience myself [of] discrimination.

PANELIST: I totally disagree. I believe people believe that, but when I look, I want people who don't jump around and I see older people as more stable, more dependable. They know what I need. I think you should show enthusiasm. Maybe it's in your mind because that comes through in the interview and that caused it.

SAME CLIENT: I talked to an employment agency over the phone and I told them I had twenty-three years' experience. They said, "Why don't you retire?"

SECOND PANELIST: Well, you don't want to work for them.

THIRD PANELIST: It's not a liability.

SECOND PANELIST: I see people and they have an attitude of "I'm old so you won't hire me." Not to say there are not companies like that, but you don't want to take a job with that company. Work ethic is better in older people.

FOURTH PANELIST: Take a look at the culture of the company. Look down the hallway. If there's lots of young people there, you don't want to work there.

In this poignant example the overwhelming power differential between employer and employee was masked by arguing with clients that if they had a choice, they would not want to work for a firm that would discriminate against them, making it seem not only that the client had agency, but that in some way employer and employee encountered each other on a level playing field.

Thus, in many subtle ways clients were taught that they had to conform to the needs of employers by happily providing the contingent labor they need. Participating as contingent labor is to be viewed as an "opportunity" by the dislocated professional. This steel curriculum lies hidden behind the velvet veneer of opportunity, choice, and agency.

STALLING

Goffman (1952, 458) analyzed techniques by which agents

> may convince the mark that there is still a slight chance that the loss has not really occurred. When the mark is stalled, he [sic] is given a chance to become familiar with the new conception of self he will have to accept before he is absolutely sure that he will have to accept it." Earlier, we saw evidence of this strategy when staff asked clients

to set aside their long-term career goals "temporarily" in order to meet short-term needs. Clients were told they do not have to "give up" their long-term goals, but must in the meantime adjust to the present circumstances of lower-status work.

The contention that the program "stalls" clients so they can adjust to their new position in life is further supported by the laxness of the program; it was strongly recommended that students *not* look for jobs while in the program. This is in stark contrast to the urgency felt by clients of welfare-to-work programs who are told explicitly that their job is to seek employment and that assistance from the government is contingent on applying for a minimum number of jobs (Miller 1983). By creating a break in the job search process, clients are given an opportunity to rethink the type of jobs they will apply for once they resume the search (after the program cools them out).

DISCUSSION

Within any system that experiences strain, conservative agencies will seek to minimize strain both to the system and the individuals affected so that social protest is prevented. Such structures will attempt to maintain motivation for participation in the system (Clark 1960). This chapter has analyzed one such example. Macroeconomic changes such as polarization of the labor market left a dearth of professional managerial jobs and created a new group of unemployed workers. In response, the local government created a program to "cool out" dislocated professionals who could not find work.

Why would a program created to help dislocated professionals align its interests with those of the capitalist class at the expense of its clients? Muzzin (chapter eight this volume) asks a similar question: What produced the schism within academic departments in the pharmaceutical sciences which led to differential rewards for faculty who pursue the development of pharmaceutical care (mostly women) and those who pursue clinical research interests (mostly men)? One piece of the puzzle can be explained by financial concerns. Specifically, the departments have become reliant upon research funding from transnational pharmaceutical producers of synthetic drugs. Thus, academics participating in this type of research attract money from these large corporations and are rewarded in terms of tenured positions and higher salaries.

Similarly, the School of Professional Development depends upon the Department of Labor (DOL) for funding. While the DOL does not give the program specific quotas, statistics on placements after graduating from the program are kept and compared to other (re)training programs they administrate. This aligns the program with the interests of local employers by making the program accountable to employer interests. This includes persuading clients to accept contingent jobs for which they are overqualified, as well as jobs that pay much less than previous jobs because these are now the jobs for which local employers are hiring.

By offering individual strategies to alleviate the clients' problems, administrators undermine structural explanations and remedies for what is occurring in the economy. This process puts the onus of change on the shoulders of the dislocated professionals, making structural changes seem as though they are really individual troubles. When viewed as individual troubles, dislocated professionals are less likely to take collective action or hold capitalists accountable for decisions to create a contingent workforce at the expense of the worker.

This chapter has advanced the literature on the hidden curriculum on two fronts. First, the theory of the hidden curriculum was applied to a new site, the retraining program. This is important because it suggests that the processes of the hidden curriculum do not simply cease at the end of schooling, but continue to occur *outside* the traditional academic setting. Second, it demonstrates how the hidden curriculum can adapt to meet the changing needs of capitalists by *resocializing* a previously socialized middle-class group of workers into accepting lower-status jobs and hence providing a new habitus from the one they originally acquired through earlier socialization experiences. As the quote in chapter two by Karen Anijar suggests, the transformative nature of the hidden curriculum accounts for part of its elusive nature: "[I]t moves. It doesn't remain constant. If it remained constant it would be easy to unearth and deconstruct and everybody would know about it and where it would occur . . ." (Gair and Mullins 2001, 24).

NOTES

1. What I classify as service jobs included supervisor, computer tape librarian, telephone representative, communications specialist, and congressional aide. Managerial and professional jobs include vice president, director of human resources, district representative, supervisor of quality assurance, and manager of customer service.

2. Prior occupations of the men included electronics engineer, engineering section manager, product control accountant, vice president, systems control engineer, methods engineer, supervisor, program manager, administrative vice president, and controller.

"Powder Puff Brigades" 8

*Professional Caring versus
Industry Research in the
Pharmaceutical Sciences Curriculum*

Linda Muzzin

There is a tug-of-war in pharmaceutical sciences between two curricula. On the one hand there is a "professionalization" model that supports a caring ethos; it is intended to prepare future pharmacists to provide drugs and care to the public. Those who do this teaching are generally clinical, part-time, or otherwise non-tenure-stream faculty. Most are women, as are most of the pharmacists and most of the students in Canada who intend to work in practice. This is actually the main curriculum; pharmacy schools prepare pharmacists for professional practice. The (not so) hidden curriculum, on the other hand, is small but powerful. This other curriculum is molecular research and biological science. It is visible in high-rise architecture, high-rise salaries, and modern laboratories. Most of the faculty are tenured and male. They teach graduate students and enjoy access to the big resources of academia: laboratories, research funding, and so on. This curriculum and the power structure that sustains it are encouraged and supported by deep-pocket drug companies. As we shall see, these powers control and are driving professional schools to the point where administrators who ignore their needs may find their schools closed or taken over. In the case of the pharmaceutical sciences, the struggle over curriculum has taken the appearance of "gender wars." Tenured male faculty with research support vie with non–tenure-stream women bolstered by a few senior women and males defending "professionalization." One of my male basic science colleagues referred to this faction as "the dean and his powder puff brigade."

After an introduction to American and Canadian pharmaceutical sciences faculties and recent curricular revisions that give lip service to the idea of "patient-centeredness," or "pharmaceutical care," I will present tables showing the distribution of men and women faculty in pharmacy academia across Canada. These data will be explained from my own standpoint as a woman "social-administrative/clinical" pharmacy professor, and will be informed by an extensive research project entitled "Making a Difference" (principal investigator Sandra Acker) funded by the Canadian government's Social Sciences and Humanities Research Council. The larger project involved interviewing faculty at various university-based professional schools. At the same time that I conducted interviews for the Acker project, I pursued a similarly funded single-investigator study of the pharmaceutical care movement in Canada. I created a sample, matching by rank and age more than half of the tenured and tenure-stream women pharmacy faculty across Canada with male professors. Between 1995 and 1998, I taped and transcribed fifty-six interviews. Men and women pharmacy academics were asked to describe in detail their teaching, research, and administrative responsibilities within the context of their overall academic careers and the "climate" of their schools. I also inquired into their orientations toward and promotion of the pharmaceutical care movement. Their structural positions in the school and the university were noted, and they were asked whether they were "making a difference" in the pharmaceutical care movement.[1]

There are nine schools of pharmacy in Canada; I visited each one in the course of my research and wrote extensive field notes at each of the sites. As Gair and Mullins and Costello point out in this volume, elements of the hidden curriculum are visible in the very design and condition of the buildings. At the time I was doing the field work I was not thinking of hidden curricula, yet in the interests of locating myself and putting some of the intense emotion that I was feeling down on paper, I wrote my personal reactions to the academic architecture. As I look back, the comment by Donald Blumenfeld-Jones (Gair and Mullins, chapter two, page 28 of this volume) rings especially true: "Looking at the building you are to have a certain attitude towards education and towards that institution that's embodied in that building."

Perhaps most intimidating for me, a unilingual anglophone, was the University of Montreal. I am sure that these politically incorrect field notes would be different in content were they made by a unilingual francophone professor approaching the University of Toronto—although I suspect that the emotion and the tone of her field notes would be similar to mine. Here is some of my edited commentary:

> [This university], for me, evokes the worst images of paternalism, which have to do with its layout, its reputation, and my personal experiences here. . . . Gender discrimination runs very deep in Québec society as we heard from the organizers of the "gender tour" when the Learned Societies Congress was at [another Montreal university, the Université du Québec à Montréal] two years ago, and it is very difficult to address—it is entrenched. [My colleague] calls the main medical building where pharmacy is housed, the "giant penis" because it has a tower which is the tallest structure on campus, several stories higher than the building to which it is attached. . . . The building sits at the top of Mount Royal, towering over the city. The building next to the medical building is the Ecole Polytechnique, where fourteen women engineering students were murdered in 1989. Entering through the wooden doors of this [phallic symbol], one walks into a huge marble vestibule where nothing is person-sized. The marble columns are oversize, as is the room itself. The main building is a quadrangle, and if you walk around inside of it, it is clear that the offices of the scientists, mostly physicists, are quite small and uncomfortable compared to the huge public entrance. The message given is that people are insignificant, SCIENCE is everything. And science, quite clearly, is MALE. (Field notes 1997)

The masculine spaces of the tenured scientists are what first impresses a visitor to these buildings, rather than any caring or patient-centered agenda, nor even any technical clinical professional presence. The University of Alberta, an anglophone school, made a similarly negative impression on me with its overtones of medical and capitalistic dominance:

> The centerpiece is the spectacular medical center with its two large cylindrical skylights on top—the largest building on campus. My sister studied here and it was she who first made me see it: a kind of hospital/Eatons Center[2] she called it, and indeed, you would think that you were in a [mall] except for the white coats and stretchers. High-tech tertiary care medicine. It was built long before the expansion of the

> Toronto General Hospital and other Toronto teaching hospitals [which also incorporate shopping malls].... On the map of the campus, on the way to the light rail transit station, it was clear to me that the health professions hold a dominant place. Education is also in the center of the campus, as are medicine, dentistry, and pharmacy ... [but] the Education, Dentistry, and Pharmacy buildings are old, with harlequin black-and-white tile floors and ivy outside. Dentistry is not to be closed, but merged with Medicine, and there was a big wall chart in the foyer showing the corporate donors who made this possible. The faculty looks considerably less affluent than the one at [the University of British Columbia]. The building in which the two professions are housed reminds me of the University of Montreal—decaying and a bit sinister. (Field notes 1996)

The dominance of androcentric science supported by corporate interests is obvious in the churchlike architecture of the medical/pharmacy building at the University of Montreal as well as the modernist architecture of the medical building at the University of Alberta. At the University of Toronto Faculty of Pharmacy where I taught from 1989 to 1997, a modernist building was constructed with approximately four million dollars donated by Shoppers' Drug Mart (SDM), the largest pharmacy chain in Canada, which is mostly owned by British American Tobacco. Laboratories were outfitted by drug manufacturers. Rows of bronze plaques festoon the walls, thanking numerous pharmaceutical corporate sponsors. In Toronto the building itself was named after the original founder of the SDM drugstore chain, Murray Koffler. Some material used in class even bears the logo of drug companies on its covers, preparing young trainees for their careers in promoting their products.

Higby and Stroud (1997) argued that the influence of both home-grown and transnational drug manufacturing corporations, firmly rooted in North American universities for decades in the form of pharmaceutical research, has grown substantially in Canada. There are many reasons for this trend. Most important, industrial support for basic science research has been pursued with increasing vigor as Medical Research Council funding has been curtailed. Despite high visibility in buildings and logos, it can be argued that this curriculum seeks to remain hidden. As one pharmacy professor turned industry executive has assured me, it is not in the best interests of pharmaceutical firms to be seen to influence the direction of such research or the interests of those scientists who perform pharmaceutical research or their students.

Much can be read in the built environment that is reproduced in the curricula of the pharmaceutical sciences. Decaying buildings, symptomatic of the retrenchment that has infected Canadian university campuses in the past few years, are intermixed with bold new steel and glass architectural spaces funded by pharmaceutical and other corporate sponsors. The decay of the dentistry/pharmacy building at the University of Alberta makes visible what happens if training of undergraduates to practice a profession (in this case, dentistry) competes with the hidden corporate curriculum that supports molecular research. Dentistry administrators faced closure, or takeover of their faculties by academic medicine, unless they hired young tenure-stream (mostly male) molecular researchers to bolster the molecular science research supported by the Medical Research Council.[3] The masculine spaces within which curricula are enacted, full of black countertops and benches, are similarly visible in the pharmaceutical sciences. The peripheral nature of "professional caring" and the centrality of "research" were evident in both the buildings and the curriculum.

Nearly three-quarters of the eighteen thousand Canadian pharmacists practice commercial pharmacy, while the rest practice non-commercial or hospital pharmacy. At least 60 percent of pharmacists are female and the proportion of females in the pharmacy workforce increases with each graduating class. Although pharmacy schools ostensibly exist to prepare future pharmacists, not to do molecular biological research, until the last decade most pharmaceutical science curricula did not emphasize training for the profession of pharmacy until the final year of study. Up to the 1990s, over 90 percent of the initial three years of the curriculum was composed of basic science courses. For the bachelor's degree in pharmacy, a key course in the first year is inorganic chemistry, followed by organic chemistry in the second year, and an emphasis on medicinal chemistry in the third year. Consistent with all this emphasis on chemistry, pharmacists are called "chemists" in many European countries. Until the past few years, little within these hallowed labs hinted that professionals, mostly women, were being trained who might "care" for patients. In Toronto, the largest Canadian school, students who had achieved the highest grades in mathematics and science courses were selected straight from high school, thus minimizing any exposure they might have had to education that included humanities or social sciences. Few electives were allowed, although students were encouraged to take the one that taught about over-the-counter (non–prescription) drugs. This course served to teach the brand and generic drug names that they would be selling when they began to practice (Muzzin 2000).

THE PERSONAL PROCESS OF GENDERING AND RACIALIZING THE PHARMACEUTICAL "CARE" CURRICULUM

A worldwide social movement started in the 1990s to put "pharmaceutical care" at the center of the curriculum. At my school in Toronto the curriculum was under constant revision during this period, just as it was in many other academic units. "Old" courses were to be regrouped around the concept of "pharmaceutical care" (Perrier et al. 1995). We were mainly white full- and part-time female clinical and social-administrative faculty, and most of us thought that the world was about to change for the better. But curriculum revision was presided over by a white male dean directing the activities of a curriculum committee whose members held little power. I was aware that most of us on the curriculum committee were untenured women, a fact that made us particularly vulnerable to the pressures exerted by the dean. But despite my feminism and critical sociological training, it was difficult to see that I was participating in the reproduction of a sexist and racially hegemonic curriculum. It is a profound testimony of the ability of these hidden curricula, as Margolis et al. (2001, 2) noted in the introduction to this volume, "to bamboozle, to pull the wool over people's eyes." At the time that I was a member of this curriculum committee I failed to notice that none of our nonwhite faculty were involved. I also failed to notice that, although there is a long history of herbal medicine and healing within the profession of pharmacy, the new curriculum focused solely on the synthetic drugs produced and sold by transnational corporations.[4]

Hepler (1987) argued, from inside American pharmaceutical science academia, that the professional discourse of "pharmaceutical care" has its own history paralleling "medical care" or "nursing care." Care discourse has its own history; I would argue that its rebirth in this context has less to do with ancient holistic conceptions of health and well-being than with new improved "window dressing" for the profession of pharmacy. It's just another suit of the emperor's new clothes. Elsewhere, I have argued that pharmacy has relatively unsuccessfully attempted to justify its existence with a series of professional ideologies (Muzzin, Brown, and Hornosty 1993). Much later, I was able to rewrite the history of the ideologies to show the contributions of women (Muzzin, Lai, and Sinnott 1999). Viewing the process through a gender lens made visible how industry appropriates so-called caring perspectives to mask the pursuit of profit through drug manufacture and sale. However, when I wrote that historical reconceptualization of pharmacy curricula I was not completely aware of *why* these successive professional ideologies packaged into new curricula were not successful in garnering widespread public support and recognition for this "challenged" profession.

My initial understanding of the political significance of "curricular reform" came not from feminist and antiracist sources but from the work of Samuel Bloom (1988), who identified the conflict between *caring* and *curing* in medical education curricula. Bloom speculated that the "caring" part of medical education is a front distracting attention from the highly profitable and hegemonic synthetic molecular research done by professors of medicine and supported by the pharmaceutical industry. Similarly, in the pharmaceutical sciences, although there is little in the way of a "caring curriculum," concepts such as pharmaceutical care give lip service to the caring discourse presented more fully in medical and nursing education, and distract outsiders (as well as most insiders) from seeing what is really happening in pharmaceutical science faculties. But pharmaceutical "care" curricula are, at best, a pale reflection of the concept of *patient autonomy,* now popular in the writings of Western ethicists, as applied to the requirements of dispensing synthetic drugs. "Caring" curricula accomplish this task by transforming the idea of "care" as it was espoused in classical literature such as that of Nightingale in *Notes on Nursing* (1859) to a context in which it is assumed that the production and marketing of drugs rather than well-being is at the center of "healthcare" and that patients require a medication expert to interpret which synthetic drugs to take.

In sum, if students and others can be convinced that they are being adequately trained for their role as "medication experts," the uncritical teaching of the molecular chemistry that supports the marketing of products of the transnational synthetic drug industry will continue to go largely unquestioned. When I interviewed faculty, I found that although the pharmaceutical care discourse has been variously espoused as a "continuation" of prior curricular practices or, alternatively, as a new professional practice that "puts the patient at the center of drug therapy," the nuts and bolts of the curriculum remain the molecular biochemistry that is based on the production and sale of synthetic drugs as the central aspect of health.

Elsewhere, I have analyzed as "dynamics without change" the process by which curriculum was revised at the University of Toronto (Muzzin 2000). Here I wish to continue the process of examining the gendered and racialized curriculum, which is shared by pharmaceutical science faculties around the world. In the process of exploring who teaches what, and where these professors are located, the basic science-clinical rift that has often been noted in professional curricula can be viewed from a feminist vantage point.

GENDER AND TENURE STATUS IN PHARMACEUTICAL SCIENCES FACULTIES

Depending upon where the pharmaceutical care unit is located geographically, the complement of the full, contractual, and part-time faculty differs, as does the way in which the term *pharmaceutical care* is interpreted. Despite these local variations, the overall picture is the same and involves the near-total marginalization of women academics. Their marginalization is problematic for students in that the profession of pharmacy in Canada is much more feminized than its U.S. counterpart. As I noted above, women make up approximately 60 percent of the practicing Canadian pharmacists and classes are frequently two-thirds or more women students.

Moreover, 40 percent of the academic workforce are women involved in pharmaceutical science education, as shown in table 8.1. This table summarizes information about the faculty employed in the nine schools of pharmacy in Canada in 1996, as listed in university calendars and in the Roster of the American Association of Colleges of Pharmacy (AACP). Of 285 names listed in these sources, 155, or just over one-third taught either clinical or so-called social-administrative topics. Clinical specialties include a hodgepodge of therapeutics,

Table 8.1 Number of Faculty in Canadian Pharmacy Schools by Appointment Type in 1996
(Showing Percentage Tenure-Stream or Tenured and Percentages of Women)
These calculations were based on calendar listings and American Association
of Colleges of Pharmacy listings in their 1996 Roster.

School/ Faculty Type	British Columbia	Alberta	Manitoba	Saskatchewan	Montreal	Toronto	Nova Scotia	Laval (Quebec City)	Newfound-land	National Totals
Total no. faculty— % women	34 (29)	28 (25)	18 (28)	24 (29)	56 (54)	35 (49)	23 (48)	49 (53)	19 (33)	285 (40)
Clinical[a] (% tenure stream)	13 (77)	11 (27)	10 (60)	13 (62)	32 (31)	22 (27)	16 (19)	32 (22)	6 (67)	155 (37)
% women	31	55	50	46	56	64	69	69	83	59
% women in the tenure stream	8	9	30	23	22	14	13	9	50	17
Basic Science (% tenure stream)	21 (81)	17 (94)	8 (100)	11 (91)	24 (58)	13 (92)	7 (86)	17 (100)	12 (100)	130 (86)
% women	29	6	0	9	21	23	29	24	8	13
% women in the tenure stream	50	0	0	100	40	100	50	100	100	65

[a]The category "Clinical" includes those who label themselves social and/or administrative faculty.

compounding and dispensing, clinical pharmacy, over-the-counter medication sales and gerontology; while social-administrative topics, with considerably fewer hours in the curriculum, introduce briefly the health care system, pharmacoeconomics, and the professional practice of pharmacy, including its business context (see Muzzin 2000). Clinical and social-administrative faculty can be considered front-line workers in the teaching of the new professional ideology of pharmaceutical care as well as its promotion in hospitals and communities across Canada.

The number of non-tenured faculty (i.e., permanent contractual, contractually-limited, and part-time) faculty who teach clinical topics in the pharmaceutical sciences are underestimated in the sources I used, since many neither join AACP nor have their names listed in university calendars. This means that my estimate that almost *two-thirds of them are non-tenured* is quite conservative. Although calculations often present the contributions of these faculty as full-time equivalents, I have chosen instead to list them as persons, even though most are part-time rather than full-time positions. I do this because I find it difficult to separate the community work done by these teachers from the contributions they make to clinical teaching in the faculty. I would maintain that there is an inherent bias in a reporting system that excludes community practice as a valid aspect of a faculty member's role in a professional school while counting molecular research done by another faculty member as a contribution to scholarship.

The "other half" of the faculty listed in table 8.1 are professors teaching basic science topics in the curriculum, including pharmaceutical chemistry, microbiology, pharmaceutics, and pharmacology. Although pharmacy education publications such as the *American Journal of Pharmaceutical Education* often discuss the friction between basic science and clinical faculty in pharmacy schools, the lopsided gender balance visible in table 8.1 has never been the object of analysis. As the shaded portions of the table show, there is a substantially higher proportion of women among the clinical and social-administrative pharmacy faculty, almost 60 percent of whom are women, than among the basic science faculty. Of 130 basic science teachers in Canada in 1996, only 15 of the 112 tenured or tenure-stream positions (or 13 percent) were filled by women. Another aspect of this gender and basic science/profession split that has not been attended to is the fact that the majority of basic science professors are tenured or tenure-stream (86 percent in 1996), while the majority of clinical and social-administrative faculty are not. In 1996, only 37 percent of clinical faculty in the pharmaceutical sciences nationally were tenured or tenure-stream.

Table 8.2 provides additional detail about the status of these clinical and social-administrative teachers. It underscores that a relatively large proportion of clinical faculty are in either contractually limited or part-time faculty positions. In 1996, 98 of 155 clinical faculty (63 percent) were part-time or contract faculty. When the gender composition of this untenured faculty group is considered nationally, 65 percent are seen to be women. (These numbers hide inequities practiced by different schools, discussed below.)

Thus, the mostly male basic science professors tend to enjoy the job security that their clinical colleagues find so elusive. Further, my interviews with faculty indicate that the basic science faculty are assigned considerably fewer teaching responsibilities, ostensibly to allow time for molecular research. However, a central and often unspoken issue is that much of what molecular research faculty could teach is inappropriate for curricula that prepare professionals for practice. Unlike disciplines such as dentistry, where part-time clinical faculty positions can be combined in a lucrative way with community practice, in pharmacy, high teaching loads for contractual and part-time faculty along with relatively low hospital salaries limit such possibilities. Thus the Canadian pharmaceutical care curriculum depends on high teaching loads of mostly untenured female faculty. High student-faculty ratios and their devotion to bring about curricular change toward pharmaceutical care mean that these faculty have limited time for applied research. To put it bluntly, pharmaceutical care teachers can be seen as a ghetto of white women academic workers, second-class citizens to male scientist colleagues, making valiant attempts to trope (Haraway 1998) the molecular-dominated curriculum toward more "patient-centeredness."

The statistics themselves do not do justice to the gender oppression being practiced in these schools. Here is an excerpt from my field notes regarding an informal interview with two women faculty at one of the schools of pharmacy:[5]

Table 8.2 Number of Full, Associate, Assistant, and Contractual/Part-time Faculty in Canadian Pharmacy Schools in 1996 by Gender and Appointment Type
(Percentages in brackets)

School/ Faculty Type	British Columbia	Alberta	Manitoba	Saskatchewan	Newfound- land	Montreal	Toronto	Nova Scotia	Laval (Quebec City)	National Totals
Full clinical professors— clinical[a] % women	0	2 (0)	0	1 (0)	2 (0)	4 (50)	3 (33)	2 (50)	2 (0)	16 (25)
Associate clinical professors— % women	3 (0)	0	2 (50)	0	5 (60)	3 (67)	2 (50)	0	2 (0)	17 (41)
Assistant clinical professors— % women	7 (14)	1 (100)	4 (50)	3 (100)	1 (0)	3 (100)	1 (100)	1 (100)	3 (100)	24 (54)
Contract or part-time clinical faculty % women	3 (100)	8 (63)	4 (50)	2 (100)	5 (60)	22 (72)	16 (69)	13 (69)	25 (72)	98 (65)
Full science professors— % women	10 (10)	11 (0)	5 (0)	2 (0)	5 (20)	10 (20)	6 (17)	2 (0)	8 (0)	59 (8)
Associate science professors— % women	4 (50)	0	2 (0)	3 (0)	5 (0)	2 (0)	5 (20)	3 (33)	4 (50)	28 (21)
Assistant science professors— % women	3 (0)	5 (0)	1 (0)	8 (13)	0	2 (0)	1 (100)	1 (0)	5 (40)	26 (15)
Contract or part-time science faculty % women	3 (68)	1 (100)	0	0	1 (0)	10 (30)	1 (0)	1 (100)	0	17 (41)

aThe category "Clinical" includes social and/or administrative faculty.

I wanted to know about gender issues, could they help me? They looked helplessly at me and called themselves "the unwashed." They pointed out that of the women in the faculty, [most] had [postbaccalaureate credentials]. They recalled that there'd [also] been a woman faculty member who'd left to "upgrade" herself but said she'd "left all her stuff behind" and "never returned. . . ." They said that she'd probably felt like they did, that things were "hopeless. . . ."

Molly [all names have been changed] pointed out that she has numerous grants and publications. . . . Molly explained that a person whom I'll call Agnes [another non–tenure-stream academic] negotiated getting her on staff. She isn't making much—I think she said $35,000 Cdn. She said that the [administration's] view on what to pay women [academics] has to do with what their husbands make. The highest paid . . . is single. The next highest paid has a relative in a position of power. . . . Sandra's husband is a [professional], so her salary is one of the lowest. When I looked at the faculty list that Molly copied from the calendar for me, I saw that one of the men who [was listed in the AACP Roster] as a male assistant professor had already been promoted to an associate professor. Molly and Sandra told me that he had "lots of [Medical Research Council] money" so managed to get a good salary. . . . Interestingly enough, when I asked whether the women had ever been proactive enough to push for hiring of another female faculty member, they said they had. . . . [Senior male academics], Molly and Sandra said, had always countered their proposals for hiring a woman with the argument that there was only a "set pot" for their salaries and that a new hire would necessitate reduction of their salaries.

We talked a bit about the work habits of these women. Molly says that she works ninety hours a week . . . and that she says "yes" to important requests when she knows no one else will do them and she is "not prepared to do anything halfway." She agreed that she has a "public service ethic" like many women. Sandra added that she did so much volunteer committee work that she even got "token pay" i.e. a "few bucks" from the local licensing board. . . .

I can see that there's only [a few tenure-stream women faculty] at [other universities] too, leading the pharmaceutical care [p.c.] curriculum movement. As I originally thought, p.c. is a kind of "feminist movement" within pharmacy. . . . The gendered aspects of the movement are really clear to me now, and that pharmacy will fail as a profession because of gender discrimination. (Field notes 1996)

Just as interesting as the overall gendered nature of faculty appointments in so-called wet lab versus clinical pharmaceutical teaching are the variations of the clinical "female ghetto" theme that are seen from school to school. As the highlighted section of table 8.2 shows, in population centers such as Montreal; Toronto; Quebec City; and Halifax, Nova Scotia, 76 of 102 of the faculty teaching pharmaceutical care courses are part-time or contractually-limited and 54, or 73 percent, are women. In these urban locations, where a supply of cheap female academic labor is readily available, only a little over a quarter of the clinical labor force is full-time tenured and tenure-stream. In "hinterland" provinces such as Newfoundland in the East along with the Western provinces, a smaller proportion of the faculty teaching pharmaceutical care courses are part time or contractual faculty (i.e., 22 of 53, or 42 percent), and of the almost 60 percent of the clinical/social-administrative faculty in these schools who are tenured or tenure-stream, only 8 of 23, or 35 percent, are women.

Thus in smaller schools, the clinical presence is smaller and male-dominated at a ratio of about two to one. This can be understood as a move by these "hinterland" schools to retain clinical faculty through awarding a slightly higher proportion of clinical positions to the tenure-stream. As if it were a law of nature, as the proportion of clinical tenured or tenure-stream faculty rises in a school, the proportion of women faculty declines. Larger schools have more clinical faculty, mostly women, plus administrative support for these pharmaceutical care initiatives, but they are marginalized in non–tenured positions. Thus, all schools demonstrate what has been called a "chilly climate" for women academics; women are frozen out of full-time tenure positions in the clinical teaching that they prefer, while their initiatives regarding pharmaceutical care are made more difficult to achieve.

THE "EMPOWERING" SENIOR WHITE MALE
PROFESSOR PHENOMENON

Although I would like to report that women faculty, whose experiences of academia awakened them to resistance, have led a revolution toward a more holistic pharmacy curriculum in Canada, sadly, this is not the case. I interviewed the senior women clinical faculty and without exception they championed the concept of pharmaceutical care. These women are not in a position to have much impact on curriculum. Indeed, I have more fingers than there are women full pharmacy professors in Canada! As table 8.2 shows, there were only 4 women full professors in clinical pharmacy in 1996 (compared to 12 men) and 5 women basic science full professors (compared to 54 men). Senior women and their largely untenured colleagues were not in a good structural position to openly lead this movement without the "mentorship" of senior male academics. This administrative support of the curricular initiatives of clinical faculty amounted to support of women in these curricular "gender wars," but that did not make these senior male professors feminists. Identifying themselves as saviors of the *profession*, they pointed out that, as I have emphasized above, pharmacy schools prepare pharmacists for professional practice and not to do molecular research. Thus these deans or former deans defined a position as apologists for "professional" interests in the curriculum, often strongly opposing those who represented "research" factions, but without adopting a feminist and holistic position. They could do this without having to advocate any structural changes vis-à-vis tenured and clinical positions.

These quantitative and structural descriptions do not begin to capture the reality of the struggle over curriculum. Nor do these descriptions and analysis do justice to the intensity of interpersonal relations within these structures of hegemony and unequal power. I will turn to some excerpts from interviews and field notes to demonstrate what exactly is at stake:

> The last interview was probably the teariest I've ever done in my life. After about an hour of straight interviewing, the woman broke down and started to cry and I stopped the interview, but she cried, basically, all through the rest of the time, and that didn't seem to bother

her. At first she didn't even want to get a tissue to wipe away all these tears, and she didn't seem to want to stop, either, even though I was worried that I was doing something bad to her, and I tried to steer the conversation away, but she clearly wanted to talk about things. [Afterwards] she gave me such a look of radiance that I thought that, in fact, it had been wonderful for her to have this cathartic experience to talk about how difficult life had been for her. Let's see if I can piece together what I know. . . .

My interpretation of what happened is that [one of the senior male academics], although he doesn't define himself as a feminist, in fact, was very facilitating of women who came into the faculty who were interested in doing clinical teaching. And that includes the woman whom I interviewed this afternoon, who was teary, and who I think has been a key player in the dissemination of pharmaceutical care. . . . He was also instrumental in bringing on and supporting other women and they perceive him as being a kind of mentor. . . . [Other senior male science professors] don't share his vision, and being basic scientists and trying to build the "research bucks" into the faculty to maintain its standing with the upper administration and plus protect it from deep budget cuts, they have failed to pay attention to the profession end of the faculty, and what comes out as male domination is this ignoring of the service end, which is what the women are interested in. . . .

Now in itself, this situation doesn't seem to be particularly evil. You can see why [science academics] would want to build up the science side in order to protect the reputation of the faculty, but it does get played out as a gender issue and the lives of these women get destroyed because they have no opportunity for getting [tenured] faculty positions or acknowledgment or competing on a level playing field with the men who are obviously going to get promoted given the number of MRC grants they win and the number of publications they make.

In fact, some of these women could be seen as real "flakes," like the one I interviewed this afternoon, because she talked in such a dedicated way about caring and teaching, that I'm sure that the men would just roll their eyes. . . . The [empowering senior male professor] is interesting because . . . he doesn't think he's mentored these women, even though they think they've been mentored by him. What he seems to have done is raise their consciousness to the point where they thought they could achieve great things and . . . they have achieved great things. . . . They've changed the teaching. They changed the curriculum. They've done a lot of liaison with the government. The person I interviewed this afternoon had done a lot of inter-disciplinary work at the university. . . . [But the senior male science administrators have] completely cut off the support of the initiatives taken by these women and their achievements are not recognized. . . . (Field notes 1996)

In retrospect, I thought that it was not accidental that some of the men involved in encouraging the pharmaceutical care curriculum in Canada had either experienced discrimination themselves and were conscious of racial and gender issues through their family backgrounds or through observations of the operation of academic coalitions at their faculties. On the basis of my interviewing of deans and associate deans of pharmacy and dentistry, I determined that such consciousness is rare among the most senior white male pharmacy academics (and indeed most senior women pharmacy academics) in Canada who are mainly involved with basic science rather than teaching about the profession.

But I had to interview administrators and faculty *outside* of the pharmaceutical sciences before I was really able to understand how the upper administration of Canadian universities and the Canadian scientific funding system supports the systemic discrimination documented here. As noted above, dentistry faculties in Canada have recently faced closures or takeovers by medicine if the upper administration deemed that too much money was being spent on preparing dentists as compared to supporting molecular research. By way of comparison, it is unlikely that too much money will be spent on "pharmaceutical care" in Canadian schools of pharmacy as compared to molecular research. However, the problem of what young molecular researchers will teach in curricula that are intended to prepare professionals for practice is the same problem that older molecular researchers have faced. Given that the funding of academic molecular science is unlikely to change in the near future, we can predict continuing discrimination and a continuing inability to make curriculum more relevant to health and healing.

DISCUSSION: A CRITICAL FEMINIST VIEW
OF "HOW THINGS WORK" IN THE PHARMACEUTICAL
SCIENCES CURRICULUM

Dorothy Smith (1987, 1994, 1999) proposed that an understanding of "how things work" should be informed by an analysis of the invisible labor of marginalized groups vis-à-vis what she terms *extra-local* relations of ruling. Critical approaches that examine these extra-local relations have for the past few decades been considered central to the sociology of the professions (e.g., Johnson 1977; Larson 1977; Noble 1977; Coburn, Torrance, and Kaufert 1983; de Montigny 1995; Krause 1996). However, in the past decade, there has been an exponential increase in the number of publications that turn a critical eye toward the situation of feminized professional groups such as nurses (Armstrong, Choiniere, and Day 1993; McPherson 1996; Reverby 1987; Street 1992) as well as women in nonfeminized professions such as law (Pierce 1995; Monture 1986), academia (Richardson 1997; Stalker and Prentice 1998), and medicine (Wear 1997; Witz 1992). Contemporary scholarship has similarly begun to focus on the intersections of gender and race in professional work (hooks 1994; Haraway 1998; Sokoloff 1992; Thornhill, 1994). This development can be contextualized as part of a vigorous feminist critique of science as androcentric and neocolonial (Shiva 1995; Harding 1991, 1994, 1998; Hubbard 1995; Bleier 1991).

This chapter contributes to the feminist critique of science and the professions by making visible the struggle over curriculum between mainstream and marginalized faculty within university pharmaceutical sciences. As such, it examines the "relations of ruling" by explicitly naming who teaches what in this curriculum and how it is valued through the awarding of permanent faculty positions. Overall, it was noted that male faculty are much more likely than female faculty to be involved in laboratory research funded by federal agencies and pharmaceutical firms. They are thus not directly involved in the teaching of pharmaceutical care. This structural imbalance relegated the "pharmaceutical care" movement to being the "poor sister" to molecular research and teaching in the pharmaceutical sciences curriculum. The poor sister position of this professional ideology limits the impact of the pharmaceutical care curriculum.

In order to appreciate the full significance of the process that I detailed in this chapter, it is necessary to consider pharmaceutical science curricula within a global context. Specifically, pharmaceutical science curricula around the world reflect the hegemony of molecular science; they teach professional work as the sale of synthetic drugs in a worldwide market. To this end, discourses of indigenous health and healing are purged or adapted to the ruling agenda. While I dealt specifically with Canada in this research, the arguments can be usefully applied to any other marginalized country with a modest market for pharmaceutical sales.[6] Canada is a particularly interesting example of the processes involved, since it has an official policy of "multiculturalism" supported by immigration policies that differentially favor the entry of professionals educated in Western ways, while at the same time largely restricting the entry of its own aboriginal population into science studies.

NOTES

1. Another fifty-five individuals outside the schools were similarly interviewed about the impact of the academic pharmaceutical care movement. These included representatives of provincial licensing boards and professional associations, independent pharmacy owners, corporate and franchise pharmacy executives, hospital administrators, government pharmacare managers, and pharmaceutical firm executives. Interviews were transcribed and are being analyzed in order to generate a theory of how gender is linked to the way pharmaceutical care is taught and the extent to which it is accepted in the communities surrounding each school.

2. Eatons, taken over by Sears in 1999, was a longstanding Canadian-owned department store, the flagship of which, still called the Eatons' Center, was built as one of the first indoor Canadian malls, located in a prominent position on the main street of Toronto.

3. This statement was made in an interview that I conducted with a dentistry dean in Canada in 1996; his identity is not revealed for reasons of confidentiality.

4. The work of Vandana Shiva (1995, 1997), a scholar writing from India who has labeled white science and technology "mono-cultural" in that it runs roughshod over indigenous cultures and concerns about the environment, has helped me to see how the global relations of ruling operate in the curriculum of pharmacy. Nonetheless, my lack of awarenes of exclusionary practices in "normal science" vis-à-vis indigenous knowledges in my curriculum committee work is all the more difficult to understand because I was at the time teaching classes in which

I assigned readings from the critical feminists who have had so much to say about the science and technology that contribute to the activities of the occidentally based transnational pharmaceutical industry and its excesses. Globally, as well as in my local Canadian situation, I taught, women have been the victims of dangerous reproductive technologies, defective breast implants, largely untested hormone replacement therapy, infant formula scams, and mind-numbing mood-altering drugs for decades (Addiction Research Foundation of Ontario 1976; Bader 1981; Coney 1994; Harding 1994; McDonnell 1986; Weiss 1996).

5. A large section of the analysis that followed was omitted because it would be possible to identify this particular school if it were included.

6. It might be considered a controversial statement that Canada is a marginalized nation because of its apparent central role in global economic discussions. Certainly it occupies a different position than countries which Amin has labeled "fourth world" because of their complete disconnection from the capitalist global economy (Amin 1997). However, with respect to the operation of the pharmaceutical industry, which is what is being examined here, a good case has been made that the Canadian government has had difficulty in "keeping up" with the task of ensuring public safety in the context of the activities of these corporations (Lexchin 1984, 1990, 1997, Regush 1993) as compared to more powerful nations (Wright 1994). Canadians like me have recently become aware, mainly through European sources, that they are part of a "post–marketing surveillance" experiment in which a large proportion of our food has been genetically modified by pharmaceutical corporations such as Monsanto and Novartis, without our approval (Nottingham 1998; HRH Prince of Wales 1998; Suzuki and Knudtson 1990). Canada thus has the dubious honor of being the first nation to become familiar with the implications of living not only in a transuranic world—one that contains synthetic elements like plutonium, patented by Dupont—but also a synthetic transgenic world—one that contains formerly discrete species, now genetically mixed by pharmaceutical industry technology, also first patented by Du Pont (Haraway 1998).

"Plotting Something Dastardly" 9

Hiding a Gender Curriculum in Engineering

Karen L. Tonso

> Several years ago, women faculty happened to sit together "down front" at a faculty meeting. When women faculty left the meeting, some of their men colleagues accused them of "plotting something dastardly" and of "conspiring against them."
>
> —A story that circulates on an engineering campus in the U.S. mid-continent

Most faculty knew the tale. No one disputed that it could have happened, yet no one was sure of the year, the women involved, or the men who spoke in these terms. It was commonly agreed that these untoward behaviors no longer occurred, and that was taken as an indication of progress; yet I wondered if this story and its retelling illuminate current practices. As a twice-told tale, it functions to establish women faculty's subordinate place on campus. The original telling by men in power equates women's entering previously male bastions to a kind of assault on a sacrosanct society. The retelling as a parable serves to consolidate the power of men by dismissing sexist practices as something "other people" had done in a bygone era. Apocryphal or not, statements like this emerge from and reinforce men's opposition to women's presence as full-fledged members of engineering education.

Late in my final semester of fieldwork, as I completed interviews with engineering faculty members, a woman professor and I were talking about what it was like to be a woman in engineering. Out of the blue, one of her colleagues stuck his head in the door to say hello. He had a reputation for treating women colleagues and students with respect and, although I had not observed his classes, I knew him informally. Turning to leave, he quipped, "Are you guys plotting something real dastardly?" Neither professor seemed to notice the exchange, but I did and began thinking about what engineering faculty and students learned to not-notice. Learning to not-notice proved crucial to my examination of sociocultural productions that favored men over women and some forms of manhood over others. In this chapter, drawn from a large-scale ethnography of an engineering campus (Tonso 1993, 1997), I describe processes for "hiding" the campus gender curriculum. Because the curricula I describe were in plain sight, like the emperor's new clothes, "hiding" means learning to not-notice.

GENDER IN ENGINEERING

Women's circumstances in engineering are among the most difficult of all scientific disciplines[1] (Carter and Kirkup 1990; McIlwee and Robinson 1992; Rossiter 1982, 1995). Three key indicators mark women's circumstances in engineering:

- Women are represented in very low numbers. At the time of my study, fewer than 8 percent of practicing engineers were women, and, women earned fewer than 17 percent of undergraduate degrees. (National Science Foundation 1996)
- Women leave engineering majors at higher rates than men and report greater alienation from the discipline than do men. (Agogino and Linn 1992, Seymour and Hewitt 1997)
- Women experience downward mobility over time in careers. Significantly, many women who start in high-status design jobs move into less prestigious jobs. (Carter and Kirkup 1990, McIlwee and Robinson 1992)

Taken together, these suggest that processes for becoming an engineer build (some) men's strengths and engineering affiliations, but not women's, alluding to a gender curriculum. However, no research had been devoted to studying how this "favoring" is accomplished. My study follows in the tradition of critical ethnography, melding sociocultural theories of learning (Chaiklin and Lave 1993; Lave and Wenger 1991; Levinson, Foley, and Holland 1996; Nespor 1994) with feminist critiques, including science (Eisenhart Finkel, Behm, Laurence, and Tonso 1998; Harding 1991; Kahle 1985; Keller 1985; Longino 1990), post–secondary education (Holland and Eisenhart 1990; O'Conor 1998), cultural relativism (Friedman 1987; Young 1990), and democratic principles (Gutmann 1987; Howe 1993).

Following Margaret Eisenhart and Nancy Lawrence, I sought to make visible the cultural model of belonging on an engineering campus:

> Cultural models, or taken-for-granted sets of ideas about how the world is *supposed to work*, are frames of reference that people use to make sense of, and debate, the meaning or interpretation of events. . . . When a cultural model is invoked, it establishes one way of interpreting an event, and in so doing it limits and simplifies the interpretations that people are likely to give to the event. . . . [A]ctual events are not determined or dictated by a cultural model, but experiences are anticipated, extrapolated, or evaluated in light of it. When someone acts or speaks in such a way as to evoke a familiar aspect of the model, people are likely to assume that other aspects of the model apply as well. (Eisenhart and Lawrence 1994, 98; emphasis added)

Thus, an action or behavior intended in one way by its performer could in fact be taken to mean something altogether different in a cultural context, just as two identical actions when performed by different persons could mean different things. Therefore, I thought it important not only to observe how it was that people acted and interacted, but also to understand the culturally salient lens through which those actions were given meaning.

Two works in sociocultural theory suggested how to study both the practical work of engineering design and the academic-science work of conventional engineering courses. First, the situated learning theory of Jean Lave and Etienne Wenger (1991) provided a starting point for thinking about the real-world, out-of-school nature of practical engineering and how design class activities might promote this kind of learning. They explained how apprentices learn a trade, such as becoming a tailor or butcher. Novices participate in the community and learning occurs through working with "old timers." According to Lave and Wenger, identities such as "expert tailor" motivate novices to learn. However, the theory seemed to assume that becoming a member of a community was somehow uncontested, that there was a single "tailor" identity being produced that was available to all novices. This seemed too simple to explain the circumstances in engineering.

Second, Jan Nespor (1994, 9) examined how academic disciplines structure professionalization in some majors. He found that physics and business majors (but not sociology and education) channeled students into prescribed, discipline-appropriate ways of belonging that constrained who belonged and what belonging entailed. For these academic disciplines, he argued:

> "Communities" aren't just situated *in* space and time, they are ways of *producing and organizing* space and time and setting up patterns of movement across space-time: they are networks of power. People don't simply *move into* these networks in an apprenticeship mode, they are defined, enrolled and mobilized along particular trajectories that *move them across* places in the network and allow them to move other parts of the world into that network. (italics in the original)

Nespor's (1990) analysis of curricular structures provided a tool to characterize the extent to which academic disciplines define and control belonging. I found that trajectories embedded in engineering coursework exerted even more control over students' futures than was true for physics and business majors; little latitude existed for student engineers to shape their academic lives. I doubted that disciplinary control was enough to create a singular entity encapsulated by the term *engineer* and wondered how such a system was revealed and produced in everyday interactions.

Dorothy Holland and Margaret Eisenhart (1990) provided insights into the ways in which interactions produce cultural ways of life. They studied women college students' proclivity to begin college with high expectations and ambitions for careers that evaporated only to be replaced by aspirations for becoming romantic partners of men. As women became disinterested in their academic work, they engaged in a campus "culture of romance." Through their participation in extracurricular, on-campus peer groups, women whose academic work contained little to inspire them learned to think of their value primarily in terms of romantic relations with men. I studied a set of engineering courses at the intersection of real-world engineering practices, academic practices, and a culture of romance.

RESEARCH METHODOLOGY

I conducted the research at Public Engineering School (PES), a state-supported college of engineering with programs typical of many engineering colleges. PES had about twenty-three hundred undergraduate students (20 percent women and 14 percent ethnic minorities) and has always been coeducational. This college stood out among engineering colleges as a place with more women students and more women professors than national averages, as well as a place with considerable collective will to change the curriculum in ways intended to address concerns about women's education in engineering.

Successful engineers need an excellent grasp of engineering, scientific, and mathematical principles, as well as a wide range of historically nonacademic and nontechnical skills. Engineering employers still call for better preparation in applying scientific and engineering principles to real-world problems, working in teams, and communicating (e.g., Dutson, Toddd, Magleby, Sorenson 1997). Engineering design courses are one way that PES responded to the industry's concerns, combining out-of-school engineering practice with in-school "book-learning." Design provides opportunities for student engineers working in teams to complete real-world projects that require not only the application of scientific, mathematical, and engineering principles to specific situations, but also gathering information from clients about their needs and interests. Students similarly must learn to communicate their ideas to teammates and to industry employees ranging from hourly laborers, to engineers, engineering managers, and nontechnical managers.

Two portions of the research project proved critical to understanding the cultural model for belonging: gathering participant-observation field-data to document actions and behaviors and eliciting categories for belonging. The research began in 1993 with a pilot study in a second-year class, then added fieldwork in first- and fourth-year classes in 1995 and 1996 (Tonso 1993, 1997). I selected classrooms taught by engineering educators known for their skills in teaching engineering design. Because the sophomore-class professor promoted a classroom climate that alienated women (Tonso 1996c), when I expanded the study, I sought professors recognized for their contributions to women's participation. Within these classrooms, I selected teams of women and men students that had more than one woman, as being the only woman on the team is known to be alienating (Agogino and Linn 1992, Tonso 1996a). I followed three teams in a one-semester, first-year engineering design class (seven women and five men), two teams in a one-semester, second-year class (four women and six men), and two teams in a two-semester, senior-year engineering design class (four women and seven men) (table 9.1). I participated as an engineering colleague on each of these seven teams, attending all of their whole-class meetings and many of their out-of-class meetings. During four semesters collecting data, I interviewed twenty-four students on teams twice, eight students on teams once, and design class professors once (four women and five men). Analysis proceeded using semantic domain techniques and an interpretive approach (Spradley 1979, 1980).

To elicit engineering-students' categories of belonging, I modeled my data collection strategies after Holland and Skinner's (1987) study of the cultural models behind Americans' talk about gender types. Using a two-stage elicit-and-sort interview protocol, I first asked seventeen student engineers (six women and eleven men) to list "all of the terms they use to refer to each other as student engineers" and to describe each of the terms in the list. After eliciting terms, I made a comprehensive list from audiotape transcripts. Of the 126 terms given, 36 occurred more frequently in interviews and field notes. In the sorting stage I asked eleven student engineers (four women and seven men) to sort the most frequently elicited terms into "categories that make

Table 9.1 Makeup of Student Teams

Design Course	Team Name	Women	Men	Students
First year,	Monday	3	2	5
one semester	Wednesday	2	1	3
	Friday	2	2	4
Total	3	7	5	12
Second year,	Team A	3	2	5
one semester	Team B	1	4	5
Total	2	4	6	10
Fourth year,	Mercury	2	4	6
two semesters	Sludge	2	3	5
Total	2	4	7	11
Grand Total	7	15	18	33

sense to you" and to "tell me why you put terms together in each group and to describe how the categories differ." The sorting interviews coincided with my fieldwork in senior design and came at the end of my final ethnographic interview with senior student engineers.

As detailed elsewhere (Tonso 1999a, 1999b), the cultural model of belonging, through which events and actions were interpreted and given meaning, was organized by two interlocking ideologies: academic-science prestige and gender status. "Recognizing" proceeded by measuring flesh-and-blood student engineers against hierarchically arrayed engineering-student images. Students talked about the kinds of engineers recognized on campus, describing how various "old-timer" identities were ordered. The culture favored men (and a few narrowly recognized women) who employed academic-science forms of practice, primarily drill-and-test, decontextualized principles without substantive applications. This "preferred" sort of engineer became the prototype against which other forms of practice were measured. Thus, men practitioners of another form of practice, one closely matched to the industry's purported needs that incorporated site-specific applications and other nonacademic and non-technical skills, came to be considered inferior. The categories of belonging were profoundly gendered (Tonso 1999b). Gender-neutral (unmarked) terms (e.g., nerd, dork, hard-core overachiever) occurred in terrain recognizing "acting like engineers" and referred only to men. Gender-marked terms such as *frat boy* and *sorority woman,* occurred only in the portion of the belonging terrain where social achievement was celebrated. Here, women were expected to be men's (subordinate) romantic partners. By not "seeing" women when they acted like engineers, the culture conserved the status quo.

Thus, campus "authorities" recognized some kinds of action as deserving respect, other action as less deserving of respect, and, when practiced by women, some actions fell outside the recognition system; that is, were invisible. It was especially distressing that the quality of engineering practices (and I take those needed for real-world engineering to be the rightful goal of engineering education) were inversely related to recognition. That is, those with the highest status exhibited virtually no real-world engineering expertise on design teams, while those with exemplary engineering skills (purportedly valued by industry employers) received limited recognition, if any. At all levels, in and out of classrooms, women's presence and potential collaboration was "recognized" as an intention to reshape the campus culture. Thus, women's actions were interpreted as threats to the survival of a hegemonic, male-centered, academic-science form of practice preferred on campus.

HIDING THE GENDER CURRICULUM

The gender curriculum was "hidden" via various cultural performances that spanned campus contexts. The examples that follow illustrate how talk about gender, codes of dress, appropriation of women students' work, faculty attention to superficial rather than substantive features of engineering practice, and the dismissal of women's interpretations of campus norms constituted a hidden curriculum that produced women as "not-engineers."

Being a Man versus Being a Woman

I asked first- and fourth-year student engineers and engineering faculty what it was like to be whatever gender they were, and then followed up by asking if they thought it would be different to be the other gender. I compared these answers to their answers to questions about treating women and men "equally." Though almost all men and women thought that everyone was treated equally, every student also gave examples of strikingly unequal campus circumstances (Tonso 1996b).

Being a man engineering student meant that people just like yourself surrounded you. Though none characterized this as "privileged," men were aware of the extent to which it made their lives easier. For instance, it meant "just being one of the guys" (freshman man), "fitting into a role where you're more accepted" (senior man), and "not being subjected to the pressure of people thinking men can't do engineering" (senior man). In the words of a freshman man, "It's about as conducive a situation as you could hope for ... because it retains the white males' approach ... [and] you're welcomed with open arms." And another freshman student, said "I would much rather be a man going to a campus like this, [because] that's what I've been prepared for ... to be a male in society."

Being a woman student meant that you had to learn to "deal with" men, that you had to work harder to fit in, and that you would associate with many more men than women. Women's remarks included that they "have to get along with men" (freshman woman) and "have to deal with guys that think women shouldn't be here" (senior woman). However, one freshman woman student thought that "being associated with men more is good for women" since that is what a woman can expect on the job. Three of the men students thought that women received preferential treatment. But most men recognized negative attitudes toward women, commenting that "women are kidded about getting 'girl points'" (senior man) and "women [have to put up with] standard-issue stereotypes of women in engineering, such as being unattractive, overweight, and picky about men" (senior man). Students thought women had to work harder to receive the same amount of respect. Men stated that women who "have avoided society's push toward art, sociology, and psychology" majors to study engineering (freshman man) must "learn a new language, a language developed by men" (freshman man). Women must be "more determined and have to prove everybody wrong" about women's lack of aptitude for engineering (senior man). Students commented on "professors grading women's work harder" (freshman woman) and on "having to try twice as hard to be heard" (senior man).

Yet, almost without exception, student engineers professed that everyone was treated equally on campus. This suggests an ideology of learning to not-notice differences in women's and men's circumstances. In fact, learning to ignore the realities was one of women's survival techniques and a key way that they "went along," which tacitly promoted the status quo. Likewise, men's learning to not-notice their privilege functioned to reinforce it. But these interview data tell little about how social interactions between and among students and faculty contributed to hiding the gender curriculum. Let us turn to a few illustrative examples.

Dressing Like Women

Professional dress was one area where women found they did not fit perceptions about engineering (Tonso 1993). Design class students were expected to wear professional dress when they met with clients and for formal presentations to faculty and other design teams. The sophomore class professor gave these instructions: "You should be at least as formal as the client. If he has on a coat and tie, you keep your coat on. If he is in a shirt and tie, you can take off your jacket." This posed dilemmas for women that did not exist for men.

First, what is the analogous form of dress for women? On Team A,

Franci wondered: "Do we have to wear hosieries? Not ya'll [the men in the group], but us [the women]." After discussing the issue further, Paul stated, "We should look nice, but not necessarily a suit and tie," and Amy immediately added, "Or a jacket and skirt." Franci suggested that "the guys could all wear a tie, white shirt, and blue jeans." Aside from the "hosieries" comment, which Doug teased Franci about by remarking that he would wear "fishnet stockings," none of the student engineers gave specific examples of women's clothing.

Second, wearing a dress on campus did not indicate that women belonged, though wearing a tie and jacket conferred belonging on men students. As they tried to decide on a time when the team could carpool to the client's office, Franci suddenly realized that she was the only team member who had another class before the design meeting. If she had to meet the group when they would usually attend design class, there would be no time to change and she would have to wear a dress to her other class. This was troublesome because "everybody hassles you in class [when you wear a dress]." Most other team members nodded or "uh-huh'd" their agreement. Franci added, "I hate for them to notice that I am wearing a dress." However, Doug disagreed, saying, "It's not that big a deal. Everybody knows you're in [this class] or have an interview." Franci was not convinced and the team alleviated her concerns by agreeing to depart ten minutes later, allowing her to change after her other class.

The explicit curriculum of faculty directives encouraging professional behavior took men's clothing for granted. This left women to interpret these directives, knowing that women's clothing was not a marker of affiliation but one of not-belonging. And in the social interactions between women and men, when women discussed the contradictions of fitting into an engineering way of life, some men (Doug in this instance) ridiculed their attempts by alluding to inappropriate forms of womanhood—fishnet stockings.

Though one woman professor worked diligently, but unsuccessfully, to incorporate guidelines for women's dress in design courses, her men colleagues steadfastly failed to see the importance of doing so. In particular, there were no avenues except the design-course organizational meetings where this issue could be discussed. In her words:

> There wouldn't be any place to go over the head of [the design
> program director]. I mean who would you go to? The [Academic]

VP [a man recently caught in a compromising situation with a staff member]. . . . That would have been a real waste of my time. So I don't think there was any place to go talk about it. I don't think it would have done any good if there was, because I would have been typecast even more than I already am as, you know, this sort of extreme fringe.

The system punished her for trying to improve circumstances for women students as behaviors of a person who did not belong at PES, someone on the "extreme fringe" who threatened engineering. Ultimately, her working for this one seemingly minor issue of women's inclusion became a reason for colleagues to doubt her expertise in her academic specialty (Tonso 2000).

Controlling and Exploiting Women's Engineering Work

Because women had limited access to the cultural machinery through which one garnered prestige, they were easy targets for exploitation. This was evident on the senior Mercury Team, comprised of two women (Carol and Pam) and four men (Carson, Pete, Samuel, and Shane). They worked for A-Tech, a small company developing environmental technology for large power plants and created a mathematical model of a proprietary technology for removing mercury from power-plant flue-gas emissions. Their project—moving gigantic volumes of flue gas (one million cubic feet per minute) through a "sorbant" bed with negligible pressure drop and amalgamating trace amounts of mercury—was a technological challenge. This technology is analogous to a car's catalytic converter, though the Mercury Team was designing a catalytic converter that would be about the size of a high school gymnasium.

On the Mercury Team, Carson routinely demanded that Pam explain all of her work to him, ostensibly so he could check it. Their rapid-fire exchange during a mid-February team meeting is representative of how he controlled her work:

CARSON: Well, are we going to be able to extrapolate the trend in the sorbant efficiency with time?
PAM: That's exactly what I'm inferring [answering him curtly].
CARSON: Well, where's the total amount of sorbant per day?
PAM: Why? [She's beginning to bristle.]

CARSON: Well, so how much?. . .

PAM: Well, the client and three professors told me to do it this way. What's the problem? [She's becoming more irritated with Carson.]

CARSON: I'm not doing heat transfer. I'm doing how much we need. [He's supposed to be doing heat transfer.]

PAM: Why? That's what I'm doing.

CARSON: So we can check each other. . . . [He turns to his calculator.]

Differences in disciplinary expertise made it highly unlikely that Carson (a mechanical engineer) would be able to "figure out what's going on" to the same extent that Pam (a chemical engineer) could. In this situation, chemical engineers worked on mass transfer, aspects of an amalgamation process moving vapor-phase mercury carried in flue gas onto the gold catalyst embedded in a porous media (a complicated form of fluid flow not covered in Carson's course work). By comparison, mechanical engineers dealt almost exclusively with the piping and equipment needed for holding and transporting flue gas streams, and for heating the catalyst to drive off amalgamated mercury. They focused on heat-transfer and corrosion characteristics of the metals and plastics used in the equipment. In spite of the fact that Pam knew what she was talking about and spent considerable time and energy studying advanced engineering texts and conferring with experts about the issue, Carson doubted her at every turn. He acted as if it were Pam's job to teach him advanced chemical engineering.

In fact, though needing to share information, neither had enough expertise in the other's specialty to check the work, and not performing heat transfer calculations precluded anyone checking Carson's work. Nonetheless, when the team met with the client, Carson took center stage and proffered information he had gleaned from Pam, as if it were his own work. Until late in the second semester, when a draft report became due, Carson's only contribution to the team's engineering work was to control Pam's work. Yet no one ever interrupted Carson's academic harassing of Pam. Ultimately, Pam doubted her expertise, though it sustained the entire team.

Carson's actions violated the engineering code of ethics distributed in class. In particular, "ethical" engineering is restricted to that which one is qualified to perform, one has performed, and which respects the expertise of engineers working in other specialties. Acting as if he were qualified in Pam's area of expertise, treating her as if she were not qual-ified, and later taking credit for her work were unethical practices. Fac-ulty contributed to reinforcing such unethical practices by failing to teach students how to apply the code of ethics and failing to use ethics as a yardstick for students' behavior.

In end-of-fieldwork interviews, Pam's teammates expressed disgust with Carson's mistreatment of her. For instance, consider Samuel's appraisal of teamwork contributions:

> Pamela's done fairly good, I think. She's been like our best member because she does stuff. I think that's the most important thing, going and doing it and then coming back to the group and saying: "This is what I found. Does this make sense? Can we talk about this? Do you have suggestions?". . . . Carson's done a fair amount. . . . It's just, like Carson's contribution is going to be to sit back and critique what other people have done, and that won't work.

Yet no one characterized Carson's behavior as unethical, affirming my growing suspicion that students could not interpret or apply ethical standards in real-world situations. Ethical behavior became just another set of "rules" to dodge, another arena where students must "dupe" faculty.

Others on the team colluded to keep Pam's engineering work from being recognized outside team meetings. In particular, when the team gave oral presentations to the design class and to their client, Pam's teammates volunteered to give presentations because "Pam has already done so much." In blatant disregard for ethical behaviors, every oral presentation except the last one was almost entirely limited to pre-senting engineering work that Pam had performed. "Teamwork," as practiced by the Mercury Team, meant Pam's work, something the fac-ulty could not discern when students successfully misrepresented their contributions.

Faculty's Pathological Control

Though design-class objectives intended students to learn to com-municate through oral and written presentations *and* engage in team-work and real-world engineering practices, evaluation of student work focused on superficial aspects of oral presentations and writ-ten work, overlooking both teamwork and the engineering work itself. Faculty grading and feedback contributed to a climate where inconsequential issues of form took center stage and issues of substance were neglected.

For instance, in the senior design class, students heard Dr. Stanley, a man and the Mercury Team's advisor, describe the form their final project was to take. The form was inexplicably patterned after National Science Foundation funding applications. In fifteen years as an engineer, I never saw this format employed, but I did recognize it from efforts to secure funding for social science research. This suggests that engineering faculty continued to model the academic way of life, precisely the set of academic-science-affiliated practices that design courses were intended to reform.

In my field notes I commented that students paid little attention to Dr. Stanley, assuming the "attentive student" position: outstretched legs crossed at the ankles, arms folded across the chest, relaxed in the chair, looking toward the professor with a blank look, and occasionally nodding. However, students referred to the report-format document repeatedly as they wrote their drafts, writing something for every heading even when they had done no work in an area. As a member of student teams, I observed that portions of reports were *boiler-housed,* an engineering term for creating the illusion of work. Faculty read the drafts, checked that all sections were in place, and marked copy-editing mistakes and formatting errors. They did not seem to be able to tell the difference between imagined and performed engineering.

Feedback on oral presentations was even more focused on superficial behavior. Two pet peeves received most attention in the senior design class: time limits and standing by the overhead projector, instead of at the front, thereby blocking the audience's line of sight. When a team exceeded the limit, they were immediately interrupted, told to sit down, and not allowed to finish. They chose between being graded down and leaving out crucial information. Though only one of the fifteen professors or guest speakers giving presentations stood by the screen, students were publicly upbraided for this transgression. Attending to trivial aspects of engineering practice was a hallmark of the PES way of life.

Taken together, faculty attention to superficial details set the tone for what counted as good engineering, and overlooked ethics, teamwork, and engineering quality. By failing to recognize bogus engineering, faculty came to be thought of as people who could be duped, a skill that high-status students used to succeed. Being easily duped established faculty as not "real" engineers. Subsequently, they could not claim students' respect, a fact that reduced faculty's ability to counter the sexist practices of powerful men students, as illustrated in the following example.

Dismissing Women's Interpretations of Sexist Practices

Marianne's circumstances on the senior Sludge Team were remarkably positive (Tonso 1997). Her teammates treated her with respect, did not exploit her considerable engineering contributions, and took her out-of-school social commitments seriously enough to balance them with her teamwork commitments. However, her otherwise progressive men colleagues failed to defend her in a whole-class setting when a vocal minority of sexist men shouted down her characterization of a sexual-harassment case study.

On the day in question, a guest speaker arrived to discuss affir-mative action and sexual harassment policies with the senior design class. As the fifty-minute session unfolded, a small group of men stu-dents sitting in the back corner began to behave in ways that violated classroom decorum standards. When the guest speaker asked what one did if he or she were discriminated against, one of these young men shouted out "SOOOO-EEE!" from the back of the room. It took me a minute to realize that this referred to filing a lawsuit. The faculty, who in other classes had set narrow behavior standards, did not inter-vene. Things quickly got out of hand and a vocal minority took over the class to shout down students and faculty alike.

After a few minutes of team conversations about a case study ostensibly illustrating a successful hostile-climate sexual-harassment claim, the guest speaker asked each team whether in their interpreta-tion of the facts the case study was sexual harassment and if so whether an example of quid pro quo or hostile climate. The first team reported: "Yes, hostile climate." Marianne spoke for the Sludge Team and gave our answer: "Yes, hostile climate." Next, an all-men team in the corner reported: "No," and a woman spoke for the fourth team: "Yes, hos-tile climate." One of the men from the all-male team stood up, placed his fists on the table, glared at the woman on the fourth team, and loudly reiterated his team's position: "This is the way things were before the woman arrived." The woman student said nothing. One of the man's teammates (also a man) stood up and said, "If they can't stand the heat, they should get out of the kitchen. That is the way it was and how come they [the men] can't keep doing this, just because she came in there?"

Marianne, sitting next to me, was the only student who argued against the vocal men's position, saying, "This is not fair. Why do I have to work in a place like that?" When they repeated what they had said earlier, she rolled her eyes, and tsk-tsked, saying (to those of us sitting near her) "I can't believe it; these men are so clueless." No other student took up the counterargument, even though three other students at our table and two other teams identified this as hostile-climate sexual harassment.

Faculty efforts to defend the sexual-harassment interpretation were likewise shouted down. Bob Thomson argued on the basis of fairness: "She's not going to be able to go to work here because of this environment? Why? Why is it that you [the men] get a different set of choices than she gets? That's not fair." When the vocal men countered that the woman who filed the claim should put up pictures of scantily clad men in sexually-explicit poses, Mary Austen replied, "Two wrongs don't make a right." These comments were not persuasive because logical argument and respectful relations had been abandoned.

Nothing seemed to be at stake for the vocal men in this class session. Acting in clearly indecorous ways and exhibiting patently anti-woman behaviors incurred no threat to their place in the campus community. There was a very lopsided logic of acceptable behavior in the senior design class. On the one hand, faculty held absolute sway over inconsequential matters related to forms of speaking and writing and, on the other hand, faculty power counted for naught in the face of entrenched sexism.

WHO IS PLOTTING SOMETHING DASTARDLY?

For a critical ethnographer, there was nothing about this curriculum that was "hidden." It was in plain view at every turn. This was not the case for insiders (Martin 1994). The sexual harassment class became a focal point of final interviews when students recalled it as one of the few classes that "stood out in their minds." Many students and professors referred to other classroom experiences by saying: "like what happened that day in the sexual harassment class." However, these lived experiences in classrooms did not extend to questioning PES as gender-biased or male-dominated. When interviewing Nate at the end of the two-semester course, we discussed the fact that campus insiders seldom talked about what happened in the senior-design sexual-harassment class. In fact, like other students, he was surprised to be talking about it during an interview. In trying to explain why no one talked about these matters, Nate said:

> It's almost like because there's that sense of, you know, everyone wants to make sure that we're all equal engineers. And when you start talking about sexual harassment, and that says, "Well, wait a minute! That treatment implies that we're not all equal." And the people say: "Well, we don't want to admit that," you know. 'Cause we are [all equal]. I think that's the biggest thing.

Learning to take for granted that "we're all equal engineers," rather than learning to notice just how unequal women student engineers' circumstances were hid the realities of gender inequality.

These findings suggest the importance of the data-collection strategies educational researchers use to examine learning settings, especially to unpacking how a "hidden" curriculum is hidden. Attempts to hide the gender curriculum at PES became most visible in the everyday social interactions between and among students and faculty. This was in marked contrast to student and faculty observations on campus life during interviews, where students and faculty seldom volunteered information indicating that they "saw" this curriculum. When I identified key examples of students and faculty not-noticing gender-biased customs, such as the sexual harassment class or Franci's comments about being hassled for wearing a dress, the gender curriculum could bubble to the surface and come under scrutiny by some insiders. But this was something that only surfaced during out-of-context interviews when I initiated the conversation. Clearly, as currently construed, PES culture provided no social spaces where an awareness of the gender curriculum could be mentioned. Moreover, as I argue elsewhere (Tonso 1999b), to notice the gender curriculum was to mark oneself as someone who did not belong. In fact, part of the dilemma of representing myself on campus as a "pretend" insider, while seeing as an outsider, was my premonition that making my observations known would limit my access to the social interactions central to the hiding processes.

Who is "plotting something dastardly" at PES? It depends on the vantage point of the person making the determination, which is what makes cultural models difficult for insiders to examine and for outsiders to change. According to the cultural model, women do not belong, except as heteronormatively subordinate partners of men. Other forms of women's participation were interpreted as coming from someone who doesn't belong, someone meddling in engineering's internal affairs. These cultural scripts, or habitus, are grooves built into everyday life. By not examining critically the gender bias encoded in custom, the gender curriculum had the same force as an antiwoman conspiracy. Recall the man engineering professor who interrupted my interview with his female colleague. He invoked a social control routine to mark a woman-only conversation as inappropriate behavior. His action, like Carson's persistent grilling of Pam, as well as the silence of men who fail to chastise colleagues for their sexist practices, were performances of social practices marginalizing women. These practices sought to establish that women belonged only to the extent that they were willing to defer to (some) men's definitions of engineering. Such a gender curriculum (re)produced male hegemony.

As I detail elsewhere (Tonso 2000), women and men senior students who expressed concerns with the unethical behaviors of their colleagues and with sexism were moved/moving to the margins of engineering or out of the discipline. All told, six of the eleven senior students did so—two women and four men, the best engineers of the lot. This further consolidated the power of engineers willing to exploit others, increased the proportion of engineers willing to be exploited, and depleted the ranks of engineers prepared for practical engineering work. McIlwee and Robinson (1992) noted that industry-employed engineers fall into two large categories: managers and engineers (who are further ranked via design/research, production, and sales/service assignments). PES elevated two sorts of student engineers: those with propensities to exploit others—possibly the sort of individual who would make a good manager—and those with academic-science skills. In spite of the industry's purported preference for engineers who can apply engineering and scientific principles to real-world situations, these were the lower-status graduates at PES. This is a more complicated reality than envisioned by class-based critical-theory research, which posits coherence between the desires of employers and the skills of "star" graduates.

As Ehrensal noted (chapter six), Bourdieu's theory posited that schooling differentiated white-collar from blue-collar workers. Thinking in these terms, Ehrensal anticipated that normative practices of college business-management studies further consolidated or unified business majors into white-collar workers. While this may be the case for business majors, it does not explain the circumstances of student engineers at PES where a group of young adults from similar, academic-achievement backgrounds and middle- to upper-middle-class circumstances entered college to prepare for a white-collar profession. While experiencing a remarkably uniform curriculum in varying ways, by deciding to affiliate with hegemonic forms of practice or not, they were differentiated into a hierarchical arrangement that ordered supposedly "similar" students along engineering-manager and engineering-worker lines.

Whose interests does such a model serve? On the one hand, PES produces managers (such as Carson) to ride herd on "unruly" engineers. PES can claim "success" from the fit between these student engineers and industry-manager models. Among engineering "workers," the preferred academic-science worker is a perfect feedstock for high-status industry jobs (design/research engineers) and for engineering graduate schools. Along this dimension, PES benefited both industry and academic institutions. On the other hand, by alienating some of the engineering students who are best prepared as practical-engineering workers, PES harmed industry by depleting the supply of qualified workers, but benefited academic institutions whose throughput must remain high to replace alienated engineers.

At Public Engineering School, women were not plotting something dastardly. However, the campus managed, through its propensity to fall into unexamined cultural practices, to conspire against women being considered to be people who belonged in engineering. By aligning the recognition system with academic-science practices that preferred prototypically masculine ways of life, social interactions became arenas where recognition conferred power to exploit others and to not-notice exploitation. Learning to not-notice became an active cultural performance that contributed to hiding the gender curriculum.

NOTE

1. After fifteen years as an engineer, I left the only career I ever really
    wanted as a survival strategy. In casting about for a meaningful way of
    life, I gravitated toward high school math teaching, the second-career
    choice of many former engineers, where I studied explanations for
    women's underrepresentation in math and science careers. I took con-
    siderable umbrage with the predominant arguments, which cast the
    dilemma in terms of what was wrong with women (critically reviewed
    in Eisenhart et al. 1998). I decided to use my engineering sense to study
    what was going on. I drew on my expertise when gathering and analyz-
    ing data and did not take on the guise of a disinterested bystander.
    Making judgments about who knows what in engineering discussions is
    technical work for which I am qualified. It matters to the analysis
    whether an engineer who claims to have things figured out can actually
    give a bona fide engineering explanation grounded in technical details.
    Seeing what goes on also requires someone who understands, but is not
    enamored with, the "watched" practices. Although no advocate of
    engineering culture, I could "pass" when it was convenient to do so.
    Moreover, being taken for an insider meant that I had access that might
    not be available to other researchers. For instance, students and profes-
    sors with incredibly sexist ways of talking believed that I agreed with
    them, and my not disrupting this assumption reinforced my insider
    status. Research strategies deepened my understandings of engineering
    culture.

Preparing to Be Privatized 10

The Hidden Curriculum of a Community College ESL Writing Class

Mary Jane Curry

SAKY: Sometimes I think I should quit my job and go to school full time, you know.

MJC: Yeah.

SAKY: And how can I eat?

MJC: Yeah, right, you have to support yourself and your family. Did you get to talk to anybody about what you would need to do to become a policeman?

SAKY: I want to [feel] more confident in myself for writing and reading first. . . . I feel ashamed of myself, you know. I don't want people to say, what the hell are you thinking about, you're not even help[ing] yourself with it.

The American education system plays a large role in assimilating immigrants and refugees (McNeil 1986, 5). Historically this social function was performed for children in K-12 schools, and for adults in high school or adult education "Americanization" classes. Today community colleges also play a role in the assimilation functions. This fragment of an interview with a twenty-five-year-old male Laotian refugee illustrates the complex set of issues that English language learners face at the community college. These students experience tensions between work and school, between supporting a family and trying to realize their dreams. Often they feel inadequate to meet these challenges, yet remain highly motivated to improve their lives. Immigrant and refugee students form an increasingly large presence at community colleges

(Arenson 1998).[1] The rise of this population in two-year colleges calls for an examination of their educational experiences—both the overt curriculum they study and the hidden curriculum embedded in "remedial" English as a second language (ESL) and writing courses.[2]

One focus of such analysis is to examine how adult education courses try to meet the stated objectives of two-year colleges, which include providing an "open door" to nontraditional students. The 1960s boom in community colleges resulted largely from the demands of racial and ethnic minorities (Brint and Karabel 1989; see also Soldatenko, chapter eleven this volume). Yet the goals of the community college have been contradictory since the inception of junior colleges early in the twentieth century (Brint and Karabel 1989; Dougherty 1994), making curriculum analysis difficult. These goals have included:

- Training workers for specific occupations (Paris 1985);
- Providing high school dropouts with a "second chance" at education;
- Protecting the prestige of four-year institutions by diverting lower-status students (Brint and Karabel 1989);
- "Cooling out" students' aspirations (Clark 1960, 1980) by propagating "a meritocratic ideology, a critical piece of the body of beliefs which sustains capitalist social relations" (Ryan and Sackrey 1984, 112); and
- Absorbing surplus labor (Shor 1980).

Historically and currently, immigrants and refugees have performed many of the agricultural, janitorial, health care, child care, and other low-level jobs that U.S. citizens disdain (Boyle 1999). In the context of current debates about the roles and rights of immigrants and refugees in U.S. society—and actions such as the recent denial of benefits like food stamps to "legal" immigrants—the contested status of the public services to which newcomers are entitled becomes salient. The educational field promises to teach English and the other academic proficiencies that these students need to pursue further education, job training, and employment. My first focus is to see whether and how these promises are fulfilled.

A second focus analyzes students' responses both to hidden and overt curricula, including the forms of resistance, mediation, and accommodation that they embrace. As Margolis, Soldatenko, Acker, and Gair (chapter one this volume) describe, many scholars have complicated the reproduction model of educational inequality to account for students' agency as they encounter the curricula, both hidden and overt. For many immigrants and refugees, ESL and composition courses function as gatekeepers to college-transfer or vocational programs (Shaughnessy 1977). These courses are therefore a pivotal locus of student preparation and enculturation into academic discourses. Students themselves recognize the importance of English language literacy to their future success, as Saky's interview, above, shows. Yet they do not accept the curriculum unthinkingly. This chapter examines the curriculum—both overt and hidden—of an ESL basic writing class, a "remedial" community college course. Ideally, the overt curriculum of an English composition course teaches the academic literacies and discourses that will enable students to undertake college-level work (Purves 1988). In this study, however, as I will demonstrate, the overt curriculum was only superficially realized. Instead, multiple lessons of the hidden curriculum carried more force. The hidden curriculum worked on three levels: the institution, the classroom, and the larger economy.

On the institutional level, historical tensions among the competing goals of two-year colleges often come to the fore in ESL programs, which serve the widest range of students. At the same time, with the increasing casualization of academic labor, community colleges hire more part-time faculty, which can shortchange students of needed services. The state crisis in educational funding produces greater need for institutions to compete for government grants to support instruction in English language and literacy. This competition has curricular and policy implications, including the threat of privatization, which is the direction in which basic education programs in New York are headed (Arenson 2000). At the college under study, ESL students themselves became a commodity; they embodied the diversity that the institution actively sought to display.

At the classroom level, ESL students confronted a well-recognized hidden curriculum of low-expectations, docility, and the internalization of failure (Morrow and Torres 1998). They were also constructed as a monolithic group with few individual differences in past histories and future goals. At the economic level, in this era of privatization and global capitalism, students were taught not to expect the social services, from schools to libraries to welfare support, that characterized the United States during much of the twentieth century (Apple 1996; Gee, Hull, and Lankshear 1996; Gewirtz, Ball, and Bowe 1995). As the relentless logic of privatization reduces public services, the gap widens between those who can afford to purchase such services and those who suffer from reductions. Nonetheless, many ESL and adult basic education courses are still funded by federal and state grants that allow programs to offer courses gratis. As this chapter shows, however, the ironic message becomes that if something is free, it must have little worth. The hidden curriculum on these three levels sends the message that in the United States, "You get what you pay for."

THE HIDDEN CURRICULUM AND FORMS OF CAPITAL

As Martin (1991) pointed out, the hidden curriculum is experienced individually; particular students receive different messages from and respond differently to the curriculum. Bourdieu's (1990) concept of various forms of capital—economic, social, and cultural—provides a theory with which to examine this process.

> Social space is constructed in such a way that agents or groups are distributed in it according to their position in statistical distributions based on the two principles of differentiation which, in most advanced societies, such as the United States, ... are undoubtedly the most efficient: economic capital and cultural capital. (Bourdieu 1998, 6)

Examining ways in which players on the educational field embody these forms of capital facilitates a subtle and complex understanding of how students and teachers grapple with both overt and hidden curricula.

The influx of nonnative speakers of English into two-year colleges highlights the contradictions of institutional missions and creates new challenges for instructors and administrators. As the demographic data about the students in this study demonstrate, adult students have varied backgrounds, histories, and educational and occupational goals. The contemporary ESL classroom includes economic immigrants, political refugees, and relatives of international students or highly skilled international workers. Students differ on the basis of race, class, gender, age, ethnicity, religion, and educational attainment. Moreover, students occupy multiple categories, which contribute forms of capital, and therefore to their ability to maneuver in the institution and achieve their goals.

MONROE TECHNICAL COLLEGE

The research took place at Monroe Technical College (MTC) (all names used here are pseudonyms), which is located in a medium-sized midwestern city that also houses a large research university. Founded in 1912, MTC, according to its mission statement, "welcomes all individuals who can benefit from the services provided . . . supports students to choose and prepare for successful careers by assessing students' skills and needs . . . offers intellectually rigorous studies facilitated by highly skilled faculty in technical and vocational skills, basic literacy, and arts and sciences." Within the college, the Alternative Learning Division (ALD) offers ESL and basic education.

I studied one semester of a Basic Writing 3 course, using ethnographic observations and semistructured interviews. Approximately eighteen students began the course, but only four stayed through the term. The students included five refugees, seven immigrants, and six students related to international students or staff at the university. In addition to the typical variety of linguistic, national, and racial backgrounds, a more unusual characteristic was the range of students' educational attainment levels. Of all students, twelve had at least bachelor's degrees; five of these had graduate degrees, including three Russian women with Ph.D.'s. Of the refugees, Saky had graduated from high school; Ahmad, twenty-three, a refugee from the civil war in Sierra Leone, was taking the GED tests. I interviewed six students (three who left and three who stayed in the course), the course instructor, the lead teacher of the ESL program, and the dean of the ALD.

I did not set out to study the hidden curriculum. Initially, my research asked about how students learn, accommodate, and resist Western-style argumentation in academic writing (Reid 1984). This focus emerged from the larger question: If two-year colleges are to fulfill the promises they make to educate the public (including immigrants and refugees), how do the curriculum and the students' experiences prepare students to transfer to academic or training programs? However, the Basic Writing 3 class touched so lightly upon argumentation that little data resulted. Instead, a new research question arose: If academic writing—the overt curriculum—was not taught in Basic Writing 3, what actually happened? The concept of the hidden curriculum provides an ideal framework with which to answer that question.

THE HIDDEN CURRICULUM AT THE INSTITUTIONAL LEVEL

The course instructor plays a pivotal role in creating and implementing both overt and hidden curricula. Instructors are institutional actors imbued with pedagogic authority (Bourdieu and Passeron 1990, 20; see also Ehrensal, chapter six this volume). The Basic Writing 3 instructor was George Cleary, a white, middle-aged man who had taught English extensively in Mexico but had had little experience in teaching second-language writing in the United States. Spring 1999 was Cleary's first semester teaching in the ALD, although he was simultaneously teaching composition in the Arts and Sciences Division, and ESL to Mexican students at satellite locations. Besides teaching courses at three locations, Cleary worked on call as a medical interpreter and had child care responsibilities. Indeed, one structural form of the hidden curriculum, hiring part-time instructors, teaches students that free courses may not offer the services associated with for-credit courses that charge tuition. Colleges thus communicate that students cannot count on having well-trained, full-time faculty who are invested in the institution and knowledgeable about its systems. Cleary's case illustrates some of the problems with this practice.

Cleary suffered from institutional policies and practices that put him in the classroom three weeks into the semester because of problems scheduling the first instructor. Being hired late deprived him of time to prepare for the course and learn ALD procedures. During the semester, Cleary received virtually no support or direction. Other than a textbook and course objectives, he was given no previous syllabi or materials, although the policy requires keeping such materials on file. Furthermore, even though he was assigned a mentor, a policy that the ALD implements to maintain certification, they never met. (See Margolis and Romero, chapter five this volume, on the nature of mentoring.)

Cleary was left in the dark about many key issues. For example, only on the last day did he learn about reporting requirements for grant and college record keeping. Cleary was supposed to follow-up with students when they missed class, and enter it on the computer system if they dropped the class. "Client reporting" data for funders requested detailed knowledge not only of students' academic competencies, but also personal information such as whether they were U.S. citizens and registered voters. Part-time instructors rarely have access to such information, and they may not want to have such intimate knowledge. On the last day, Cleary also learned that the Basic Writing course was non-credit, which he noted was "a real letdown," as it created "a big problem in a course like that as far as getting students to follow through."

Cleary was not given an office, so he had nowhere on campus to store materials or read student papers. Nor did the ALD assume that Cleary would meet with students outside of class. In addition, lead teacher Maureen Powell had informed part-time instructors that they were not required to attend meetings. The labor union contract specifies that mandatory meetings and student conferences must be paid; by releasing part-time instructors, the ALD saved money but increased the isolation of instructors and kept them ignorant of institutional policies, procedures, and issues. These problems alienated Cleary from the ALD administration and his students. As a result of these conditions and the high dropout rate, Cleary characterized the semester as unsuccessful: "The class was not a success. . . . If you're going to be honest about it and measure it accurately, it wasn't." He identified as reasons "daily pressures" on students, the course's lack of clear expectations for students, and little institutional support. However, he noted that:

> The major problem that anybody in my situation is going to come into is that your being a part-time instructor, you're going to be in off the street to give your class, and you're going to be gone. That's the fallacy in doing the part-time instructor. I think that's a very difficult role to play . . . because there's no feedback, [or] making contact with people in the department.

In his view, a key factor was that ALD courses were free. Cleary believed that students would be more attentive and responsible if they had to pay. "If you're giving something for free, it's worthless. People don't appreciate when things are given away for free." Charging students for courses "creates a commitment." Buying a textbook, for example, is "an investment." Cleary commented to students about the $38 textbook: "It's an expensive textbook. But education is expensive." Here the instructor—not necessarily consciously—promulgated the hidden curriculum of the privatization of education.

Cleary's comments raise the issue of student expectations, using a consumer model. Cleary stated: "You pay more money for something and you expect a better product and you're more proud of what you've done." In discussing the private language academy he ran in Acapulco, Cleary used the discourse of consumerism and contemporary business practices:

> The philosophy at our school, when we train teachers, is that the student is your boss, really. You must satisfy the student, for everything ordinary. . . . You're there to serve the student and you must have results. And to do that you focus on strategies that are efficient, straightforward, so sort of the Japanese model, keep it simple and keep it functional.

However, it is not solely the instructor's responsibility to get such "results." On paper, the ALD provides student services to support classroom teaching. According to the dean of the ALD, Ricardo Garcia, students are supposed to develop Personal Education Plans (PEP), a "road map" for their academic futures. Both full- and part-time faculty help students create PEPs, yet part-time instructors are not compensated for the extra work. Likewise, the ALD's Transition Committee helps students who are planning to transfer into academic or vocational programs. It relies on instructors to identify likely candidates for the program. But because of the haphazard way that these services are implemented, no PEPs were developed for students in Basic Writing 3, nor were students directed to the Transition Committee.[3] As a part-time instructor, Cleary thus received little support, yet found the ALD placing high expectations that he would be a conduit to student services.

The trend toward part-time faculty is not limited to adult education courses. "Part-timers now make up over 40 percent of the faculty in institutions of higher education, and about two-thirds at two-year colleges. And their share of teaching jobs continues to grow, almost doubling since 1970" (Brill 1999, 38). These statistics match the proportion of ALD part-timers, according to the president of the MTC part-time instructors' union. Part-time instructors who do not receive benefits or job security obviously save the institution money and offer other benefits. Dean Garcia noted his preference for part-timers because, despite requiring more paperwork, it allows for "flexibility" in securing workplace education contracts.

THE COMMODIFICATION OF STUDENTS

Institutional factors constitute one part of the hidden curriculum— that non–paying students may receive a lesser quality education. Also of interest is the role that the physical bodies of ESL students played in institutional politics related to minority students. Garcia highlighted the importance of good minority enrollment figures: "What we've been trying to get [the other college division administrators] to see is that when you need students, you can get them from us. . . . When you need to improve your retention numbers, guess who can do that." Although MTC does not keep statistics on ALD student retention, Garcia claimed that ESL students are "the most consistent attenders. . . . They come back the most."[4] High retention rates help secure and retain grant funds. Perhaps this is why, although Garcia claimed that "it is not the intention of the program" to serve international students, about one-third of the students in Basic Writing 3 were related to students or staff at the state university. The cultural capital that such students possess enables them to negotiate the rules that exclude them from free courses at MTC. At the same time, the ALD benefits from their presence in its ESL courses.

DISCOURSES OF DIVERSITY

Like many institutions, MTC's concern with diversity results in a commodification of the bodies of ESL students as an integral part of its curriculum. Diversity is codified in its Core Abilities program. A pamphlet for students proclaims that "[MTC] teaches eight Core Abilities that support you as a life-long learner on the job, at home, and in the community."[5] The Core Ability particularly relevant to this study is global awareness. Interestingly, the institution appears less concerned with developing global awareness among the ALD students themselves, and more with using ALD students to provide global awareness to others. The Transition Committee's 1999–2000 report stated that "[b]asic skills education students are promoted to the college as a source of global awareness and well-prepared and successful degree-credit program students." Thus in a curious twist, the ALD promotes "diverse" students who embody global awareness to the rest of the predominantly white institution.

THE OVERT CURRICULUM AT THE CLASSROOM LEVEL

Before describing the details of the hidden curriculum, I want to discuss what the course intended to teach explicitly. Basic Writing 3 serves "adults who have writing skills at a high school level and who want to improve their writing skills for further education, employment, or life." As the range of goals included in this statement indicates, students' goals varied considerably. In the Basic Writing class, three of the refugees were retired Russian Jews who had no further educational plans. Two younger Russian women were married to American citizens. Katarina, one of my interviewees, had trained as an engineer and planned to study accounting at MTC. The younger refugees, Saky and Ahmad, hoped to become a police officer and a lawyer, respectively. Some students with university connections wanted to obtain second bachelor's or graduate degrees. Four middle-class students were applying to the state university system, including Minji, a thirty-five-year-old Korean woman with a bachelor's degree from a Korean university, and the Hasans, two young Palestinian sisters and a brother who had grown up in the United Arab Emirates and had completed high school.

The course emphasized English grammar, pronunciation, and isolated skills. Writing assignments were intentionally short, partly to reduce Cleary's (uncompensated) grading time and partly because of his teaching philosophy. Cleary believed in a product model of composition pedagogy, that if a student "conform[s] to a certain model in English . . . that transition will be almost automatic. . . . The best way to learn writing is just a classical simple, simple model. Read good examples and imitate those examples, and do a variety of writing practices." However, learning to write in a new language requires more than plugging in new vocabulary and grammatical structures or imitating other writers. Rather, cultures express their styles, values, and expectations for writers and readers in the rhetorical structures, use of evidence, and citing of authorities (Kaplan 1966; Leki 1991). Developing familiarity with the various roles and genres of text is also crucial to becoming a competent academic writer. However, the curriculum was not related to students' cultural backgrounds, nor did it examine genres of writing or relate the writing in this course to future academic or other writing tasks. In this way the overt curriculum helped reduce the level of academic expectations for students.

Cleary's espousal of an outdated methodology reflected his own situation, that after ten years in Mexico he was not current with ESL composition pedagogy. His lack of training and supervision communicated to students not to expect the most current pedagogy and methods in this free course. In addition, the absence of discussions of textual and rhetorical differences from the curriculum contributed the message that ESL students are a monolithic population, without distinguishable identities, histories, and goals. Further, the lack of discussion of academic discourse evidenced low expectations for students. Indeed, putting the onus on them, Cleary noted that teaching these students was "sort of an endless battle. And they need a lot of work. A tremendous amount of work." The instructor's reliance on the exercises in the book, the teacher-centered mode of instruction, and the traditional physical setup of the classroom with chairs and desks in front-facing rows created a pedagogy that, although perhaps familiar and comfortable to students, did not foster learning to write in preparation for college. (See Costello, chapter three this volume, for the messages sent by educational spaces.) The failings of the overt curriculum contributed to the high dropout rate and overall dissatisfaction of the students.

At the same time, it is important to recognize that Cleary's curriculum occurred in conjunction with administrative structures and demands. Such "defensive teaching" (McNeil 1986, 88) can result from a complicated mixture of factors. "Even well-trained teachers are often unable to teach ideally in the face of the organizational systems controlling their workplace" (McNeil 1986, 161). Like Cleary, the high school teachers McNeil (1986, 176) studied "felt that neither the support nor the financial reward was commensurate with the out-of-class time needed to preparing learning activities adequately, or to read and comment on the student essay tests or written assignments."

THE HIDDEN CURRICULUM IN THE CLASSROOM

Cultural models, which operate as "tacit theories" (Gee 1996, 17) are useful constructs in studying the operation of hidden curricula. Such models "involve (usually unconscious) assumptions about models of simplified worlds" (Gee 1996, 87). They function as schemas, metaphors, and stereotypes that can motivate behavior. Cleary's discourse about his students evidenced his cultural model of the "good student," which had implications for the interactions in the class. Cleary viewed students in interpersonal terms, as "wonderful, they're marvelous people . . . very motivated." Compared with his native-English-speaking students, whom Cleary found distant, the ESL students "are much more eager, much more sociable, they're easier to teach . . . because they're friendlier. . . . And they know how to be good students." To Cleary, "good students" are "interested in your presentation. . . . They're not falling asleep, they're not distracted. They don't look disinterested, just the opposite, they look very interested. They enjoy being here." Cleary's upbeat assessment of the students glossed over much of their resistance, which I will discuss shortly.

Although Cleary became frustrated at the low level of academic performance of the ESL students, in daily interactions he communicated a hidden curriculum of docility, passivity, and low expectations that included the following points:

- *Listen politely.* Cleary praised the students as "wonderful people that go along with whatever's being presented." He acknowledged the high proportion of the time he spent lecturing, often digressing with stories of his life in Mexico. In contrast, when he teaches for-credit courses, Cleary claims, "There's no wasted time. You know, I don't talk about my life." The Basic Writing 3 students did not openly challenge this "waste of time." Yet Katarina, for one, was dissatisfied: "[The class] wasn't interesting. Again, because like Mr. Cleary, he was explain[ing] us all his experiences when he had been to Mexico a couple of times. It's not an English class. I think a teacher should make some kind of plan before."

- *Maintain hierarchical distinctions.* By introducing himself using the title "Mr.," Cleary established his authority in the classroom. Supporting this role, he wore a necktie and pressed trousers to class. (See Tonso, chapter nine this volume, on the gender aspects of dress.) Reflecting on the course, Cleary used the analogy of teacher as parent. "Coming in the middle of the course . . . it's like changing parents halfway." Like parents, such teachers exert authority over their students, even if they happen to be adults with much life experience.

- *Conform to traditional gender roles.* Not only did Cleary consistently call the female students "girls," even older women with children, he frequently commented on their appearance. In a humorous manner, he also ascribed romantic motives to students' absences—although he included men in this, too. When Rosa, a young Dominican student, returned after missing three classes, Cleary said, "I thought you had a new boyfriend." She later dropped the class for good, although she did not discuss with me her reasons.

- *Participate by asking questions about grammar.* Students who asked about specific grammar points or pronunciation received positive feedback. Because the well-educated students knew grammatical terminology as well as the metalinguistic practices of language classrooms, it was easy for them to participate.

- *Select "nice" topics to write about.* Students were assigned to write a research paper, but Cleary controlled their topics. For instance, when Susie, a Taiwanese student who wanted to get a master's degree in special education, suggested suicide as her topic, Cleary replied, "That's not very happy. Now why would you choose suicide?" After this feedback, Susie did not return to the class.

- *Don't give your opinion.* Related to his dislike for emotional topics, Cleary criticized the author of a textbook reading on divorce for providing his opinion:

  You think it's his opinion, and that he's not being objective.... The author is talking, he's mad, he's angry, yeah, he's very angry.... I don't want to hear from this author. And I didn't like it.... Because then I go against him. And I don't believe what he says. Yeah, I want an author to be very neutral.... Just give me the facts. Be objective and just give me the facts.... Don't get emotional.... I want you to be very logical.

Cleary's commentary presented some elements of good sense about academic writing. Basic writers often need to learn to turn their opinions into arguments supported by evidence, especially on topics that evoke strong emotions. However, in preparing students for academic writing, this message of neutrality and docility does students a disservice. Students need to learn to substantiate their opinions, not to suppress them, in arguing a position and promoting an opinion.

STUDENT RESISTANCE TO THE CURRICULUM

Early in the semester, students began to show discontent with the course. Some responded to the failings of the overt curriculum, others to their perceptions of the hidden curriculum. They ignored Cleary during class, mildly disrupted the class, listened to him passively, carried on conversations on the side; skipped homework, complained to Cleary, and dropped out of the course. Saky saw that Cleary was unavailable in and outside the class. Despite Saky's frequent confusion, he was reluctant to ask for clarification: "He [the instructor] explain[s] but sometime we need, there's too many students asking, you know. And it gonna be my turn, second turn, time's up already." The students who stayed reduced their expectations of the course. Minji recognized the instructor as a novice in this environment. She commented:

> I know he is the lecturer, not the regular professor at the university, I mean, MTC, so he is not responsib[le]. . . . I mean, that if there's a regular professor at the MTC, he . . . [has] more experience and everything for the teaching. But he just teach the class, so he [does] not that much have responsibility about [doing] something for the . . . students.

The range of resistant behaviors included the silent resistance of the high school students that McNeil (1986) documented. Likewise, it paralleled the junior high students in Everhart's (1983) study, who carried on simultaneous unrelated conversations while completing their classwork. Unlike these pupils under compulsory school attendance, however, the Basic Writing 3 students had the option of leaving, and most of them took it. Ultimately, dropping out of the course (or the institution) constituted the fundamental form of resistance for three-fourths of the class. Of the eighteen students who began the course, eight students attended regularly at midsemester; by the last day, only four showed up.

The first two students to leave the class, Saky and Ahmad, were young male refugees who worked full time or more and had the lowest previous educational attainment levels. These students conformed least to the hidden curriculum of docility and passivity, at times by sitting in the back of the room and muttering comments. They cited time constraints that prevented attending and doing homework, and they lacked the word-processing skills that were an unstated prerequisite for the course. Ahmad, the only black student, also felt that Cleary made racist comments and discriminated by not accepting handwritten work.

That these students did not attend class regularly or complete assignments allowed them to be blamed for their own failure—or to blame themselves. As with the resistance that African-American community college students manifested in Lois Weis's (1985) *Between Two Worlds*, dropping out became a contradictory response that negatively affected students even as it demonstrated their agency (see also Willis 1977). Indeed, Saky and Ahmad's goals were deferred indefinitely. A year later, neither had finished additional courses in the ALD; nor had Ahmad passed the GED tests.

The four students heading to four-year universities remained the longest, along with the retired Russians. These students were most compliant in their comportment and behavior toward Cleary. For instance, Ali Hasan consistently appended "sir" to his questions. Thus students with more cultural capital—higher levels of education, better language skills, better connections in the institution, and more familiarity with using services—benefited most from the community college's courses and services.

THE ECONOMIC LEVEL OF THE HIDDEN CURRICULUM

The lack of a challenging curriculum constitutes one form of the hidden curriculum; it embodies the dearth of institutional confidence in and expectations for these students. It also represents the "cooling out" of immigrant and refugee students, which functions as one mechanism for keeping them in the low-paying labor force. In the case of Basic Writing 3, however, few students were prevocational, as most had or were planning to earn bachelor's degrees. Indeed, given the mixture of students, few were working for pay or seeking work. Of those working, Saky's supervisors at the plastics manufacturing company were pressuring him to further his education so he could assume more responsibility. Ahmad held jobs more typical for recent immigrants, cleaning at a bakery and driving a taxi. He characterized his work as usual low-level immigrant work: "the only work I think it's capable for us here, so we have to do it. . . . Most of the immigrant[s] that comes here . . . even if you are a doctor, you have to start afresh."

In the current economic "boom," with its low unemployment rate, other rationales must be found for the continued existence of these programs. Brint and Karabel (1989) argue that community colleges evolved in partnership with local businesses as a result of the empire-building goals of administrators. The success of the ALD in attracting state and federal grant funds as well as private workplace education contracts bolsters this thesis (see also Childress, chapter seven this volume, for strong support). Moreover, Apple (1996, 88) noted the government's need for legitimacy in the face of economic policies that foster the shift of manufacturing jobs to off-shore locations. It is not surprising, therefore, that after the passage of NAFTA the federal government funded courses through the Economic Dislocation and Worker Adjustment Assistance Act designed to retrain workers who had lost their jobs to Mexico (Merrifield 1997, 274). Along the same lines, the government seeks legitimacy in absorbing the demands of minorities for education and other services. Weis (1985, 10) noted that "increased access to education is a political response to racial contest in the state sector." In fact, federal funding for adult basic education increased twelvefold between 1965 and 1997 (National Center for Educational Statistics 1997), as the economy underwent a fundamental shift from a manufacturing to a service base.

DISCUSSION: THE STUDENT AS PRODUCT

In the final analysis, basic education programs that attract government grants and workplace contracts may be more successful at shoring themselves up than at achieving their stated mission of preparing students to transfer to vocational programs, community colleges, or four-year universities. In this process, these institutions create a new type of product—student bodies—in the same way that the mass media sells the audience to advertisers. The "student body" is the accumulation of individual students who contribute to the body count demonstrating that the services for which grant funders pay are being provided. Likewise, the ESL student body provides a source of diversity for an institution concerned about minority enrollments. In this scenario, if a student drops out of one class but resurfaces in another, in the long run the institution's student count remains unaffected, although retention rates for individual classes suffer. Of course, individual teachers and administrators often care passionately about student outcomes.

An institutional-level analysis, however, challenges the extent to which individuals can effect large-scale change in the face of these structural goals and pressures.

On the economic level the hidden curriculum (re)produces the commodification of student bodies, a phenomenon that furthers the sweep of privatization, including vouchers and charter schools in public education. Currently, privatization is poised to take over remedial education at the college level, as the proposal to seek outside bids to teach basic education at the City University of New York demonstrates (Arenson 2000, 6). The hidden curriculum of the Alternative Learning Division, that you get what you pay for, helps prepare students—and the rest of us— to accept the privatization of basic education. Unlike the socialization of costs strategy that produced common schools and state universities with low tuition, in this model those who cannot afford to pay are left out. Students with more capital—of all types—benefit from educational institutions at all levels.

However, all types of students assert agency when they find themselves in substandard situations. Many of the students in the Basic Writing 3 course refused the various ways in which their bodies were commodified. Ironically, they learned the lesson of consumerism—that the customer is always right. Students actively refused the lesser "product" they were offered in the Basic Writing 3 course, despite the fact that it was free.

NOTES

1. Since the 1970s, more students have begun their college careers at two-year community colleges than at four-year colleges and universities (Brint and Karabel, 1989, v). In higher education overall, the share of students at two-year colleges continues to rise, reaching almost 40 percent in 1996 (National Center for Educational Statistics 1999).

2. The term *English as a second language* is problematic, given that many learners, including some in this study, are multilingual. However, as the program under study uses this term, I will follow suit.

3. The lack of PEPs may be detrimental to some students, but since the "cooling-out" function often occurs through the offices of counselors and other agents attempting to reduce students' aspirations, such services can also have deleterious effects.

4. Statistics on adult education retention rates are difficult to obtain. The National Center for Educational Statistics (NCES) does not track the retention of ESL students in ABE courses.

192 • Mary Jane Curry

The NCES adult education questionnaire, which is a component of the National Household Education Survey, collects data on individuals who do and do not participate in ABE and ESL classes in the twelve-month period prior to the interview. Since we never know whether the adult will take any more ABE or ESL classes, we never know whether they are a dropout or not. It is difficult to know when an adult 'completes' their ABE or ESL classes. Hence it is difficult to calculate a dropout rate" (Peter Stowe, NCES, personal communication, November 8, 1999). In fact, lead teacher Powell contradicted the dean's claims, noting that while ABE students in general have a 50 percent dropout rate, the rate for ESL students is higher, as in this course.

5. The Core Abilities are: communication, critical thinking, ethics, global awareness, mathematics, science and technology, self-awareness, and social interaction.

Radicalism in Higher Education 11

How Chicano Studies Joined the Curriculum

Michael Soldatenko[1]

The greatest failure of Chicano studies[2] was its complicity with the hidden curriculum in U.S. higher education. The desired radical utopia of establishing an oppositional space within the academy became, at best, an alternative among a number of confined spaces (African American, Asian American, Native American, ethnic, cultural, and women's studies, etc.). Chicano studies fell victim to the only "political correctness" that has ever existed in higher education: management of potential disruptive elements. In this chapter I examine how the university's hidden curriculum contained the activism of Chicano(a) students.

INTRODUCTION

Students of color transformed the university curriculum by institutionalizing ethnic studies in the late 1960s. While most of these programs were about student services, they also sought to establish courses that delved into their particular ethnic, racial, and class experience. (Later, gender was added when women challenged patriarchal practices among students of color.) Students assumed that these courses could subvert the intellectual colonial apparatus. In these classes, students of color would learn who they were; recapture their culture and history; learn about oppressive colonial, class, or national systems of control; and, most importantly, develop a political ideology and organization to fight these systems of oppression.

While many activists recognized the university as part of the process of domination, they did not grasp the operation of institutional power. Therefore they battled over university policies (admissions, requirements); they criticized personalities (faculty, deans); they attacked the apparent bifurcation of university and outside world as well as internal divisions between student services. They never noticed the hidden curricula that structure academic life and were designed to channel oppositional practices into mere alternative choices (Williams 1977, Williams 1989, Said 1983, Ross 1991, Schürmann 1994, Soldatenko 1998).

Radicals fell victim to the very mythology of higher education they wanted to challenge. The resolution of student protest was to accept academic practices. While many activists acknowledged the need to negotiate an end to the protests, they also hoped that the new "studies" programs could foster a critical practice. Instead, hidden curricula disciplined the oppositional curriculum into acceptable alternatives. The protests of the late 1960s and early 1970s did not fundamentally challenge, much less overturn, the hidden curriculum. Rather the new programs were schooled by the logic of academic practice.

THE HIDDEN CURRICULUM AND U.S. HIGHER EDUCATION

The works of Michael Apple and others displayed the covert mechanisms through which education reproduces and legitimates unequal class, race, and gender divisions. Now visible, now hidden, these curricula occur at multiple places and times during schooling but overall are what Peter McLaren (1988, 223) called "a pedagogy of submission." Simultaneously, schools, while sites of domination, can also be seen as locations of contestation and resistance (Margolis, Soldatenko, Acker, Gair this volume).

While acknowledging the possibility of resistance within the hidden curriculum, this chapter emphasizes the limitations of contestation. Both Apple and Giroux left ample ambiguity in their writing to allow us to reexamine the structuralist "reproduction" arguments that drove the original thinking on hidden curricula. While sympathetic to the possibility of resistance, my analysis demonstrates the function and power of the hidden curriculum to manage contestation. The history of curricular development in higher education reveals the permanent structure of the hidden curriculum and its ability to devour, as far as I can see, all expressions of opposition.

Daniel Bell observed that Columbia University, like other colleges and universities, faced three challenges that led to the general education movement in the early twentieth century: discontent with the German tradition in U.S. universities and its professional emphasis; abandonment of a sterile classicism; a change in the character of the student body, particularly the inclusion of children of non–traditional immigrants (Bell 1966, Veysey 1965, Hsi-En 1940). Throughout the first half of the twentieth century, these concerns led to an effort to develop a general education program. Typically the general education movement pushed in two directions: establishing liberal arts programs and linking education to the needs of society and democracy. The marriage was never easy (Bell 1966, 13–15).

The general education movement was reactionary, a return to an earlier tradition in U.S. higher education. Old collegiate values were reasserted against modern approaches based on the German ideal of electives (Rudolph 1965, 449).[3] The early-twentieth-century humanists contested the individualism, materialism, and scientificism fostered by the university with the fundamental goodness of men. Thus the full, free, undisciplined chaos of the elective curriculum was seen as the consequence of the substitution of the science of men for the service of God (Rudolph 1965, 452). The humanists demanded a return to stability—the need for established standards:

> The general education movement, as the effort to redefine and enforce a common curriculum has been called, began as a response to the sense of bewilderment with which many young students faced the freedom of the elective course of study. It received clarification during and after World War I, when a consciousness of Western values and national problems found expression in courses designed to orient students to their cultural inheritance and their responsibilities as citizen. And, like all impossible dreams, the general education idea was carried along from decade to decade, receiving new encouragement in one institution or another, the product of a quixotic conviction that the limits of essential knowledge could be defined. (Rudolph 1989, 236–37)

The quixotic quest manifested itself as a repeating pattern, first present in the general education movement at Columbia University in 1919. "General education proposed to restore some balance, to revitalize the aristocratic ideal of the liberal arts as the passport to learning" (Rudolph 1965, 455). From the beginning the general education movement "was an attempt to capture some of the sense of a continuing intellectual and spiritual heritage that had fallen victim to the elective principle" (Rudolph 1965, 456). The hope of the humanist reform movement was to bring knowledge under control as they hypostatized that it was before the United States became a dominant capitalist and imperialist power.

While the debate over the design of liberal arts—survey courses or great books—dominated the early general education movement, the second theme of societal needs progressively overtook the attempted institutionalization of liberal arts programs. The rise of a national society and a national economy, the growth of the regulatory state, the creation of a national popular culture, the growing demands of international affairs, and changes in student composition pushed this second concern to the fore (Bell 1966, 69–87). By the 1940s, the central question had become: how could higher education serve the needs of U.S. society? In particular, how could the "American" be constructed; that is, a united citizenship with shared values and belief in capitalism. This opened the way for further specialization through the academic "major" (Rudolph 1989, 229). This ran counter to the humanist push for liberal arts programs, often by turning to the great books (Levine 1981, chapter 1; Erskine 1928, chapter 1; Hutchins 1936).

The triumph of societal needs over liberal arts with the turn to specialization resulted in a third feature in higher education—the department. The general education movement assisted the shift of power from the university to the department. The department, defined by "faculty lines" rather than any larger entity, fixed the content of courses. "Whether this is a vice or virtue, the consequence has been that the interests, slants, and prejudices of the departments, rather than any central or unified source, have shaped the curriculum" (Bell 1966, 25). This institutional transformation was reinforced by the growth of research within the university, with the increasing role of extramural funding and therefore prestige (Ross 1991, 161). The department, through the leadership of the discipline's national associations, began to establish academic standards and credentials for those within the department. The accreditation process additionally fortified uniformity. In the process the role of the professor changed from educator to researcher within a discipline. His or her success was measured by discipline-bound publications, recognition within national associations, and mobility.

As disciplinary-fettered faculty came to control departments and associations, the professionalization of the professorate served to secure faculty's pedagogic authority (Ross 1991, 160; Ehrensal, chapter six). To join the ranks of this guild and receive this authority, the adept had to participate in a long apprenticeship during which he or she acquired a particular cognitive base—the discipline's tradition. This valued knowledge was contained within a canon that each acolyte had to master (Wilshire 1990, 48; Robinson 1983, 83). As the adept became initiated and credentialized, she or he reproduced the same power and authority relationship through her or his management of the curriculum (Viswanathan 1989, Margolis and Romero chapter five). The apprenticeship process manufactured consent among the players even before the game had started: "[C]onsent is first created in people's heads and then reinforced by the playing of the game" (Ehrensal, Ehrensal 2000, 97).

Departments and associations mainstreamed all within the discipline. Publications, presentations, invitations, and funding became the measure of success, further reinforcing professionalization. The ability to survive mainstreaming could result in choice positions at research institutions, followed by tenure, and promotions (Cohen 1993, 35). Prestige begat more visibility and prestige. A few achieved superstardom, invited to present to larger groups of fellow initiates (Cohen 1993, 57). With professionalization, academic freedom became simply the right to be an academic and any endeavor to enter public dialogue was frowned upon (Jacoby 1987, 119, 130). "[U]niversity employment often prevents professors (among others) from speaking their mind" (Cohen 1993, xix). To discover an "engaged" or "critical intellectual" among the professorate became increasingly rare. "The idea of the intellectual as adversary of the dominant culture is utterly foreign to current arrangements . . ." (Aronowitz and Giroux 1988, 177). Jacoby stated this quite clearly: "[A]cademic careers undermined academic freedom . . . the institution neutralizes the freedom it guarantees" (Jacoby 1987, 118–19).

Establishing the liberal arts at the center of undergraduate study became an increasingly distant aspiration as specialization for the major became central. Higher education was subsumed by and came to reflect the larger social, economic, and political concerns of consensus building and Americanization. This transformation was evident in the different views on general education between Columbia (1919), Reed (1921), Chicago (1924), and Harvard's *General Education in a Free Society*, the famous Redbook of 1945 that was an important blueprint for the postwar university. The Redbook defined "General education, as education from an informed responsible life in our society, has chiefly to do with ... the question of common standards and common purposes" (*General Education* 1945, 4). In the Redbook, education had two goals: to help a person fulfill individual purpose and help students fit into a common culture they share as citizens. This last goal, as I read the report, predominated.

While the Harvard report discussed the need to develop the abilities of effective thinking, communication, and judgement, the final aim was to understand the proper role of education in maintaining a free society (Harvard Committee 1945, 73). Implied was the need to make education play the role of creating and reinforcing the new American citizen who could properly function in the postwar society. It broke from the past and to read the Harvard report as part of a continuum from Columbia to the Redbook would completely reverse its purpose. I suggest that the Harvard reform movement did little to challenge the discipline, department, major, and role of the faculty. (Note the differences between the Redbook and the 1939 Harvard student council report [Kridel 1989].) Upton Sinclair's (1922, 18) condemnation of education was equally true of policies advocated by the Redbook:

> Our educational system is not a public service, but an instrument of special privilege; its purpose is not to further the welfare of mankind, but merely to keep America capitalist.

The 1950s curriculum, in fact, was more openly defined by the goal of producing a citizenship united by the bounds and logic of the market than ever before (Rudolph 1989, 247; Veblen 1965; Sinclair 1922). According to Lucas, the academic institution differed little from business enterprises seeking to survive in the marketplace (Lucas 1994, 238). The push to create a bond among citizens was to turn to the logic of the market (Henderson 1944). The attempt to corral electives, under a romanticized notion of the liberal arts, corresponded to the emergence of a corporate structure and mentality in higher education. The *new* general education movement, increasingly centered on the major (and therefore the discipline), was no longer about "liberal learning" but about serving demands that business, government, and the military had placed on the university—or what Clark Kerr, chancellor of the University of California at Berkeley, coined the "multiversity" (Bell 1966, 95).

> Corrupted by populism, professionalism, and assembly-like scholarship, universities had allegedly given themselves over to turning students to specialized professional careers as quickly as possible. (Lucas 1994, 269)

The universities[4] became knowledge factories satisfying the demands of business and the state, creating a new unholy alliance (Lucas 1994, 278):

> The American university had committed itself to all that was objective, countable, precise, and verifiable. Its focus, once again, was upon knowledge as a commodity, packaged for consumption in tidy little bundles called credit units, hours, and courses. (Lucas 1994, 269)

The humanist dream of a Socratic education was replaced with the ideologically, driven demands for consensus, reinforcement for specialization, discipline-centered knowledge, and professionalization of the professorate to serve the capitalist order.

> The university in the United States had become largely an agency for social control. . . . The custodian of popular values comprised the primary responsibility of the American university. It was to teach its students constructively rather than with an imprudent and disintegrative independence. (Veysey 1965, 440)

The humanists' demand for liberal arts had been incorporated into the very mechanism of specialization and electives they had criticized. Interests that were outside education— business and the state— drove the counterrevolutionary challenge that became part of the program of education. While liberal arts became requirements, they served merely as a preparation for the more important task of the major discipline. The hidden curriculum had subjugated the humanist agenda.

Paralleling the rise of departments and associations, a particular intellectual perspective came to forge "academic knowledge." Dorothy Ross, a noted U.S. historian, examined the origins of "American social science." Ross (1991, 28) traced the dynamic interaction between "American exceptionalism" and U.S. institutions of higher learning. She noted that American exceptionalism "was a nationalist ideology" that created a particular vision of the American experience that permeated all forms of discourse. By the turn of the century, this exceptionalist ideal was invigorated by the rise of a new liberalism, rooted in the academy, which contested ideologies that tried to confront American exceptionalism. These liberal scholars formulated paradigms, such as neoclassical economics, liberal economic interpretations of history, a sociology and ideology of social control, and pragmatism, which "laid the groundwork for twentieth-century social science" (Ross 1991, 143). In the process, these Progressive Era social scientists found a new way to comprehend the American experience and its future progress. "America's ideal future could be attached to the great engines of modern progress: the capitalist market, social diversification, democracy, and scientific knowledge" (Ross 1991, 149). The capitalist market furthermore provided the model of truly free acting individuals.

The aim of this vision together with the reconstitution of American exceptionalism was to respond to challenges of the early twentieth century by constructing a science of social control (Ross 1991, 319). Pragmatism, in particular Dewey's work, presented "the method of natural science . . . as the model for all kinds of knowing" (Ross 1991, 328). Science became the only authoritative discourse (Ross 1991, 162). For Dewey, the social sciences could "produce the kind of positivist knowledge that could establish rational control over society and history" and therefore life (Ross 1991, 252). The ambiguities of earlier academic thinking were brushed aside as scientific models became central to the training of future generations of scholars. Furthermore, this view of knowledge defended American exceptionalism—now intimately linked to capitalism (Ross 1991, 386–87). "Social science was to be an autonomous body of knowledge, pursued in a way to develop its scientific character, yet it was to be directed at and constituted in accordance with the technological capacity for control" (Ross 1991, 400). In the end, instrumentalist rationality and technique became the prize medium for research:

[I]nstrumental positivism and neoclassical economics with its offshoot of social and public choice theory, the paradigms that most closely embody the individualistic and atheoretical premises of liberal exceptionalism. . . . (Ross 1991, 473)

Academic knowledge, just like the department, association, and faculty, developed its own logic of production and presentation. Riddled with jargon, often obscurantist, research was defined not by the "quality" of result but by whether the process was properly followed. Even in the most legalistic of institutions, candidates were denied tenure because of lack of "collegiality" (Cohen 1993, 36). Scholarship was deemed successful when the producer repeated established patterns, adjusted to reviewers and editors, and fit their piece within the constraints of journal-writing. This process augmented specialization, bound by academic cultural dogma and procedures, creating a particular knowledge and jargon whose purpose was social control (Lucas 1994, 252; Ross 1991; Schürmann 1994). This was made further confusing by a style of writing that reinforced "officiality." Conservative, liberal, and Marxist academics, Russell Jacoby argued, suffer from a tortuous style of writing (1994, chapter 6). C. Wright Mills's criticism of Talcott Parsons's writing remains valid today:

In many academic circles today . . . anyone who tries to write in a widely intelligible way is liable to be condemned as a "mere literary man" or, worse still, "a mere journalist." (cited in Jacoby 1994, 169)

Sadly, reading scholarship did not even provide the joy of cracking a puzzle; rather, its very pedestrian repetition leaves one, as Jacoby (1987, xiii) suggested, simply bored.[5]

At the dawn of a new century the battle over curriculum burns anew. Late-twentieth-century humanists demand a return to an imaginary past when higher education, successfully guided by a liberal arts program, taught students "American values." Allan Bloom and his followers harken back to a mythical past in which liberal arts and general education stood at the heart of higher education. They presented themselves as defenders of the liberal arts against the disruptive and anti-intellectual relativism of activist faculty who imposed political views on students, colleagues, and administrators, vanquishing the general education curriculum that was essential for a free society (Bloom 1987, Hirsch 1987, Heilman 1987).

To paraphrase Marx, all great humanist traditions in U.S. higher education appear twice, "the first time as tragedy, the second time as farce" (1963, 15). It is difficult to give credence to their rhetoric. A summary history of U.S. higher education makes clear that the failure of the general education movement and the inability to establish liberal arts programs occurred long before the 1960s. Moreover, the radical "takeover" of U.S. higher education was primarily the product of the imaginations of hacks like Dinesh D'Souza, Roger Kimball, and Charles Sykes. To look back, U.S. higher education enjoyed fifty years of stable growth based on a hidden curriculum that reproduces capitalist America. Even the challenges of the 1960s were not that profound. Much of the 1960s curricular agenda was already present in the general education structure (Brubacher and Rudy 1997, 284). Rudolph (1989, 270) argued that the student movement of the 1960s wrought no great transformation in the curriculum. Even the more utopian dream of social justice quickly dissipated (Giroux 1983, 43). As Russell Jacoby (1987, 135) put it, "The New Left that remained on campus proved industrious and well-behaved. Often without missing a beat, they moved from being undergraduates and graduate students to junior faculty positions and tenured appointments." Instead of a threat, tenured radicals remained disengaged and merely served to legitimate U.S. higher education.

What drives this new humanist farce, then? Many humanists were simply unhappy, as Bloom maintained, with the arrival of a new student population with distinct economic and cultural backgrounds whose intellectual curiosity led them to play (temporarily) with a variety of ideas and perspectives. Following the footsteps of Jews, women, and working-class Anglos, the entry of students of color temporarily disequilibrated the academy. Their presence interrogated American exceptionalism and briefly exposed the hidden curriculum. The newcomers, constructed as they were by academic knowledge, denied any positive existence, voided of history, culture, and self-determination, briefly made visible the hidden curriculum and contradictions of U.S. higher education. They brought memory to bear on what had been suppressed; as Cohen (1993, 21) explained, these students tried "to deacademicize the devices and apparatus of memory." For this reason, after all the ink and fury of the humanist *Kulturkampf* of the 1990s, all that was left was an attack on affirmative action.[6] Their problem was not any particular intellectual tradition, text, or ideology; it was not even the dream of a utopian transformation. Rather, their fear was simply the presence of these people and memory.

Ironically the humanists had little to fear. The students of the 1960s, including those of color, never recognized the nature of their challenge. They spent their energies in battles that either resulted in their expulsion from the academy or their transformation into academics. Militancy mutated into constituency. The hidden curriculum (re)instituted society's particular reading of human nature and the wisdom of the hidden hand—the common good regulated by the laws of the market, free competition, private ownership, and profitability (Apple 1993, 26–31; Boyer 1986). Traditional instrumentalist logic was recycled and repackaged (Giroux 1983, 43). The interests of business and the state (both becoming more difficult to distinguish) were again pervasive.

STUDENT PROTEST AND THE FORMATION OF CHICANO STUDIES IN CALIFORNIA, 1967 TO 1970

The student efforts of the 1960s had a profound impact on the formation of Chicano studies as an academic discipline. While the Los Angeles high school "blowouts" in March 1968 were the first major Chicano(a) student protest, the university strikes at San Francisco State (SFS) and the University of California at Berkeley (UCB) (1968 to 1969) were central to the genesis of Chicano studies in California. The student protesters' political visions formed the background for the establishment of Chicano studies programs in the academy.

Social and political unrest in the Bay Area preceded Chicano(a) activism. Ever since the 1964 Free Speech Movement, student activism was a constant activity at UCB and at times on other campuses in the Bay Area. The developing antiwar and hippie movements together with the transforming Civil Rights Movement/Black Power Movement accentuated campus protests (Caute 1988). Chicano(a) protests rapidly followed in the wake of these other movements. Even though their numbers were small, Chicano(a) students established the first organizations on many campuses in the Bay Area (*La Raza* 1:7).

At both SFS and UCB Chicanos(as) and Latinos(as) participated with African American and Asian American students to organize the

Third World strike with the goal of recruiting students and faculty of color to set up ethnic studies programs on their campuses (Barlow and Shapiro 1969, 290; "The Fifteen TWLF Demands" 1971). For example, at UCB the Third World Liberation Front (TWLF) demanded a college controlled by Third World people:

> The TWLF is asking for a college run by minority group administrators, taught by minority group professors and deals with the political and cultural understanding of these long neglected and oppressed people. (Chicanos on the Move 1968)

Behind these demands, as Conchita (1969, 6) stated, was the hope of self-determination, liberation, and a relevant education: "What the students demand can be summed up in two words: liberation and relevancy." Roger Alvarado of the SFS TWLF stated: "We don't want equality, we want self-determination" (Barlow and Shapiro 1969, 292). For protesters at UCB and SFS, self-determination and a relevant education aimed at creating an institution within the academy that could serve their home communities. This oppositional space would be under the control of students, faculty, and staff of color with representation of community groups.

In the wake of these student strikes some Chicano(a) students, faculty, staff, administrators, and community came together to formulate a political manifesto based on the demand for self-determination. The Third World strikers sought to use the university to transform their communities and "strive toward the ideal of 'participatory democracy' and radical social change" (Barlow and Shapiro 1971, 62). In *El Plan de Santa Bárbara*, Chicanos(as) furnished the political vision for a strategic use of the university against the oppression of Mexican Americans. The university could become "a vital institutional instrument of change" (Rochin 1973, 888). Chicano power could be achieved through the political application of university resources—channeled through Chicano studies and other campus programs.

In *El Plan*, Chicano(a) activists proposed that Chicanos(as) build institutions within the academy under Chicano control in order to wage the wider struggle for self-determination. Through institutions Chicano power would be realized on campus and university services could be directed to the Chicano(a) community (Chicano Coordinating Council on Higher Education 1970, 13). To secure the autonomy of these institutions, *El Plan* proposed to integrate students, staff, and community with faculty to govern these programs. This balance, it was assumed, could mitigate the rise of Chicano(a) faculty's self-interest or interference from administration. Simultaneously, collective leadership could assure that courses, while fulfilling an academic role, would prepare students for political and social responsibilities. Following *El Plan*, Reynaldo Macías, Juan Gómez-Quiñones, and Raymond Castro (1971, 32) argued that Chicano studies must be institutionalized within the university where it should be given sufficient latitude to achieve the goals of self-determination and self-definition.

El Plan, however, did not fully confront the second theme of the Third World strikes: a relevant education. At best the authors saw the development of courses that could serve the political battle with dominant society (Gómez-Quiñones 1990, 140). To search for the academic roots of Chicano studies one has to turn to *El Grito: A Journal of Contemporary Mexican American Thought*, the first sustained Chicano challenge to dominant intellectual paradigms. Octavio Romano's and Nick Vaca's essays developed a Chicano critical perspective at the periphery of the academy (Garcia 1992, 6). These authors proposed an intellectual framework to question and overturn the social myths of Mexicans and Mexican Americans and began an exploration of the Chicano(a) experience. As their critique developed, they moved from criticism of stereotypes and bad analysis toward a more honest appraisal of the Mexican American experience.

In attempting to uncover the Mexican American experience, some writers in *El Grito* began to question the entire academic project. Their work problematized academic knowledge. In the essay "Social Science, Objectivity and the Chicanos," for instance, Romano began by tracing the intellectual origins of "objectivity" in order to contextualize the concept, demonstrate its meaning, and reveal its biases. For Romano (1970, 5), objectivity demanded an artificial (and false) separation of mind and body. In a later piece, Romano (1980, 10) reiterated his point:

> If there is a cohesive configuration of cultural themes and overriding values which characterize the historical development of American society and its West European intellectual, philosophical

and political heritage, then that configuration can best be summarized as an analytical orientation toward the empirical, physical, and
cultural world accompanied by a pervasive belief in the separability
of reality into its constituent parts and elements.

Thus, personal self-consciousness—who we are—was banished from
academic knowledge. In rejecting dualism, Romano concluded that the
only way to "do" Chicano studies was to commence from the "self-
image" of the Chicano(a) himself or herself. Given the impossibility of
objectivity, Chicanos needed to reclaim and rewrite themselves:

> If this self-image is rejected by non-Chicano social scientists, then, in
> effect, they will have rejected summarily the rationality of the Chi-
> cano. (Romano 1970, 12)

While students eventually achieved the creation of alternative institutions, the larger goal of community liberation was lost. The SFS
strike had modest results: several new departments were organized
under ethnic studies and stronger support given to recruiting and
admitting minority students. The new departments were to be gov-
erned by a collective of students, staff, faculty, and some people from
the community. Students, however, quickly grew disenchanted with
the results. Even as *La Raza* studies program was instituted, SFS students realized they had been unable to achieve their goal (Smith 1970,
chapter 18; Barlow and Shapiro 1971, 320–21). The UCB strike
evolved in a similar demoralizing pattern. The strike also resulted in
the establishment of an ethnic studies program, but concessions were
small compared to the dream of an autonomous Third World College
as a center of political action (Kim n.d.). Chicano studies programs,
whether at SFS or UCB, were abandoned by students and fell into the
hands of faculty who had little choice but to follow academic procedures. William Wei noted a similar situation for Asian American
studies at UCB: "By the late 1970s, students and community involve-
ment had all but disappeared, and power was wholly in the hands of
faculty" (Wei 1993, 135).

The compromise for an ethnic studies department necessarily
deemphasized the activist agenda that had been part of the Third
World strikes. Instead "the main route to curricular legitimacy was the
liberal model . . ." (Padilla 1974, 157). In order to establish Chicano

studies, the protesters accepted the rules of the academy. This led to the changing of the goals for Chicano studies from community transformation to self-preservation in the academy:

> What began as a Chicano studies goal of people-community development based on the use of university resources changed to sheltering students from an alien and inhospitable university environment. (Padilla 1974, 48)

Why did this occur? Student protests exemplified the difficulty in challenging the operation of the university and its hidden curricula. Oppositional voices faced two institutional defenses. First the students' challenge was presented as irrational and lacking validity. In the academy there were proper ways of challenging the institution and the students' complaint had to fit the criteria of "rationality." For example, at SFS, administrators used a combination of negotiation (fit your request on the proper form), dismissal (you don't make sense), and repression to dismiss the protest (Karagueuzian 1971; McEvoy and Miller 1970; Smith 1970, chapter 16).

A second response was co-optation. The academy's self-regulating system provided mechanisms to translate oppositional challenges into more acceptable alternative choices. Self-determination was mutated into the liberal ideology of abstract tolerance (Marcuse 1969)— rendered into the language of institutional rights; in particular, that of academic freedom. Students misunderstood the multiple mechanisms through which higher education reproduced the existing social, political, economic, and ideological order. The students' criticism of particular institutions, individuals, and programs missed the covert mechanism that is part of the academy and activists were unprepared for the subsumption of their oppositional demands.

Chicano studies, as a concrete manifestation of the protests, itself became an element of hidden curricula. This institutionalization of Chicano power at the university transformed Chicano(a) faculty into agents of colonization, and thrust them between students and the institution. Whatever their rhetorical posture, faculty operated under institutional rules, articulating the institution. Faculty compradors differed little from Fanon's (1967, 1968) description of the "native bourgeoisie" who "adopted unreservedly and with enthusiasm the ways of thinking characteristic of the mother country." More importantly,

Chicano(a) faculty began to mold students into future academics. Chicano(a) faculty became just as adept as their non-Chicano(a) counterparts in manufacturing consent. They, too, came to accept publications, presentations, association meetings, professionalization, and the search for prestige as the *non plus ultra*. It should not be surprising that some critical students quickly acknowledged Chicano(a) faculty as part of the institution and came to despise them—unaware that this was their future as well.

More devastating, from my perspective, was the intellectual failure of Chicano studies. The goal of a relevant education, with its critique of academic knowledge, was channeled into the traditional disciplines, and the oppositional curriculum was brought under control. Like cultural studies in Britain, initially one could discern a zeal to relate Chicano studies to "life-situations . . . outside the established educational system" (Williams 1989, 152). However, like Raymond Williams's analysis of cultural studies, the academic institution supplanted the bond with life situations with knowledge reproduced in the image of the institution. Like cultural studies, Chicano studies became disassociated from its community and its development was reduced to textual analysis—and academic jargon. "At the very moment when that adventurous syllabus became a syllabus that had to be examined, it ceased to be exciting" (Williams 1989, 156). Williams (1989, 157) noted that at this point of institutionalization:

> a body of theory came through which rationalized the situation of this formation on its way to becoming bureaucratized and the home of specialist intellectuals.

For cultural studies this meant the arrival of theories that "tended to regard the practical encounters of people in society as having relatively little effect on its general progress" (Williams 1989, 157). For Chicano studies, it meant acceptance of academic methods and principles later followed by acceptable theoretical alternatives (colonial theory and Marxism) (Soldatenko 1998, 4–5).

El Grito's critical call to challenge Anglo research and to uncover knowledge of Mexican Americans came to naught. The hidden curriculum established the "how" and "why" of research, and to reject academic knowledge production made it impossible to establish a relationship within the academy. Attempts to "research" outside established paradigms and processes resulted in self-publication or fiction. This reinforced the journal's move toward the arts. Vaca and Romano had not developed the methodology and theoretical apparatus to produce knowledge outside the bounds of the pre-established procedures of the academy. Unable to get around the hidden curriculum, *El Grito* lost its voice as the organ of Mexican American contemporary thought.

With the failure of *El Grito*, the vacuum was filled by Chicano(a) scholars who accepted academic practices albeit with a radical rhetorical tinge. The first journal to jump into the gap was *Aztlán: Chicano Journal of the Social Sciences and Arts*. The editors of *Aztlán*, though critical of social science literature, retained an ambivalent relationship with academic knowledge (Soldatenko 1999). The editors and some writers, trained within proper research procedures, could not resolve the tension between "scholarship" and "activism." Activist scholarship became simply a mixture of acceptable academic work and rhetoric—often couched as interdisciplinary, transdisciplinary, multidisciplinary, or comparative work. Instrumentalist logic dominated much of the research in *Aztlán*; most essays shared an epistemological framework that turned on various interpretations of structures of domination (Rocco 1977). These structuralist approaches, typically based on a variety of mixtures of internal colonialism and Marxism, were acceptable in the academy.

Sliding into the academy, Chicano scholarship demanded its own particular paradigm, journal, and association—all the accruements of any disciplinary endeavor. Though challenged by peripheral journals, such as *De Colores: Journal of Emerging Raza Philosophies*; *El Cuaderno*; *Con Safos*; *Calmecac*; and *Caracol*, only *Aztlán* was able to integrate into "American social science." In 1973 the National Association of Chicano studies (NACS) developed similar to other disciplines. All in all, Chicano studies replicated all the traditional practices and institutions of academic disciplines.

Like the struggle for self-determination, relevant education floundered on the shoals of the hidden curriculum. Attempts to challenge legitimate knowledge resulted, at best, in the process of "mentioning." Chicano(a) scholarship became part of the acceptable intellectual mix. Within Chicano studies, canon formation occurred, as in other disciplines. As the canon was being constituted, some Chicano(a) faculty were groomed to enter the professoriate. Eschewing activism, a few became "divas," blessed with "superstardom" and allowed to articulate their "uncompromising" positions as public intellectuals. The end result was departments that were no different than other departments. And like other academic pursuits, Chicano studies could not provide any way to engage the world; it, too, was ethically dead.

DISCUSSION

Less than five years after the SFS and UCB Third World strikes, Chicano studies programs were under siege by students who felt the promise had been abandoned. Thirty years later students remain critical of Chicano studies for distorting the strikers' and the Chicano Movement's goals. At a recent conference organized by the Southern California FOCO [center] of the National Association of Chicana and Chicano studies, while faculty celebrated their programs maturing into departments with increasing numbers of majors, students called attention to how Chicano studies had abandoned its ideals. Students complained: Chicano studies had no organic tie to the community, student services were bureaucratic machines, student and academic services were depoliticized, student input was minimal, and classes reinforced traditional methodologies and epistemologies.

No one at the conference named the hidden curricula or confronted limitations that academic structures and functions imposed on Chicano studies. Chicanos(as) were content to embrace the mystical power of the academic Oz, affirming its mythology and rituals as their own. While faculty and students differed on interpretation, all desired Chicano studies to be part of the academy. Therefore the blueprint was still to establish Chicano studies programs where none existed: if the campus had a program, then struggle to make it a department; and if the campus had a department, then add a research unit.[7] The goal was faculty lines, the only manifestation of institutional power. Chicano studies consented to the bondage of disciplines to become like any other field in the social sciences or the humanities.

In this way Chicano scholars became academics, schooled by the institutions (university, discipline, professional society) into (re)producing themselves as the ivory-tower intellectuals they distrusted or despised. They struggled to publish in mainstream journals, raised grant money, held each other to the tenure requirements, sat in judgment "on each other" in search committees, applied standards of "objective" knowledge, used citation indices, ranked journals on academic criteria like rejection rates and prestige, built good old boy (and good old girl) networks, promoted their friends, built publishing empires, became superstars. . . . They practiced the rituals with the same conviction and ability as any of the adept, disdaining threats from outside and destroying the careers of potential challengers. Chicano studies failed not because it had not properly implemented *El Plan* or any other vision, but because it was successful in grafting itself onto the academy.

What I find most distressful is how Chicano studies wields academic knowledge. Chicano(a) scholars were rewarded for "doing social science" on their own communities. By the logic of the hidden curriculum they had to objectify/quantify—to study: the smoking rates of . . . ; teenage pregnancy of . . . ; disfunctional families of . . . ; youth violence of . . . ; dropout rates of . . . ; their community. What generations of Anglo social scientists did to Mexican and Chicano communities, Chicano(a) scholarship continues. Nor have fields like history, literature, or the arts escaped this intellectual subordination. Sadly, this is the only way to make careers in academia, build reputations, create departments, gain academic capital . . . survive.

By ignoring and/or denying the socialization power of hidden curricula designed to reproduce academia with its twin goals of serving capitalist markets and non–participatory democracy, Chicano(a) students and faculty became coparticipants in the reproduction of class, gender, sexual, and racial inequality in the United States. Many of us came to the academy because of discontent with the social, political, and economic realities and became active in academic pursuits in order to address questions of social justice. We believed that we had a responsibility to our community, the world at large, and ourselves. Yet in the academy these issues were intellectualized: disciplines compartmentalized knowledge, responsibility was diffused, justice and social responsibility were subordinated to the abstract search for knowledge. In the process, personal and collective responsibility was brushed aside, replaced with abstract notions of justice and tolerance.[8] Dreams of a different world were exchanged for tenured positions. If the modern university has lost its moral compass and the meaning of being human (Wilshire 1990), Chicano studies was no different. This is indeed what Burton Clark (1968) so eloquently called the "cooling-out function," as it is employed in higher education in capitalist society.

NOTES

1. I would like to thank Eric Margolis for his intellectual vision and leadership. Without his work, this project would never have occurred.
2. I use the term *Chicano studies* to denote the discipline constructed by activists of the 1960s that replicated the academy's patriarchal and homophobic disposition. This same discipline continues in the present albeit with variations in nomenclature.
3. Ironically, the imposition of the elective system broke the hold of the classics and created the modern U.S. university. As Rudolph argued, the tradition of liberal learning and the purposes of the German university were incompatible. The European elective system permitted rigorously and liberally educated graduates of the gymnasium and lyceé to design appropriate professional programs. In the United States the same program created confusion and disorientation (Rudolph 1989, 206; Lucas 1994, 210).
4. This discussion of the "American university" was really about a limited number of research institutions (Jacoby 1994). These institutions had instituted the research model with specialized fields (creating more faculty positions). Or as Cohen (1993, 62) reminded us: "The 'research' model is undoubtedly a colossal piece of narcissism."
5. Cohen (1993, 4) argued that academic writing, directed to metatheory and metalanguage, fortified the trinity of pedantry, self-satisfaction, and academicism—reinforcing the "narcissism of insiders." This writing reflected domesticated and tame thought, often reduced to rank and authority.
6. Affirmative action, Bloom (1987, 94) asserted, admitted many who were unqualified and unprepared. Some of these students went on to create programs, like black studies, that were destructive to the curriculum. Hirsch (1987, 21–22) agreed with Bloom when he argued that affirmative action undercut the cultural literacy that was inclusive and democratic.
7. An example was the 1993 UCLA protest by students of color. The protest began as a criticism of the nature of education at UCLA (Nevins 1993, Sacks 1993, Mabalon 1993, Shapiro et al. 1993). Unfortunately, a nativist, nationalist, *"chingon"* politics came to the fore, transforming the initial protest into a struggle over the formation of a Chicano studies department—a return to *El Plan*. The protest eventually achieved its goal: domestication.
8. Marcuse (1965, 96–97) argued that intellectuals have a responsibility to preserve historical possibilities, which appear utopian, by understanding the concreteness of oppression. In a capitalist society we entertain an abstract tolerance by which we accept established attitudes, ideas, and critiques. "Consequently, persuasion through discussion and the equal presentation of opposites (even where it is really equal) easily lose their liberating force as factors of understanding and learning; they are far more likely to strengthen the established thesis and to repel the alternative." Abstract tolerance is merely the neutralization of opposites, not transcendence.

Bibliography

Acker, S. 1981. No-Woman's Land: British Sociology of Education 1960–1979. *Sociological Review* 29:77–104.

———. 1994. *Gendered Education*. Buckingham and Philadelphia: Open University Press.

———. 1999. Students and Supervisors: The Ambiguous Relationship. Perspectives on the Supervisory Process in Britain and Canada. In *Supervision of Postgraduate Research in Education. Review of Research in Education No. 5*, edited by A. Holbrook and S. Johnston. 75–94. Coldstream, Victoria: Australian Association for Research in Education.

Acker, S., and G. Feuerverger. 1996. Doing Good and Feeling Bad: The Work of Women University Teachers. *Cambridge Journal of Education* 26:401–22.

Acker, S., T. Hill and E. Black. 1994. Thesis Supervision in the Social Sciences: Managed or Negotiated? *Higher Education* 28:483–98.

Acker, S., S. Transken, T. Hill, and E. Black. 1994. Research Students in Education and Psychology: Diversity and Empowerment. *International Studies in Sociology of Education* 4:229–51.

Acker, S., and M. Webber. 2000. Pleasure and Danger in Academics' Feelings about Their Work. In *Annual Meeting of the American Educational Research Association*. New Orleans, La.

Addiction Research Foundation. 1976. *Women and Psychoactive Drugs*. Toronto, Ontario: Addiction Research Foundation.

Agogino, A. M., and M. Linn. 1992. Retaining Female Engineering Students: Will Design Experiences Help? *NSF Directions 5*.

Althusser, L. 1971. Ideology and Ideological State Apparatuses. Notes towards an Investigation. In *Lenin and Philosophy and Other Essays*. 127–86. New York: Monthly Review Press.

Amin, S. 1997. *Capitalism in the Age of Globalization. The Management of Contemporary Society*. London: Zed Books.

Anyon, J. 1980. Social Class and the Hidden Curriculum of Work. *Journal of Education* 162:67–92.

Apple, M. W. 1982. *Cultural and Economic Reproduction in Education: Essays on Class, Ideology, and the State*. Boston: Routledge and Kegan Paul.

———. 1982. *Education and Power*. Boston: Routledge and Kegan Paul.

———. 1988. *Teachers and Texts: A Political Economy of Class and Gender Relations in Education*. New York: Routledge.

———. 1993. *Official Knowledge: Democratic Education in a Conservative Age*. New York: Routledge.

———. 1996. *Cultural Politics and Education*. New York: Teachers College Press.

Apple, M. W., and N. R. King. 1977. What Do Schools Teach? In *Humanistic Education*, edited by R. H. Weller. 29–63. Berkeley, Calif.: McCutchan Publishing Corporation.

———. 1977. What Do Schools Teach? *Curriculum Inquiry* 6:341–58.

Arenson, K. 1998. Classes Are Full at Catch-up U. *New York Times*. Section 4, 4. New York.

———. 2000. CUNY to Seek Bids to Teach Remedial Classes. *New York Times*. Section B, 6.

Armstrong, P., J. Choiniere and E. Day. 1993. *Vital Signs. Nursing in Transition*. Toronto: Garamond.

Arnot, M., and G. Weiner, ed. by 1987. *Gender and the Politics of Schooling*. London: Hutchinson.

Aronowitz, Stanley and Henry A. Giroux. 1988. Schooling, Culture, and Literacy in the Age of Broken Dreams: A Review of Bloom and Hirsch. *Harvard Educational Review* 58:172–94.

Aspland, T. 1999. Struggling with Ambivalence Within Supervisory Relations. In *Supervision of Postgraduate Research in Education. Review of Australian Research in Education No. 5*, edited by A. Holbrook and S. Johnston. 95–111. Coldstream, Victoria: Australian Association for Research in Education.

Aspland, T., and T. O'Donoghue. 1994. Quality in Supervising Overseas Students? In *Quality in Postgraduate Education*, edited by O. Zuber-Skerritt and Y. Ryan. 59–76. London: Kegan Page.

Astin, A. W. 1993. *What Matters in College? Four Critical Years Revisited*. San Francisco: Jossey-Bass.

Bader, M. 1981. Breastfeeding: The Role of Multinational Corporations in Latin America. In *Imperialism, Health and Medicine. Policy, Politics, Health and Medicine*, edited by V. Navarro. 235–52. Farmingdale, N.Y.: Baywood Publishing Company.

Baird, L. 1990. The Melancholy of Anatomy: The Personal and Professional Development of Graduate and Professional School Students. In *Higher Education: Handbook of Theory and Research*, edited by J.C. Smart. 361–92. New York: Agathon Press.

Ball, S. 1981. *Beachside Comprehensive: A Case-study of Secondary Schooling*. Cambridge: Cambridge University Press.

Bannerji, H. 1991. But Who Speaks for Us? Experience and Agency in Conventional Feminist Paradigms. In *Unsettling Relations*, edited by L. Carty, H. Bannerji, K. Delhi, S. Heald, and K. McKenna. 67–107. Toronto: Women's Press.

———. 1995. *Returning the Gaze*. In *Beyond Political Correctness*, edited by S. Richer and L. Weir. 220–36. Toronto: University of Toronto Press.

Barlow, B., and P. Shapiro. 1969. The Struggle for San Francisco State. In *Black Power and Student Rebellion*, edited by James McEvoy and Abraham Miller. 277–297. Belmont: Wadsworth Publishers.

———. 1971. *An End to Silence: The San Francisco State College Student Movement in the '60s*. New York: Pegasus.

Barnard, C. I. [1938] 1968. *The Functions of the Executive*. Cambridge, Mass.: Harvard University Press.

Barton, Len, Roland Meighan and Stephen Walker, ed. 1980. *Schooling, Ideology, and the Curriculum*. Sussex, England: Falmer Press.

Becker, H. S. 1961. Schools as Systems of Stratification. In *Education, Economy, and Society*, edited by Jean Floud A. H. Halsey, and C. Arnold Anderson. 93–104. New York: The Free Press.

Bell, D. 1966. *The Reforming of General Education: The Columbia College Experience in its National Setting*. New York: Columbia University Press.

Bennett, L. 1972. *The Challenge of Blackness*. Chicago: Johnson Publishing Company.

Bergenhenegouwen, G. 1987. Hidden Curriculum in the University. *Higher Education* 16:535–43.

Bernstein, B. 1977. *Class, Codes, and Control*. Vol. 3. 2d ed. London: Routledge and Kegan Paul.

1998. Best Graduate Schools. *U.S. News and World Report*.

Black, B. 1997. Attitudes Toward International Issues: Influences of Social Work Education. *Social Work and Social Sciences Review* 7:39–52.

Blackwell, J. E. 1989. Mentoring: An Action Strategy for Increasing Minority Faculty. *Academe* 78:8–14.

Bleier, R., ed. 1991. *Feminist Approaches to Science*. New York: Columbia University Teachers College Press.

Bloom, A. 1987. *The Closing of the American Mind*. New York: Simon and Schuster.

Bloom, S. 1988. Structure and Ideology in Medical Education: An Analysis of Resistance to Change. *Journal of Health and Social Behaviour* 29:294–306.

Bonilla, J., C. Pickron, and T. Tatum. 1994. Peer Mentoring Among Graduate Students of Color: Expanding the Mentoring Relationship. In *Mentoring Revisited: Making an Impact on Individuals and Institutions*, edited by Marie A. Wunsch. San Francisco: Jossey-Bass.

Booth, W. 1994. Beyond Knowledge and Inquiry to Love, or "Who Mentors the Mentors?" *Academe*: 29–36.

Bourdieu, P. 1973. Cultural Reproduction and Social Reproduction. In *Knowledge, Education, and Social Change*, edited by R. Brown. 71–112. London: Tavistock.

———. 1977. Cultural Reproduction and Social Reproduction. In *Power and Ideology in Education*, edited by Jerome Karabel and A. H. Halsey. 487–511. New York: Oxford University Press.

———. 1990. *The Logic of Practice*. Palo Alto, Calif.: Stanford University Press.

———. 1991. Authorized Language: The Social Conditions for the Effectiveness of Ritual Discourse. In *Language and Symbolic Power*, edited by J. B. Thompson. Cambridge, Mass.: Harvard University Press.

———. 1998. *Practical Reason*. Palo Alto, Calif.: Stanford University Press.

Bourdieu, P., and J. Passeron. 1977. *Reproduction in Education, Society, and Culture*. Beverly Hills: Sage Publications.

———. 1990. *Reproduction in Education, Society, and Culture.* 2d. ed. Newbury Park, Calif.: Sage.

Bowles, S., and H. Gintis. 1976. *Schooling in Capitalist America: Educational Reform and the Contradictions of Economic Life.* New York: Basic Books.

Boyer, E. L. 1986. *College: The Undergraduate Experience in America.* New York: Carnegie Foundation.

Boyle, M. 1999. Immigrant Workers and the Shadow Education System. *Educational Policy* 13:251–79.

Brah, A., and R. Minhas. 1985. Structural Racism or Cultural Difference: Schooling for Asian Girls. In *Just a Bunch of Girls,* edited by G. Weiner. Milton Keynes, England: Open University Press.

Brill, H. 1999. False Promises of Higher Education: More Graduates, Fewer Jobs. *Against the Current* 35:34–39.

Brim Jr., O. G. 1966. Socialization Through the Life Cycle. In *Socialization After Childhood: Two Essays.* 1–51. New York: John Wiley and Sons.

Brint, S., and J. Karabel. 1989. *The Diverted Dream: Community Colleges and the Promise of Educational Opportunity in America, 1900–1985.* New York: Oxford University Press.

Brubacher, J. S., and W. Rudy. 1997. *Higher Education in Transition: A History of American Colleges and Universities.* New Brunswick, N.J.: Transaction Publishers.

Bryan, B., S. Dadzie, and S. Scafe. 1987. Learning to Resist: Black Women and Education. In *Gender Under Scrutiny,* edited by G. Weiner and M. Arnot. 90–100. London: Hutchinson.

Burgess, R. 1983. *Experiencing Comprehensive Education.* London: Methuen.

Buroway, M. 1979. *Manufacturing Consent: Changes in the Labor Process Under Monopoly Capitalism.* Chicago: University of Chicago Press.

Calvert, K. 1992. *Children in the House: The Material Culture of Early Childhood, 1600–1900.* Boston: Northeastern University Press.

Carpenter, M. 1996. Female Grotesques in Academe: Ageism, Antifeminism, and Feminists on the Faculty. In *Antifeminism in the Academy,* edited by V. Clark, S. N. Garner, M. Higonnet, and K. Katrak, 141–65. New York: Routledge.

Carter, R., and G. Kirkup. 1990. *Women in Engineering: A Good Place to Be?* London: Macmillan Education, Ltd.

Carty, L. 1991. Black Women in Academia: A Statement from the Periphery. In *Unsettling Relations,* edited by L. Carty, H. Bannerji, K. Delhi, S. Heald, and K. McKenna. 13–44. Toronto: Women's Press.

Caute, D. 1988. *Sixty-eight: The Year of the Barricade.* London: Hamish Milton.

Chaiklin, S., and J. Lave, ed. 1993. *Understanding Practice: Perspectives on Activity and Context.* New York: Cambridge University Press.

Channell, J. 1990. The Student-Tutor Relationship. In *The Learning Experiences of Overseas Students,* edited by M. Kinnell. 63–81. Milton Keynes, England: Open University Press.

Chicano Coordinating Council on Higher Education. 1970. *El Plan de*

Santa Bárbara: A Chicano Plan for Higher Education. Santa Barbara, Calif.: La Causa Publications.

1968. Chicanos on the Move. *Bronze* 1:2.

Chubb, J. E., and T. M. Moe. 1990. *Politics, Markets, and American Schools*. Washington, D.C.: Brookings.

Clark, B. R. 1960. The Cooling-out Function in Higher Education. *American Journal of Sociology* 65:569–76.

———. 1968. The Cooling-out Function in Higher Education. In *Education, Economy, and Society*, edited by Jean Floud A. H. Halsey, and C. Arnold Anderson. 513–23. Glencoe, Ill.: Free Press.

———. 1980. The Cooling-out Function Revisited. In *Questioning the Community College Role*, edited by G. Vaughan. San Francisco: Jossey-Bass.

Clarricoates, K. 1978. Dinosaurs in the Classroom: A Re-examination of Some Aspects of the "Hidden Curriculum" in Primary Schools. *Women's Studies International Quarterly* 1:353–364.

Coburn, D., G. Torrance, and J. Kaufert. 1983. Medical Dominance in Canada in Historical Perspective: The Rise and Fall of Medicine? *International Journal of Health Services* 13:407–32.

Cohen, S. 1993. *Academia and the Luster of Capital*. Minneapolis: University of Minnesota Press.

Collins, R. 1971. Functional and Conflict Theories of Educational Stratification. *American Sociological Review* 36:1002–1019.

Conchita. 1969. The Student as Revolutionary. *Chicano Student News* 1:6.

Coney, S. 1994. *The Menopause Industry. How the Medical Establishment Exploits Women*. Alameda, Calif.: Hunter House.

Crabb, P. B., and D. Bielawski. 1994. The Social Representation of Material Culture and Gender in Children's Books. *Sex Roles* 30:69–79.

Cyert, R. M., and J. G. March. 1963. *A Behavioral Theory of the Firm*. Englewood Cliffs, N.J.: Prentice-Hall.

David, M. E. 1993. *Parents, Gender, and Education Reform*. Cambridge, England: Polity Press.

de Montigny, G. 1995. *Social Working. An Ethnography of Front Line Practice*. Toronto: University of Toronto Press.

Deem, R., ed. 1980. *Schooling for Women's Work*. London and Boston: Routledge and Kegan Paul.

Dilthey, W. 1961. *Pattern and Meaning in History: Thoughts on History and Society*. New York: Harper and Row.

DiMaggio, P., and M. Useem. 1982. The Arts in Class Reproduction. In *Cultural and Economic Reproduction in Education: Essays on Class, Ideology, and the State*, edited by M. Apple. 181–202. Boston: Routledge and Kegan Paul.

Dougherty, K. 1994. *The Contradictory College: The Conflicting Origins, Impacts, and Futures of the Community College*. Albany: SUNY Press.

Dreeben, R. 1967. The Contribution of Schooling to the Learning of Social Norms. *Harvard Educational Review* 37:211–37.

———. 1968. *On What is Learned in School*. Reading, Mass.: Addison-Wesley.

DuBois, W. E. B. 1989. Double Consciousness and the Veil. In *The Souls of Black Folk*. 1–9. New York: Bantam.

Durkheim, E. [1897] 1951. *Suicide*. New York: The Free Press.

———. [1922] 1956. *Education and Sociology*. Glencoe, Ill.: The Free Press.

———. [1925] 1961. *Moral Education*. New York: The Free Press.

Dutson, A. J., R. H. Todd, S. P. Magleby, and C. D. Sorenson. 1997. A Review of Literature on Teaching Engineering Design Through Project-oriented Capstone Courses. *Journal of Engineering Education* 86:17–28.

Edwards, R. 1979. *Contested Terrain: The Transformation of the Workplace in the Twentieth Century*. New York: Basic Books.

Egan, J. M. 1989. Graduate School and the Self: A Theoretical View of Some Negative Effects of Professional Socialization. *Teaching Sociology* 17:200–8.

Ehrensal, K. 1999. Establishing Pedagogic Authority: Accreditation and Staffing of (US) University Business Schools. In *Pierre Bourdieu: Language, Culture, and Education*, edited by M. Grenfell and M. Kelly. 235–45. Bern and New York: Peter Lang.

Eisenberg, A. F. 1999. Forms of Socialization: Graduate Education and the Graduate Seminar. *Teaching Sociology* 27:187–91.

Eisenhart, M., and N. Lawrence. 1994. Anita Hill, Clarence Thomas, and the Culture of Romance. In *Sexual Artifice: Persons, Images, Politics*, edited by K. Short, A. Kibbey, and A. Farmanfarmaian. 94–121. New York: New York University Press.

Eisenhart, M. A., E. Finkel, L. Behm, N. Lawrence, and K. Tonso. 1998. *Women's Science: Learning and Succeeding from the Margins*. Chicago: University of Chicago Press.

Eisner, E. W. 1985. *The Educational Imagination: On the Design and Evaluation of School Programs*. New York: Macmillan Publishing.

Epstein, S. 1997. *Law at Berkeley: The History of Boalt Hall*. Berkeley: Institute of Government Studies Press.

Erickson, E. H. 1963. *Childhood and Society*. 2d ed. New York: W. W. Norton.

Erskine, J. 1928. *The Delight of Good Books*. London: Eveleigh, Nash, and Grayson.

Etzkowitz, H., A. Webster, and P. Healey. 1998. *Capitalizing Knowledge: New Intersections of Industry and Academia*. New York: State University of New York Press.

Evans, C. 1988. *Language People*. Milton Keynes, England: Open University Press.

Everhart, R. 1983. *Reading, Writing, and Resistance: Adolescence and Labor in a Junior High School*. New York: Routledge.

Faison, J. J. 1996. The Next Generation: The Mentoring of African American Graduate Students on Predominantly White University Campuses. In *American Educational Research Association (AERA)*. New York, NY.

Fanon, F. 1967. *Black Skin, White Masks*. New York: Grove Press.

———. 1968. *The Wretched of the Earth*. Preface by Jean-Paul Sartre. 1st Black Cat ed. New York: Grove Press.

Ferguson, R. 1990. Introduction: Invisible Center. In *Out There: Marginalization and Contemporary Cultures*, edited by M. Gever R. Fergson, T. Minh Ha, and C. West. 9–14. New York: New Museum of Contemporary Art and M.I.T. Press.

Fineman, S., and Y. Gabriel. 1994. Paradigms of Organizations: An Exploration of Textbook Rhetorics. *Organization* 1:375–99.

Foucault, M. 1979. *Discipline and Punish: The Birth of the Prison*. New York: Vintage Books.

Freire, P. 1973. *Pedagogy of the Oppressed*. New York: Seabury Press.

———. 1982. *Education for Critical Consciousness*. New York: Continuum.

———. 1994. *Pedagogy of Hope*. New York: Continuum Publishing Company.

Freire, P., and D. Macedo. 1987. *Literacy: Reading the Word and the World*. South Hadley, Mass.: Bergin and Garvey.

Friedman, N. 1987. *Mentors and Supervisors*. New York: Institute for International Education.

Fuller, M. 1980. Black Girls in a London Comprehensive School. In *Schooling for Women's Work*, edited by R. Deem. 52–65. London: Routledge and Kegan Paul.

———. 1982. Young, Female, and Black. In *Black Youth in Crisis*, edited by E. Cashmore and B. Troyna. 87–99. London: George Allen and Unwin.

Fury, K. 1979. Mentor Mania. In *Savvy*. 42–47.

García, R. A. 1992. Creating a Consciousness, Memories and Expectations: The Burden of Octavio Romano. In *Chicano Discourse: Selected Conference Proceedings of the National Association for Chicano Studies*, edited by Tatcho Mindiola Jr. and Emilio Zamora. 6–31. Houston: Mexican American Studies Program.

Gaskell, J. 1992. *Gender Matters from School to Work*. Buckingham, England and Philadelphia: Open University Press.

Gee, J. P. 1996. *Social Linguistics and Literacies: Ideology in Discourses*. 2d ed. London: Taylor and Francis.

Gee, J. P., G. Hull, and C. Lankshear. 1996. *The New Work Order: Beyond the Language of the New Capitalism*. Boulder, Colo.: Westview Press.

Gewirtz, S., S. Ball, and R. Bowe, ed. 1995. *Markets, Choice, and Equity in Education*. Buckingham, England; Philadelphia: Open University Press.

Giroux, H. A. 1981. Hegemony, Resistance, and the Paradox of Educational Reform. *Interchange* 12:3–26.

———. 1983a. *Theory and Resistance in Education: A Pedagogy for the Opposition*. New York: Bergin and Garvey.

———. 1983b. Theories of Reproduction and Resistance in the New Sociology of Education: A Critical Analysis. *Harvard Educational Review* 53:257–93.

Goffman, I. 1952. On Cooling the Mark Out: Some Aspects of Adaptation to Failure. *Psychiatry: Journal for the Study of Interpersonal Relations* 15:451–63.

Gouldner, A. 1970. *The Coming Crisis of Western Sociology*. New York: Basic Books.

Gómez-Quiñones, J. 1990. *Chicano Politics: Reality and Promise 1940–1990*. Albuquerque: University of New Mexico Press.

Grant, B., and A. Graham. 1994. Guidelines for Discussion: A Tool for Managing Postgraduate Supervision. In *Quality in Postgraduate Education*, edited by O. Zuber-Skeritt and Y. Ryan. 165–177. London: Kegan Page.

Grant, C., and C. Sleeter. 1986. *After the School Bell Rings*. Philadelphia: Falmer Press.

Grant, L. 1992. Race and the Schooling of Young Girls. In *Education and Gender Equality*, edited by J. Wrigley. 91–113. London: Falmer Press.

Green, B., and A. Lee. 1999. Educational Research, Disciplinarity and Postgraduate Pedagogy: On the Subject of Supervision. In *Supervision of Postgraduate Research in Education, Review of Australian Research in Education No. 5*, edited by A. Holbrook and S. Johnston. 207–222. Coldstream, Victoria: Australian Association for Research in Education.

Griffith, A., and D. E. Smith. 1987. Constructing Cultural Knowledge: Mothering as Discourse. In *Women in Education: A Canadian Perspective*, edited by J. Gaskell and A. McLaren. 87–103. Calgary, Alberta, Canada: Detselig.

Guillory, J. 1987. Canonical and Non-Canonical: A Critique of the Current Debate. ELH 54:483–527.

Guinier, L., M. Fine, and J. Balin. 1997. *Becoming Gentlemen: Women, Law School and Institutional Change*. Boston: Beacon Press.

Gutmann, A. 1987. *Democratic Education*. Princeton, N.J.: Princeton University Press.

Hamper, B. 1992. *Rivethead: Tales from the Assembly Line*. New York: Warner Books.

Haraway, D. 1998. *Modest_Witness@Second_Millennium*. New York: Routledge.

Harding, J. 1994. Social Basis of the Over-prescribing of Mood-modifying Pharmaceutics to Women. In *Women, Medicine, and Health*, edited by B.S. Bolaria and R. Bolaria. 157–80. Halifax, Nova Scotia: Fernwood.

Harding, S. 1991. *Whose Science? Whose Knowledge? Thinking from Women's Lives*. Ithaca, N.Y.: Cornell University Press.

———. 1994. Is Science Multicultural? Challenges, Resources, Opportunities, Uncertainties. *Configurations* 2:301–10.

———. 1998. *Is Science Multicultural?: Postcolonialisms, Feminisms, and Epistemologies*. Bloomington: Indiana University Press.

Hargreaves, D. H. 1967. *Social Relations in a Secondary School*. London: Routledge and Kegan Paul.

Harrison, B., and B. Bluestone. 1988. *The Great U-turn: Corporate Restructuring and the Polarizing of America*. New York: Basic Books.

Harvard Committee. 1945. *General Education in a Free Society: Report of the Harvard Committee*.

Harvey, J. B. 1988. *The Abilene Paradox and Other Meditations on Management*. Lexington, Mass.: Lexington Books.

Heilman, R. B. 1987. Semicentennial Retrospections: The Past as Perspective. *The Georgia Review* 41:304–14.

Henderson, A. D. 1944. *Vitalizing Liberal Education: A Study of the Liberal Arts Program*. New York: Harper and Row Publishers.

Hepler, C. 1987. The Third Wave in Pharmaceutical Education: The Clinical Movement. *American Journal of Pharmaceutical Education* 51:1–17.

Herman, E. S., and N. Chomsky. 1988. *Manufacturing Consent: The Political Economy of the Mass Media*. New York: Pantheon Books.

Higby, G., and E. C. Stroud. 1997. *The Inside Story of Medicines. A Symposium*. Madison, Wis.: American Institute of the History of Pharmacy.

Hill, T., S. Acker, and E. Black. 1994. Research Students and Their Supervisors in Education and Psychology. In *Postgraduate Education and Training in the Social Sciences: Processes and Products*, edited by R. Burgess. 53–72. London: Jessica Kingsley.

Hirsch, E. D. 1987. *Cultural Literacy: What Every American Needs to Know*. Boston: Houghton Mifflin.

Holland, D., and M. Eisenhart. 1990. *Educated in Romance: Women, Achievement, and College Culture*. Chicago: University of Chicago Press.

Holland, D. C., and D. Skinner. 1987. Prestige and Intimacy: The Cultural Models Behind Americans' Talk about Gender Types. In *Cultural Models in Language and Thought*, edited by D. Holland and N. Quinn. Cambridge: Cambridge University Press.

Holly, L., ed. 1989. *Girls and Sexuality: Teaching and Learning*. Milton Keynes, England: Open University Press.

Homer, *Odyssey*, Book 2, line 225. English translation by A. T. Murray in 2 vols. Cambridge, Mass.: Harvard University Press; Londond: Heinemann. Quotation found at the Perseus site:<http://www.perseus.tufts.edu/>

hooks, b. 1988. *Talking Back*. Toronto: Between the Lines.

———. 1989. *Talking Back: Thinking Feminist, Thinking Black*. Boston: South End Press.

———. 1994. *Teaching to Transgress: Education as the Practice of Freedom*. New York: Routledge.

Horton, J. 1968. Order and Conflict Theories of Social Problems. In *Radical Perspectives on Social Problems*, edited by Frank Lindenfeld. London: Macmillan.

Howe, K. R. 1993. Equality of Educational Opportunity and the Criterion of Equal Educational Worth. *Studies in Philosophy and Education* 11:329–37.

Hsi-En, C. 1940. *Developing Patterns of the College Curriculum in the U.S.* Los Angeles: University of California Press.

Hubbard, R. 1995. *Profitable Promises. Essays on Women, Science and Health*. Monroe, Minn.: Common Courage Press.

Hulbert, K. D. 1994. Gender Patterns in Faculty-Student Mentoring Relationships. In *Gender and Academe: Feminist Pedagogy and Politics*, edited by S. Deats and L. Lenter. 247–63. Lanham, Md.: Rowman and Littlefield.

Hutchins, R. M. 1936. *The Higher Learning in America*. New Haven, Conn.: Yale University Press.

Jackson, P. W. 1968. *Life in Classrooms*. New York: Holt, Rinehart, and Winston.

———. 1990. Preface. In *Life in Classrooms*. xxi. New York: Teachers College Press.

Jacobi, M. 1991. Mentoring and Undergraduate Academic Success: A Literature Review. *Review of Educational Research* 61:505–32.

Jacoby, R. 1987. *The Last Intellectuals*. New York: Basic Books.

———. 1994. *Dogmatic Wisdom: How the Culture Wars Divert Education and Distract America*. New York: Doubleday.

Jenkins, R. 1992. *Pierre Bourdieu*. New York: Routledge.

Johnson, T. 1977. *Professions and Power*. London: Routledge.

Johnson, C. S. 1989. Mentoring Programs. In *The Freshman Year Experience: Helping Students Survive and Succeed in College*, edited by John N. Gardner, M. Lee Upcraft, and Associates. 118–128. San Francisco: Jossey-Bass.

Johnson, P., and J. Gill. 1993. *Management Control and Organizational Behaviour*. London: Paul Chapman.

Kahle, J. B. 1985. *Women in Science: A Report from the Field*. Philadelphia: Falmer Press.

Kanter, R. 1993. *Men and Women of the Corporation*. New York: HarperCollins.

Kaplan, R. 1966. Cultural Thought Patterns in Inter-cultural Education. *Language Learning* 16:1–20.

Karagueuzian, D. 1971. *Blow It Up! The Black Student Revolt at San Francisco State College and the Emergence of Dr. Hayakawa*. Boston: Gambit.

Karamcheti, I. 1995. Caliban in the Classroom. In *Pedagogy: The Question of Impersonation*, edited by J. Gallop. 138–46. Bloomington: Indiana University Press.

Keller, E. 1985. *Reflections on Gender and Science*. New Haven, Conn.: Yale University Press.

Kelly, G. P., and A. S. Nihlen. 1982. Schooling and the Reproduction of Patriarchy: Unequal Workloads, Unequal Rewards. In *Cultural and Economic Reproduction in Education: Essays on Class, Ideology and the State*, edited by Michael Apple. 162–80. Boston: Routledge and Kegan Paul.

Kelly, L. 1992. Not in Front of the Children: Responding to Right Wing Agendas on Sexuality and Education. In *Voicing Concerns: Sociological Perspectives on Contemporary Education Reforms*, edited by M. Arnot and L. Barton. 20–40. Oxford: Triangle Books.

Kenway, J., and S. Willis. 1997. *Answering Back: Girls, Boys, and Feminism in Schools*. St. Leonards, New South Wales, Australia: Allen and Unwin.

Kessler, S., D. Ashenden, R. W. Connell, and G. W. Dowsett. 1985. Gender Relations in Secondary Schooling. *Sociology of Education* 58:34–48.

Kim, E. n.d. Interview. In *Perspectives on the Third World Strike*, edited by Gary Kawaguchi. UCLA Chicano Studies Research Center Library Collection.

Knox, P. L., and T. V. McGovern. 1988. Mentoring Women in Academia. *Teaching of Psychology* 15:39–41.

Krause, E. 1996. *Death of the Guilds. Professions, States, and the Advance of Capitalism, 1930 to the Present.* New Haven, Conn.: Yale University Press.

Kridel, C. 1989. *Curriculum History: Conference Presentations from the Society for the Study of Curriculum History.* Lanham, Md.: University Press of America.

Kuhn, T. S. 1970. *The Structure of Scientific Revolutions.* 2d enlarged ed. Chicago and London: University of Chicago Press.

Lacey, C. 1970. *Hightown Grammar.* Manchester: Manchester University Press.

———. 1977. *The Socialization of Teachers.* London: Methuen Press.

Ladner, J. A., ed. 1973. *The Death of White Sociology.* New York: Vintage Books.

Lareau, A. 1989. *Home Advantage: Social Class, and Parental Intervention in Elementary Education.* London: Falmer Press.

Larson, M. 1977. *The Rise of Professionalism.* Berkeley: University of California Press.

Lave, J., and E. Wenger. 1991. *Situated Learning: Legitimate Peripheral Participation.* Cambridge: Cambridge University Press.

Lawrence, C. R. III, and M. J. Matsuda. 1997. *We Won't Go Back: Making the Case for Affirmative Action.* Boston and New York: Houghton Mifflin.

Leki, I. 1991. Twenty-five Years of Contrastive Rhetoric: Text Analysis and Writing Pedagogies. *TESOL Quarterly* 25:123–43.

Levine, A. 1981. *Handbook on Undergraduate Curriculum.* San Francisco: Jossey-Bass.

Levinson, B. A., D. E. Foley, and D. C. Holland. 1996. *The Cultural Production of the Educated Person: Critical Ethnographies of Schooling and Local Practice.* Albany: State University of New York Press.

Levinson, D. J., C. N. Darrow, E. B. Klein, M. A. Levinson, and B. McKee. 1978. *The Seasons of a Man's Life.* New York: Knopf.

Levy, F. 1987. *Dollars and Dreams: The Changing American Income Distribution.* New York: Russell Sage Foundation.

Lexchin, J. 1984. *The Real Pushers. A Critical Analysis of the Canadian Drug Industry.* Vancouver, British Columbia, Canada: New Star Books.

———. 1990. Drug Makers and Drug Regulators: Too Close for Comfort. A Study of the Canadian Situation. *Social Science and Medicine* 31:1257–63.

———. 1997. Enforcement of Codes Governing Pharmaceutical Promotion: What Happens When Companies Breach Advertising Guidelines? *Canadian Medical Association Journal* 156:351–356.

Liston, D. P. 1988. *Capitalist Schools: Explanation and Ethics in Radical Studies of Schooling.* New York: Routledge.

Longino, H. 1990. *Science as Social Knowledge: Values and Objectivity in Scientific Inquiry.* Princeton, N.J.: Princeton University Press.

Lucas, C. L. 1994. *American Higher Education: A History.* New York: St. Martin's Press.

Luna, G., and D. L. Cullen. 1996. Empowering the Faculty: Mentoring Redirected and Renewed. In *ASHE-ERIC Higher Education Report*

No. 3. ix–97. Washington D.C.: The George Washington University Graduate School of Education and Human Development.

Mabalon, D. 1993. A Student Rally for Library Programs. In *UCLA Daily Bruin.*

Mac an Ghaill, M. 1994. *The Making of Men: Masculinities, Sexualities, and Schooling.* Buckingham, England; Philadelphia: Open University Press.

MacDonald, M. 1980a. Socio-Cultural Reproduction and Women's Education. In *Schooling for Women's Work,* edited by Rosemary Deem. 13–25. London and Boston: Routledge and Kegan Paul.

———. 1980b. Schooling and the Reproduction of Class and Gender Relations. In *Schooling, Ideology, and the Curriculum,* edited by Len Roland Meighan Barton, and Stephen Walker. Sussex, England: Falmer Press.

Macías, R., J. Gómez-Quiñones, and R. Castro. 1971. Objectives of Chicano Studies. *Epoca* 1:31–34.

Maddox, R. 1997. Bombs, Bikinis, and the Popes of Rock and Roll: Reflections on Resistance, the Play of Subordinations, and Liberalism in Andalusia and Academia, 1983–1995. In *Culture, Power, Place: Explorations in Critical Anthropology,* edited by Akhil Gupta and James Fergerson. Durham, N.C. and London: Duke University Press.

Marcuse, H. 1960. *Reason and Revolution: Hegel and the Rise of Social Theory.* Boston: Beacon Press.

———. 1965. Repressive Tolerance. In *A Critique of Pure Tolerance,* edited by Barrington Moore, Robert Paul Wolff, Jr., and Herbert Marcuse. 81–123. Boston: Beacon Press.

———. 1966. *One Dimensional Man: Studies in the Ideology of Advanced Industrial Countries.* Boston: Beacon Press.

———. 1969. Repressive Tolerance. In *A Critique of Pure Tolerance,* edited by Barrington Moore, Robert Paul Wolff, Jr., and Herbert Marcuse. Boston: Beacon Press.

Margolis, E. 1994. Video Ethnography: Toward a Reflexive Paradigm for Documentary. *Jump Cut* 39:122–31.

Margolis, E., and M. Romero. 1998. The Department Is Very Male, Very White, Very Old, and Very Conservative: The Functioning of the Hidden Curriculum in Graduate Sociology Departments. *Harvard Educational Review* 68:1–32.

———. 2000. Dissed in the Department: Women of Color Graduate Students Talk About Integrating Sociology. In *Self-Analytic Sociology: Essays and Exploration in the Reflexive Mode,* edited by L. Reynolds. Rockport, Tex.: Rockport Institute Press.

Martin, J. R. 1994. What Sould We Do With a Hidden Curriculum When We Find One? In *Changing the Educational Landscape: Philosophy, Women, and Curriculum.* 154–69. New York and London: Routledge.

Marx, K. [1852] 1935. *The Eighteenth Brumaire of Louis Bonaparte.* New York: International Publishers.

Mazzuca, J. 2000. Italian-Canadian Women Graduate Students "Crossing the Border" in Graduate Studies *Department of Sociology and Equity Studies in Education.* Toronto: University of Toronto.

McDonnell, K. 1986. *Adverse Effects. Women and the Pharmaceutical Industry*. Toronto: The Women's Press.

McDowell, L. 1999. *Gender, Identity and Place: Understanding Feminist Geographies*. Minneapolis: University of Minnesota Press.

McEvoy, J., and A. Miller. 1970. The Crisis at San Francisco State. In *Campus Power Struggles*, edited by Howard S. Becker. 61–81. Chicago: Aldine Publishing Company.

McGinnis, R., and J. S. Long. 1980. Mentors Have Consequences and Reap Returns in Academic Biochemistry. *ERIC Document Reproduction Service* No. ED 193 082.

McIlwee, J. S., and J. G. Robinson. 1992. *Women in Engineering: Gender, Power, and Workplace Culture*. Albany: State University of New York Press.

McLaren, P. L. 1988. Culture and Canon? Critical Pedagogy and the Politics of Literacy. *Harvard Educational Review* 58:213–34.

———. 2000. *Che Guevara, Paulo Freire, and the Pedagogy of Revolution*. 33. Lanham, Md.: Rowman and Littlefield.

McLaren, P. L., and H. A. Giroux. 1994. *Between Borders: Pedagogy and the Politics of Cultural Studies*. London and New York: Routledge.

McNeil, L. M. 1986. *Contradictions of Control: School Structure and School Knowledge*. New York: Routledge.

McPherson, K. 1996. *Bedside Matters. The Transformation of Canadian Nursing, 1900–1990*. Toronto: Oxford University Press.

McRobbie, A. 1978. Working Class Girls and the Culture of Femininity. In *Women Take Issue*, edited by Women's Studies Group. 96–108. London: Hutchinson.

Mehan, H., A. Hertweck, and J. L. Meihls. 1986. *Handicapping the Handicapped: Decision Making in Students' Educational Careers*. Stanford: Stanford University Press.

Merrifield, J. 1997. If Job Training Is the Answer, What Is the Question? In *Changing Work, Changing Workers: Critical Perspectives on Language, Literacy, and Skills*, edited by G. Hull. 273–294. Albany: SUNY Press.

Miller, G. 1983. Holding Clients Accountable: The Micro-politics of Trouble in a Work Incentive Program. *Social Problems* 31:139–51.

Mills, C. W. 1956. *The Power Elite*. New York: Oxford University Press.

———. 1959. *The Sociological Imagination*. New York: Oxford University Press.

Mirriam, S. 1983. Mentors and Protégés: A Critical Review of the Literature. *Education Quarterly* 33:161–73.

Mirza, H. S. 1992. *Young, Female, and Black*. London: Routledge.

———. 1993. The Social Construction of Black Womanhood in British Educational Research: Towards a New Understanding. In *Feminism and Social Justice in Education*, edited by M. Arnot and K. Weiler. 32–57. London: Falmer Press.

Monture, P. 1986. Ka-Nin-Geh-Heh-Gah-E-Sa-Nonh-Yah-Gah [How Flint Women Do]. *Canadian Journal of Women and the Law/Rifd*: 159–71.

Morrow, R. A., and C. A. Torres. 1998. Education and the Reproduction of Class, Gender, and Race: Responding to the Postmodern Challenge. In

Sociology of Education: Emerging Perspectives, edited by C. A. Torres and T. R. Mitchell. 19–46. Albany: SUNY Press.

Muzzin, L. 2000. Academic Capitalism and the Not-So-Hidden Curriculum in the Pharmaceutical Sciences. In *The Political Economy of Health in Canada*, edited by Hugh Armstrong, Pat Armstrong, and David Coburn. Oxford: Oxford University Press.

Muzzin, L., G. Brown, and R. L. Hornosty. 1993. Professional Ideology in Canadian Pharmacy. *Health and Canadian Society* 319–45. Reprinted as chapter 13, pages 379–98, in D. Coburn, C. D'Arcy, and G. Torrance, ed. (1988). *Health and Canadian Society*. Sociological Perspectives. 3d ed. Toronto: University of Toronto Press.

Muzzin, L., C. Lai, and P. Sinnott. 1999. Pawns Among Patriarchies: Women in Pharmacy. In *Challenging Professions. Historical and Contemporary Perspectives on Women's Professional Work*, edited by Paula Borne, Elizabeth Smythe, Alison Prentice, and Sandra Acker. 296–314. Toronto: University of Toronto Press.

Natanson, M. 1962. *Literature, Philosophy, and the Social Sciences: Essays in Existentialism and Phenomenology*. The Hague: Martinus Nijhoff.

National Center for Educational Statistics. 1997. *Digest of Educational Statistics 1997*. Washington, D.C.: Department of Education.

———. 1999. *Condition of Education 1999*. Washington, D.C.: Department of Education.

National Science Foundation. 1996. *Women, Minorities, and Persons with Disabilities in Science and Engineering—1995*. Arlington, Va.: National Science Foundation.

Nelson, C. 1997. *Manifesto of a Tenured Radical*. New York: New York University Press.

Nespor, J. 1990. Curriculum and Conversions of Capital in the Acquisition of Disciplinary Knowledge. *Journal of Curriculum Studies* 22:217–32.

———. 1994. *Knowledge in Motion: Space, Time, and Curriculum in Undergraduate Physics and Management*. London: Falmer Press.

Nevins, J. 1993. Dear Regents: Don't Chop at the Top, Don't Cut Waste, Raise Our Fees Instead. In *UCLA Daily Bruin*.

Newman, K. S. 1988. *Falling from Grace: The Experience of Downward Mobility in the American Middle Class*. New York: Free Press; London: Collier-Macmillan.

Ng, R. 1993. A Woman Out of Control: Deconstructing Sexism and Racism in the University. *Canadian Journal of Education* 18:189–205.

———. 1997. A Woman Out of Control: Deconstructing Sexism and Racism in the University. In *Radical Interventions: Identity, Politics, and Differences in Educational Praxis*, edited by Suzanne de Castell and Mary Bryson. 39–59. Albany: State University of New York Press.

Nightingale, F. [1859] 1946. *Notes on Nursing: What It Is and What It Is Not*. Philadelphia: J. B. Lippincott Company.

Noble, D. 1977. *America by Design. Science, Technology and the Rise of Corporate Capitalism*. Oxford: Oxford University Press.

Noddings, N. 1988. An Ethic of Care and Its Implications for Instructional Arrangements. *American Journal of Education* 96:215–30.

Nottingham, S. 1998. *Eat Your Genes. How Genetically Modified Food is Entering Our Diet*. New York: St. Martin's Press.

O'Conor, A. 1998. *The Cultural Logic of Gender in College: Heterosexism, Homophobia, and Sexism in Campus Peer Groups*. Unpublished doctoral dissertation, University of Colorado-Boulder.

Packard, V. O. 1957. *The Hidden Persuaders*. New York: D. McKay Co.

Padilla, R. 1974. Chicano Studies at the University of California, Berkeley: En Busca Del Campus y La Comunidad. In *School of Education*. Berkeley: UC Berkeley.

Paris, K. 1985. *A Political History of Vocational, Technical, and Adult Education in Wisconsin*. Madison: Wisconsin Board of Vocational, Technical, and Adult Education.

Parry, S., and M. Hayden. 1999. Experiences of Supervisors in Facilitating the Induction of Research Higher Degree Students to Fields of Education. In A. Holbrook and S. Johnston, Supervision of Postgraduate Research in Education, *Review of Australian Research in Education No. 5*. 35–53. Coldstream, Victoria: Australian Association for Research in Education.

Parsons, T. 1959. The School Class as a Social System: Some of Its Functions in American Society. *Harvard Educational Review* 29:297–313.

Parsons, T., and G. M. Platt. 1973. *The American University*. Cambridge, Mass.: Harvard University Press.

Pearson, M. 1996. Professionalising Ph.D. Education to Enhance the Quality of the Student Experience. *Higher Education* 32:303–20.

Peiss, K. 1996. Making Up, Making Over: Cosmetics, Consumer Culture and Women's Identity. In *The Sex of Things*, edited by Victoria de Grazia and Ellen Furlough. 311–36. Berkeley: University of California Press.

Perrier, D., N. Winslade, J. Pugsley, and L. Lavack. 1995. Designing a Pharmaceutical Care Curriculum. *American Journal of Pharmaceutical Education* 59:113–25.

Pierce, J. 1995. *Gender Trials. Emotional Lives in Contemporary Law Firms*. Berkeley: University of California Press.

Plutzer, E. 1991. The Protestant Ethic and Spirit of Academia: An Essay on Graduate Education. *Teaching Sociology* 19:202–7.

Pounds, A. W. 1989. Black Students. In *The Freshman Year Experience: Helping Students Survive and Succeed in College*, edited by John N. Gardner, M. Lee Upcraft, and Associates. 277–86. San Francisco: Jossey-Bass.

Pride, W. M., R. J. Hughes, and J. R. Kapoor. 1993. *Business*. 4th ed. Boston: Houghton Mifflin.

Prince of Wales, HRH. 1998. Seeds of Disaster. Article originally appearing in the *Daily Telegraph* which was intended to be reprinted in the *Ecologist* 28 (5): September/October The Monsanto Files. Can We Survive Genetic Engineering? 1998. (Did not appear because the issue was retrieved from publication.)

Purves, A. C. 1988. *Writing across Languages and Cultures: Issues in Contrastive Rhetoric*. Newbury Park, Calif.: Sage.

Rawles, B. A. 1980. *The Influence of a Mentor on the Level of Self-actualization of American Scientists*. Columbus, Ohio: Ohio State University.

Regush, N. 1993. *Safety Last. The Failure of the Consumer Health System in Canada*. Toronto: Key Porter Books.

Reid, J. 1984. ESL Composition: The Linear Product of American Thought. *College Composition and Communication* 35:449–52.

Rendon, L. 1992. From the Barrio to the Academy: Revelations of a Mexican American "Scholarship Girl." In *First Generation Students: Confronting the Cultural Issues. New Directions for Community Colleges*, edited by L. S. Zwerling and H. B. London. 55–64. San Francisco: Jossey-Bass.

Rendon, L., and Justiz. 1989. Hispanic Students. In *The Freshman Year Experience: Helping Students Survive and Succeed in College*, edited by John N. Gardner, M. Lee Upcraft, and Associates. 261–75. San Francisco: Jossey-Bass.

Reverby, Susan. 1987. *Ordered to Care. The Dilemma of American Nursing: 1850–1945*. Cambridge: Cambridge University Press.

Richardson, L. 1997. *Fields of Play. Constructing an Academic Life*. Newark: Rutgers University Press.

Riddell, S. I. 1992. *Gender and the Politics of the Curriculum*. London and New York: Routledge.

Robinson, L. S. 1983. Treason Our Text: Feminist Challenges to the Literacy Canon. *Tulsa Studies in Women's Literature* 2:83–98.

Rocco, R. 1977. A Critical Perspective on the Study of Chicano Politics. *Western Political Quarterly* 30:558–73.

Rochin, R. 1973. The Short and Turbulent Life of Chicano Studies. *Social Science Quarterly* 54:884–94.

Romano-V., O. I. 1970. Social Science, Objectivity, and The Chicanos. *El Grito del Sol: A Journal of Contemporary Mexican-American Thought* 4:4–16.

Romano-V., O. I. 1980. Constitutional Issues and the Rise of the Professional Class in the United States. *El Grito del Sol: A Journal of Contemporary Mexican-American Thought* 5:9–24.

Romero, M., and D. Storrs. 1994. Is That Sociology? The Accounts of Women of Color Graduate Students. In *Women's Leadership in Education: An Agenda for a New Century*, edited by Diane M. Dunlap and Patricia Schmuck. 72–86. Albany: State University of New York Press.

Romero, M., and E. Margolis. 1999. Integrating Sociology: Observations on Race and Gender Relations in Sociology Graduate Programs. *Race and Society* 2:1–24.

———. 2000. Dissed in the Department: Women of Color Graduate Students Talk about Integrating Sociology. In *Self-Analytic Sociology: Essays and Exploration in the Reflexive Mode*, edited by Larry Reynolds. Rockport, Tex.: Rockport Institute Press.

Roomkin, M. J., ed. 1989. *Managers as Employees: An International Comparison of the Changing Character of Managerial Employment*. New York: Oxford University Press.

Ross, D. 1991. *The Origins of American Social Science*. Cambridge: Cambridge University Press.

Rossiter, M. 1982. *Women Scientists in America: Struggles and Strategies to 1940*. Baltimore: Johns Hopkins Press.

————. 1995. *Women Scientists in America: Before Affirmative Action, 1940–1972.* Baltimore: Johns Hopkins Press.

Roth, J. 1955. A Faculty Conception of Success in Graduate Study. *Journal of Higher Education* 26:50–56, 98.

Rudolph, F. 1965. *The American College and University: A History.* New York: Alfred A. Knopf.

————. 1989. *Curriculum: A History of the American Undergraduate Course of Study Since 1636.* San Francisco: Jossey-Bass.

Ryan, J., and C. Sackrey. 1984. *Strangers in Paradise: Academics from the Working Class.* Boston: South End Press.

Sacks, K. 1993. Murphy Hall Goes Marching In! In *UCLA Daily Bruin.*

Said, E. 1983. *The World, the Text, and the Critic.* Cambridge: Cambridge University Press.

Sartre, J. P. 1960. *Search for a Method.* New York: Alfred A. Knopf.

Schürmann, R. 1994. Concerning Philosophy in the United States. *Social Research* 61:87–113.

Schwartz, M., ed. 1987. *The Structure of Power in America: The Corporate Elite as a Ruling Class.* New York: Holmes and Meier.

Scott, M., and S. Lyman. 1968. Accounts. *American Sociological Review* 33:46–62.

Seymour, E., and N. M. Hewitt. 1997. *Talking about Leaving: Why Undergraduates Leave the Sciences.* Boulder, Colo.: Westview Press.

Shapiro, K., et al. 1993. Letter. In *UCLA Daily Bruin.*

Sharp, R., and A. Green. 1975. *Education and Social Control.* London: Routledge and Kegan Paul.

Shaughnessy, M. 1977. *Errors and Expectations: A Guide for the Teacher of Basic Writing.* New York: Oxford University Press.

Shiva, V. 1995. *Monoculture of the Mind. Perspectives on Biodiversity and Biotechnology.* London: Zed Books.

————. 1997. *Biopiracy. The Plunder of Nature and Knowledge.* Toronto: Between the Lines.

Shor, I. 1980. *Critical Teaching and Everyday Life.* Boston: South End Press.

Sinclair, U. 1922. *The Goose-Step: A Study of American Education.* Pasadena, Calif.: Upton Sinclair.

Slaughter, S., and L. L. Leslie. 1997. *Academic Capitalism: Politics, Policies, and the Entrepreneurial University.* Baltimore: Johns Hopkins University Press.

Smith, D. E. 1987. *The Everyday World as Problematic.* Toronto: University of Toronto Press.

————. 1990. *Texts, Facts, and Femininity: Exploring the Relations of Ruling.* London and New York: Routledge.

————. 1990. Women's Work as Mothers: A New Look at the Relation of Class, Family, and School Achievement. In *Feminism and Education: A Canadian Perspective,* edited by M. O' Brien, F. Forman, J. Haddad, D. Hallman and P. Masters. 219–44. Toronto: Centre for Women's Studies in Education, Ontario Institute for Studies in Education.

————. *Conceptual Practices of Power.* Toronto: University of Toronto Press.

———. 1999. *Writing the Social*. Toronto: University of Toronto Press.

Smith, P. C. 1993. Grandma Went to Smith, All Right, But She Went from Nine to Five: A Memoir. In *Working-class Women in the Academy*, edited by M. Tokarczyk and E. Fay. 126–39. Amherst: University of Massachusetts Press.

Smith, W. J. 1994. Comment on of Dinosaurs and Sacred Cows: The Grading of Classroom Participation. *Journal of Management Education* 18:237–240.

Sokoloff, N. 1992. *Black Women and White Women in the Professions*. New York: Routledge.

Soldatenko, M. 1998. The Origins of Academic Chicano Studies 1967–1970: The Emergence of Empirical and Perspectivist Chicano Studies. *Latino Studies Journal* 9: 3–25.

———. 1999. Empirical Chicano Studies: The Formation of Academic Chicano Studies, 1970–1975. *Latino Studies Journal*: 67–97.

Spender, D., and E. Sarah. 1980. *Learning to Lose: Sexism and Education*. London: The Woman's Press.

Spradley, J. P. 1979. *The Ethnographic Interview*. New York: Holt, Rinehart, and Winston.

———. 1980. *Participant Observation*. Orlando, Fla.: Holt, Rinehart, and Winston.

Spring, J. H. 1972. *Education and the Rise of the Corporate State*. Boston: Beacon Press.

Stalker, J., and S. Prentice. 1998. *Illusion of Inclusion. Women in Post-Secondary Education*. Halifax, Nova Scotia: Fernwood.

Stewart, A. H. 1991. The Role of Narrative Structure in the Transfer of Ideas: The Case Study and Management Theory. In *Textual Dynamics of the Professions: Historical and Contemporary Studies of Writing in Professional Communities*, edited by C. Bazerman and J. Paradis. Madison: University of Wisconsin Press.

Street, A. F. 1992. *Inside Nursing: A Critical Ethnography of Clinical Nursing Practice*. Albany: SUNY Press.

Suzuki, D., and P. Knudtson. 1990. *Genethics. The Ethics of Engineering Life*. Rev. ed. New Data Enterprises. Cambridge, Mass.: Harvard University Press.

Sykes, C. J. 1988. *Profscam: Professors and the Demise of Higher Education*. Washington, D.C.: Regnery Gateway.

Thorne, B. 1993. *Gender Play: Girls and Boys in School*. New Brunswick, N.J.: Rutgers University Press.

Thornhill, E. 1994. Focus on Racism. Legal Perspectives from a Black Experience. *Analytical Legal Study* 8:153–62.

Third World Liberation Front. 1971. The Fifteen TWLF Demands. In *An End to Silence: The San Francisco State College Student Movement in the '60s*, edited by W. Barlow and P. Shapiro. 67–97. New York: Pegasus.

Tierney, W., and E. M. Bensimon. 1996. *Promotion and Tenure: Community and Socialization in Academe*. Albany: SUNY Press.

"Time of Studies and Statistics Over." *La Raza* 1:7.

Tonso, K. L. 1993. Becoming Engineers While Working Collaboratively:

Knowledge and Gender in a Nontraditional Engineering Course. Part of Margaret Eisenhart's Final Report to the Spencer Foundation: the Construction of Scientific Knowledge Outside School.

———. 1996a. Student Learning and Gender. *Journal of Engineering Education* 85:143–50.

———. 1996b. Creating Engineers: Processes That Exclude Women. In *Proceedings of the National Conference of the Women in Engineering Program Advocates Network*, June 1–4. Denver.

———. 1996c. The Impact of Cultural Norms on Women. *Journal of Engineering Education* 85:217–25.

———. 1997. Constructing Engineers Through Practice: Gendered Features of Learning and Identity Development. Unpublished doctoral dissertation, University of Colorado, Boulder.

———. 1999a. Theorizing Mature Practitioners in Communities of Practice: Student Engineers Performing Practical Work in Teams. Paper presented at the Annual Meeting of the American Educational Research Association, Montreal, Canada.

———. 1999b. Engineering Gender—Gendering Engineering: A Cultural Model for Belonging. *Journal of Women and Minorities in Science and Engineering* 5:365–404.

———. 2000. Plotting Something Dastardly in Engineering Education: Consciousness Raising, Collective Action, and Reform. New Orleans.

Trenchard, L., and H. Warren. 1987. Talking about School: The Experiences of Young Lesbians and Gay Men. In *Gender Under Scrutiny: New Inquiries in Education*, edited by G. Weiner and M. Arnot. 222–30. London: Hutchinson.

Turner, C., and J. Thompson. 1993. Socializing Women Doctoral Students: Minority and Majority Experiences. *Review of Higher Education* 16:355–70.

Vallance, E. 1973/74. Hiding the Hidden Curriculum: An Interpretation of the Language of Justification in Nineteenth Century Educational Reform. *Curriculum Theory Network* 4: 5–21.

Valli, L. 1986. *Becoming Clerical Workers*. Boston: Routledge.

Van Den Berghe, P. 1963. Dialectic and Functionalism: Toward a Theoretical Synthesis. *American Sociological Review* 28:695–705.

Veblen, T. 1965. *The Higher Learning in America: A Memorandum on the Conduct of Universities by Business Men*. New York: Augustus M., and Kelley Bookseller.

Veysey, L. R. 1965. *The Emergence of the American University*. Chicago: University of Chicago Press.

Viswanathan, G. 1989. The Empire Within: How the Canon Divides and Conquers. *Voice Literary Supplement*.

Walker, S., and L. Barton, ed. 1983. *Gender Class and Education*. Sussex, England: Falmer Press.

Wear, D. 1997. *Privilege in the Medical Academy. A Feminist Examines Gender, Race and Power*. New York: Teachers College Press.

Wei, W. 1993. *The Asian American Movement*. Philadelphia: Temple University Press.

Weiler, K. 1988. *Women Teaching for Change: Gender, Class, and Power.* South Hadley, Mass.: Bergin and Garvey.

Weis, L. 1985. *Beyond Two Worlds: Black Students in an Urban Community College.* Boston: Routledge and Kegan Paul.

Weis, L., and M. Fine. ed. 1993. *Beyond Silenced Voices: Class, Race, and Gender in United States Schools.* Albany: State University of New York Press.

Weiss, R. 1996. A Critical Re-Examination of Tranquilizer Use by the Elderly. A Secondary Data Analysis of the 1990 Ontario Health Survey. In *Department of Public Health Sciences.* Toronto: University of Toronto.

Wexler, P. 1992. *Becoming Somebody: Toward a Social Psychology of School.* London: Falmer Press.

Wheeler, S. 1966. The Structure of Formally Organized Socialization Settings. In *Socialization after Childhood: Two Essays.* 52–113. New York: John Wiley and Sons.

Williams, R. 1977. Marxism and Literature. Oxford: Oxford University Press.

————. 1989. The Future of Cultural Studies. In *The Politics of Modernism: Against the New Conformists*, edited by Raymond Williams. 151–62. London: Verso.

Williamson, B. 1974. Continuities and Discontinuities in the Sociology of Education. In *Educability, Schools, and Ideology*, edited by Michael Flude and John Ahier. 10–11. London: Halstead.

Willis, P. [1977] 1981. *Learning to Labor: How Working Class Kids Get Working Class Jobs.* Rev. ed. New York: Columbia University Press.

Willmott, H. 1994. Management Education: Provocations to a Debate. *Management Learning* 25:105–36.

Wilshire, B. 1990. *The Moral Collapse of the University: Professionalism, Purity, and Alienation.* Albany: State University of New York Press.

Witz, A. 1992. *Professions and Patriarchy.* London: Macmillan.

Women's Studies Group. 1978. *Women Take Issue.* London: Hutchinson.

Woods, P. 1979. *The Divided School.* London: Routledge and Kegan Paul.

————. 1983. *Sociology and the School.* London: Routledge and Kegan Paul.

Wright, C. 1987. The Relations between Teachers and Afro-Caribbean Pupils: Observing Multicultural Classrooms. In *Gender Under Scrutiny*, edited by G. Weiner and M. Arnot. 173–86. London: Hutchinson.

Wright, S. 1994. *Molecular Politics. Developing American and British Regulatory Policy for Genetic Engineering, 1972–1982.* Chicago: University of Chicago Press.

Young, I. M. 1990. Polity and Group Difference: A Critique of the Ideal of Universal Citizenship. In *Feminism and Political Theory*, edited by C. Sunstein. 117–41. Chicago: University of Chicago Press.

Young, M. F. D., ed. 1971. *Knowledge and Control.* London: Collier-Macmillan.

Contributors

Eric Margolis is a sociologist and Assistant Professor in the Division of Educational Leadership and Policy Studies, Arizona State University College of Education. Recent publications include "The Department is Very Male, Very White, Very Old, and Very Conservative": The Functioning of the Hidden Curriculum in Graduate Sociology Departments" (with Mary Romero), *The Harvard Educational Review* (vol. 68, 1998) and "Class Pictures: Representations of Race, Gender and Ability in a Century of School Photography," *Visual Sociology* (vol. 14, 1999), reprinted in *Education Policy Analysis Archives* (vol. 8, no. 31, July 4, 2000). Online at http://epaa.asu.edu/epaa/v8n31/

Sandra Acker is a sociologist of education and Professor and Chair of the Department of Sociology and Equity Studies in Education, Ontario Institute for Studies in Education of the University of Toronto. Recent publications include The *Realities of Teachers' Work: Never a Dull Moment (1999)* and (co-edited with Elizabeth Smyth, Paula Bourne, and Alison Prentice) *Challenging Professions: Historical and Contemporary Perspectives on Women's Caring Work* (1999).

Linda Muzzin is Associate Professor and Coordinator of the Higher Education Graduate Program in the Department of Theory and Policy Studies in Education at the Ontario Institute for Studies in Education of the University of Toronto. She also has active cross-appointments to the Faculty of Pharmacy as well as to the Public Health Sciences and the Center for Bioethics in the Faculty of Medicine at the University of Toronto.

Karen L. Tonso is Assistant Professor of Educational Anthropology and Philosophy, Wayne State University. She specializes in the social construction of peer groups in learning settings, especially historically male-identified scientific communities.

Carrie Yang Costello is Assistant Professor of Sociology and Urban Studies, University of Wisconsin-Milwaukee. Her research interests include race/class/gender/sexuality, the sociology of identity, and the sociology of organizations.

Michael Soldatenko is Professor of History, Santa Monica College. He is currently developing a manuscript that analyzes the genesis and development of contemporary Chicana and Chicano academic thought.

Marina Gair is a doctoral student in the Educational Leadership and Policy Studies Program, Arizona State University. Her academic interests include educational anthropology, visual and critical ethnography, critical theory, and the social and philosophical foundations of education.

Caroline Childress is a doctoral candidate in the Department of Sociology, State University of New York at Stony Brook. Her dissertation research explores the (re)production of class and gender in government-funded retraining programs.

Guy Mullins is a Video Production and Integration Specialist with the Department of Information Technology, Instruction Support, Arizona State University. Guy's academic interests include interactive networked video integration, visual and critical ethnography, and human interface design, implementation, and aesthetics.

Kenneth N. Ehrensal is Associate Professor of Management at Kutztown University. He has graduate degrees in both anthropology and organizational studies. His primary research interest focuses on the control of the labor processes of white-collar and professional workers.

Mary Jane Curry is a research fellow at the Center for Language and Communication, School of Education, The Open University. She earned her Ph.D. in curriculum theory at the University of Wisconsin in 2000, her M.A. teaching English as a second language from the University of Massachusetts-Boston in 1994, and her B.A. English from Cornell University in 1983.

Mary Romero is Professor of Justice Studies in the College of Public Programs, Arizona State University. She is the author *of Maid in the U.S.A.* (Routledge, 1992) and co-editor of *Women's Untold Stories: Breaking Silence, Talking Back, Voicing Complexity* (Routledge, 1999), *Challenging Fronteras: Structuring Latina and Latina Lives in the U.S.* (Routledge, 1997), and *Women and Work: Exploring Race, Ethnicity and Class* (1997).

Index

dislocated professionals *(continued)*, and downskilling the resume, 124–125; and structural conformity, 128–131; lowering expectations of, 18; resocialization of, 133
division of labor, employees' consent to, 97–99
downward mobility, and learning to be flexible, 115, 122–123; resocialization for, 119–120
Dreeben, R., 5, 6, 15, 24, 25
Durkheim, E., 5, 6, 15, 24, 25

Eisenhart, M., 18, 99, 157, 158, 174
Eisner, E., 3, 105
elaborated linguistic code, 8
engineering curriculum, and plotting something dastardly, 170–173
engineering school, and learning to not-notice, 156, 163, 173; and pathological control of work, 167–169; and sexist practices, 169–170; hiding a gender curriculum in, 155–173
Everhart, R., 13, 188

faculty, and consequences of opposition, 32–33; and incompatible class habits, 31; and racism, 30–33; and sexism, 30–33; Chicano(a) and "cooling out", 211; Chicano(a) as agents of colonization, 207–210; Chicano(a) as coparticipants in reproduction of inequality, 211; disempowerment of, 32–33; feminist and minority, 30–33; in pharmaceutical sciences, 142–149
Fine, M., 13
Freire, P., 15, 17

Gair, M., 1, 44, 133, 136, 140
gender, and "culture of romance", 158; and pharmaceutical sciences, 142–152; in engineering school, 156–174; theoretical analyses of, 11–12
Gintis, H., 7, 11, 15, 28, 99
Giroux, H., 12, 14, 15, 16, 17, 39, 86, 194, 202, 203

Goffman, I., 116, 119, 131

habitus, 3, 49, 53, 57, 62, 77, 103-105, 108-109, 133, 172; and academic performance in graduate school, 18; definition of, 8
hermeneutics, definition of, 2
hidden curriculum, and "cooling out" the mark, 116–117; and architectural investments, 27–30; and British Sociologists of Education, 9–12; and British sociologists of education, 9–12; and construction of legitimate knowledge, 14; and Critical Theorists in the U.S., 12–15; and dialectical critique, 15; and differential outcomes, 12–15, 25; and differentiation by social class, 12–13; and dissertation advising, 61, 77; and examination of gender inequality, 11–12; and functionalist origins, 4–6; and hiddenness, 1–3, 21, 26 ; and higher education, 18–19, 21; and institutional differentiation, 34–35; and intentional socialization practices, 33–35; and manufacturing consent, 98; and Marxist perspectives, 6–9, 25; and mentoring, 79–96; and new sociology of education, 9; and physical environment, 27–30, 43–60; and reproduction of class status, 30–33; and reproduction of gender divisions, 32–33; and resistance theory, 15; and resocialization to lower status jobs, 133; and retraining programs, 115–134; and role of physical environment, 22; and socialization of business students, 109–111; and thesis advising/supervision, 62; and transformation, 16; and values, 23; as "hiding in plain sight", 1–2, 21, 23; as manifested in the body, 30–33; as manifested in the physical environment, 27–30; as necessary socializing mechanism,